Colored No More

WOMEN, GENDER, AND SEXUALITY IN AMERICAN HISTORY

Editorial Advisors:
Susan K. Cahn
Wanda A. Hendricks
Deborah Gray White
Anne Firor Scott, Founding Editor Emerita

A list of books in the series appears at the end of this book.

Colored No More

Reinventing Black Womanhood in Washington, D.C.

TREVA B. LINDSEY

UNIVERSITY OF ILLINOIS PRESS
Urbana, Chicago, and Springfield

© 2017 by the Board of Trustees
of the University of Illinois
All rights reserved
1 2 3 4 5 C P 5 4 3 2 1
∞ This book is printed on acid-free paper.

Library of Congress Cataloging-in-Publication Data
Names: Lindsey, Treva B., 1983- author.
Title: Colored no more: reinventing black womanhood in Washington, D.C. / Treva B. Lindsey.
Other titles: Reinventing black womanhood in Washington, D.C.
Description: Second edition. | Urbana, IL: University of Illinois Press, [2017] | Series: Women, gender, and sexuality in American history | Includes bibliographical references and index.
Identifiers: LCCN 2016045891 (print) | LCCN 2016056612 (ebook) | ISBN 9780252041020 (cloth : alk. paper) | ISBN 9780252082511 (pbk. : alk. paper) | ISBN 9780252099571 (e-book : alk. paper) | ISBN 9780252099571 (E-book)
Subjects: LCSH: African American women—Washington (D.C.)—History. | Women, Black—Race identity. | African American women—Washington (D.C.)—Social life and customs. | African American women—Political activity—Washington (D.C.)—History—20th century. | Women—Suffrage—Washington (D.C.)—History—20th century. | Women—Washington (D.C.)—History. | Washington (D.C.)—Social life and customs—20th century. | Washington (D.C.)—Politics and government—20th century. | Salons—Washington (D.C.)—History—20th century. | Washington (D.C.)—Intellectual life—20th century.
Classification: LCC E185.93.D6 L56 2017 (print) | LCC E185.93.D6 (ebook) | DDC 305.48/8960730753—dc23
LC record available at https://lccn.loc.gov/2016045891

For Relisha Rudd

Contents

Acknowledgments

I never dreamed of writing a book. Even as a graduate student in the Department of History at Duke University, I did not foresee using my research on black women living in Washington, D.C., during the early twentieth century for any kind of manuscript. The amazing women of my birth city, however, ended up enveloping my life. I could not put them or their stories away without digging deeper into what it meant to be a black woman moving through the city that gave me life. I would see their names on schools, on street signs, and on buildings throughout the city. I wondered. I mused about their lives—their untold stories. I knew I walked among greatness every time I set foot on Howard University's campus, strolled along U Street in search of the best after-hours spot, or indulged in a little retail therapy in Georgetown. I also knew violence, pain, discrimination, inequality, and loss inscribed the lives of generations of black women before me. The legacy of slavery, Jim Crow, race riots, and postindustrialization was visible throughout the city. By the time I was born, the ravages of the War on Drugs, mass incarceration, white flight, and resegregation were evident on my street corner across from the Shrimp Boat in northeast Washington and on far too many corners throughout the nation's capital. This was Chocolate City, and she had many stories to tell.

My parents encouraged me to pursue my research interest in Washington. They never doubted the significance of this project. Without knowing much about the manuscript-writing process, they helped me see the project that would become this book. Like so many other moments of my life, my parents advised and inspired me. They cheered for me and told me to follow my heart. Throughout graduate school and my tenure as a professor, Anthony and Treva Lindsey were my rocks. They were my biggest cheerleaders and unabashedly my greatest "fans," and I could not imagine a single page of this book being written without their love and continued support at every stage of my life. I have to thank my godparents Cheryl and Kevin Brown and Cheryl and Tony Santos for always being there. Uncle Stan Jackson and Auntie Nicey Jackson were my "other" parents from day one. They never fail to tell me how proud they are of me. To my sisters: Talia, Chenise, and Miracle—I am grateful for all of you. To my brothers, Stanley and Marcus Jackson—thank you for always riding for me. My aunts, Sarah McCrae, Louise Hodge, and Linda Blunt, and my Uncle Hayves have always cheered the loudest for me. My grandmothers, Lula Pearl, Bertha Lindsey, and Ella Ruth Streeter, instilled lifelong lessons of humility, tenacity, and kindness into me. I hope this book is a testament to the unconditional love I hold for my family.

My advisors also provided me with invaluable guidance, mentoring, and tough love. Laura Edwards, Adriane Lentz-Smith, Davarian Baldwin, and Mark Anthony Neal were the best committee members one could hope for. Laura worked closely with me on every chapter, offering critical feedback and generous line editing. Her support of my work did not cease after I graduated. Adriane joined my committee soon after she arrived at Duke University, and I could not be more grateful. Her thoughtful feedback and incisive questions on each chapter sharpened my voice as an author. I am so glad she came to Duke when she did. Reading Davarian's book on New Negroes in Chicago changed the game for me. I was ecstatic when he agreed to serve on my committee and overjoyed at how engaged he remained with my project at every stage. Last, but certainly not least: Mark. There are no words to describe how much I value him as an advisor, colleague, and mentor. He added something so special to my process and to this book. I could never overstate how amazing it was and is to have this wonderful group of scholars invested in me.

At Duke, I also had the pleasure to learn from, study alongside, and work with amazing graduate students and faculty members. I want to thank my informal cohort of amazing graduate-school peers, including Tami Navarro, Alexis Gumbs, Bianca Williams, Jenny Woodruff, Marti Newland, Britt Russert, Alisha Gaines, Micah Gilmer, Reena Goldthree, Danielle Terrazas-Williams, Felicity Turner, Kinohi Nishikawa, and Samantha Noel for all of their brilliance and kindness during one of the toughest journeys of my professional life. Faculty members Wahneema Lubiano and Maurice Wallace sharpened my skills as critical thinker. The Department of African and African

American Studies at Duke provided a second home for me at the university. This department also pushed me to develop into an interdisciplinary scholar. The entire faculty and staff of AAAS at Duke enhanced my experiences as a graduate student. I want also to thank the John Hope Franklin Scholars Program and the Reginaldo Howard Scholars program for allowing me to serve as graduate assistant during my time at Duke. Both of these programs helped me become a more well-rounded scholar.

Prior to arriving at Duke for graduate study, I had the pleasure of learning from some of the most amazing scholars in the world at Oberlin College. I did not consider a career as a professor until I had the pleasure of taking classes and studying with Drs. Meredith Gadsby, Caroline Jackson-Smith, and Pamela Brooks. These three women changed the game for me. Seeing such brilliant and fly black women scholars inspired me. They each encouraged me to think seriously about graduate school and pointed me toward the Mellon Minority (now Mays) Undergraduate Fellowship program. I had no idea applying for and being accepted into the MMUF program would literally change my life. Thank you Monique, Janene, and Clovis for making me part of the MMUF family. This program taught me how to do graduate level research, funded summer research, assisted me in applying for graduate school, provided crucial financial support during my tenure as a graduate student, helped me write a proposal, and guided me through the academic job-market process. Additionally, being part of the MMUF program made me part of a family. Two of my most prized interlocutors and dear friends came from MMUF—Drs. Jessica Johnson and Uri McMillan. You are my rocks and have been for more than a decade.

The community at my first job in the professoriate at the University of Missouri–Columbia graciously supported the transformation of my research into a book project. A person could not ask for a better department to begin her career than the Department of Women's and Gender Studies at Mizzou. Joan Hermsen, Srirupa Prasad, Rebecca Dingo, Rebecca Martinez, Julie Elman, Minnie Chiu, Tola Pearce, Mary Jo Neitz, Elisa Glick, and Zakiya Adair—thank you for being such wonderful colleagues. Our departmental staff, including Jessica Jennrich and Shelda Eggers, made the transition from graduate student to professor manageable and pleasurable. Faculty in Black Studies including Wilma King, April Langley, Stephanie Shonekan, and Bryana French lovingly supported my work during my three years at Missouri. Colleagues and friends in other departments such as Libby Cowgill and Joi Moore kept me laughing during my revision process. The MU Women's Center gave me numerous opportunities to present my work, for which I am also grateful. I had the pleasure of having tremendous students while at Mizzou. My graduate and teaching assistant of three years, Dr. Erica Campbell, amazed me with her work and her commitment to my work as well. She kept me on my toes and helped me grow as a scholar-teacher-advisor. I would not have finalized and submitted the first draft of my book manuscript without the love and support of my writing and travel buddy/colleague Sarah Diem. I miss my Mizzou community and know that my book would not exist without the intellectual support I found in mid-Missouri.

My Ohio State University community assisted me greatly in revising the book into what it is today. My department, Women's, Gender, and Sexuality Studies, has been with me at every step of the arduous revision process. Shannon Winnubst, Mary Thomas, Cricket Keating, Juno Parreñas, Wendy Smooth, Guisela Latorre, Cindy Burack, Jennifer Suchland, Mytheli Sreenivas, Lynn Itagaki, Corinne Reczek, Linda Mizejewski, Katherine Marino, and Jill Bystydzienski are incredible colleagues who challenge me to be a better scholar. Our departmental staff Lynaya Elliott, Tess Pugsley, Andy Cavins, and Jackie Stotlar are the best in the world. Colleagues across departments such as Daniel Rivers, Pranav Jani, Wendy Hesford, Koritha Mitchell, Tanya Saunders, and Elaine Richardson have been incredibly helpful in offering mentorship and providing feedback on my work. My exemplary students at OSU sharpened my work as well. I am particularly grateful to Tay Glover, Sierra Austin, Deja Beamon, and Sai Isoke for their close work with me as graduate research assistants.

When I moved to OSU, I was uncertain about whether I would find a community of folks outside of my university, yet I surely did, and they helped me push through the more challenging aspects of work. I want to thank Sandra Enimil, Erica Butler, Tyiesha Shorts, Marshall Shorts, David Butler, Speak Williams, Tiffany Williams, Damia Smoot, Brittney Gray, Darrell Gray, Kristen, Joanne Devaney, Michael Mandel, Mercedes Bender, Renee Dion, Eric Jefferson, Amna Akbar, Melissa Crum, and Yusef Abdul-Zahir for their friendship and love. I never expected to meet such a creative and warm community.

I have had the pleasure of being part of two amazing collectives of scholars throughout my career. My S.P.A.C.E. folks: Angelique Nixon, Marlo David, Marlon Moore, C. Riley Snorton, L. H. Stallings, Rachel Robinson, Mecca Jamilah Sullivan, and Darius Bost read drafts of my work as it moved from draft to book. This group does not hold back on the critique, but they always offer what they have in the most generative and loving ways. I am eternally grateful for S.P.A.C.E. and all that this group of folks does to make me a better scholar. In 2013, Joan Morgan invited to be a part of a collective she formed, the Pleasure Ninjas. Along with Morgan, Brittney Cooper, Esther Armah, Yaba Blay, and Kaila Story have become my partners in scholarly crime and domestic and global travel. The joy these women brought into my life pulled me through some of the darkest moments of my adult life. This book exists in part because these women believed in me and would not let me give up on these New Negro women.

The academy has taught me many things, but I am most grateful for the friendships and mentors it gave me. To my scholar squad and friends, Bettina Love, Regina Bradley, Tanisha Ford, Tabitha Chester, Marc Lamont Hill, Nadia Brown, Justin Hansford, Vanessa Perez, Guthrie Ramsey, James Peterson, Jeffrey Ogbar, Erica Williams, Elizabeth Todd-Breland, Emery Petchauer, Chris Emdin, and Samir Meghelli, thank you for being so dope. Our friendships may have started because of the academy, but they thrive because they have all been magnificent friends. Mentors such as Drs. Michelle Scott, Shanna Benjamin, Joshua Guild, E. Patrick Johnson, and Tiffany Gill provided me with priceless feedback on my work and essential advice of navigating the academy.

I consider anyone I call a friend family. Thankfully, I have a large and boisterous chosen family. My friend of more than thirty years, Sia Barnes, is one of the few people I always knew I would work with when I became an adult. Her talents as a writer helped me find my own voice as a writer. My friend of more than twenty-five years, Olivia Fenty has been my rock and my sister. She encourages me whenever we talk. She also gave me the gift of being godmother to three wonderful children: Aliyah Fenty, Elijah Thompson, and Kamiyah Beckles. My crew of more than twenty years emerged from my days at Sidwell Friends School. Amir Jenkins, Nyia Noel, Robynn Nichols, Rebeca Wolfe-Balbuena, Britney Williams, Laura Williams, Brookes Gore, Sara Madavo Jean-Jacques, and Shaba Lightfoot have been by my side every step of the way in finishing college, graduate school, and this book. The homies of more than fifteen years came from college. Sederia Bond, Hope Fisher, Dazlynn Smith, Lena Anderson, Franchesca Medina, Netisha Currie, Chinara Lucas, Stephanie Beasley, Lisa Merriweather Tichy, Amber Coleman-Mortley and Julius Hill hold such a special place in my heart. During graduate school at Duke I had pleasure of meeting and building lifelong friendships with folks outside my department and in Durham. Marco Harris, Yendelela Neely, and Michelle Gordon provided me with endless laughs that made the whole grad school process more doable. I thank Charlene Blake, my fellow DD, for being my sister and sistah scholar who showed me a new level of ambition and of friendship. Maya Jackson is my heart and her daughters/my goddaughters Nona Bliss and Brooklyn Hendricks make me smile from the inside out. While completing my research in Washington, I found a circle of new friends in the DMV to make sure I was not all work and no play. Thank you to Lauren Madlock, Marco Hardie, Trey Stanback, Shaun Koiner, Julia Scrivens, Lesley Cothran, K. J. Mburu, Eric, Julia Spraggins, and David Greene.

This project received support from numerous institutions and foundations. Thank you to the Social Science Research Council; the Woodrow Wilson Foundation; the Andrew Mellon Foundation; Emory University's Manuscript, Archives, and Rare Book Library; the University of Missouri–Columbia Research Council; and the Franklin Humanities Institute at Duke University. I would also like to extend my deepest gratitude to the librarians and archivists at The Moorland-Spingarn Research Center at Howard University; the Washington, D.C., Historical Society; the Martin Luther King Jr. Library in Washington, D.C.; and those at Oberlin College, Duke University, Emory University, and Ohio State University. This book would not have been possible without considerable financial and research support from these institutions. I am deeply indebted to them all. Thank you to University of Minnesota Press for allowing me to reprint a significant portion of my chapter, "Climbing the Hilltop: In Search of a New Negro Womanhood Ethos at Howard University," from the amazing edited collection (eds. Davarian Baldwin and Minkah Makalani) *Escape from New York: The "Harlem Renaissance" Reconsidered.*

My heartfelt thanks go to the editorial staff I worked with at the University of Illinois Press. Dawn Durante's patience, thoughtful engagement with my work, and sincere belief in the value project were instrumental. She made sure my vision was fully realized, and the entire staff from design to copyediting to marketing made this first-time author feel as if I could really do this. They are an incredible group of folks, and I am grateful to have had the opportunity to work with them.

Finally, I would like to thank all of my foremothers in Chocolate City and all of the amazing black womyn still fighting for justice across the globe. I hope this book is a testament to how much I value the undervalued and unrecognized work of black women. Our freedom struggles continue, but I believe that we will win.

Colored No More

Introduction

By a sort of national common consent, she has had no place in the Republic of free and independent womanhood of America. Slavery left her in social darkness, and freedom has been slow in leading her into the daylight of the virtues.

—Fannie Barrier Williams

"All through the darkest period of the colored women's oppression in this country her yet unwritten history is full of heroic struggle, a struggle against fearful and overwhelming odds, that often ended in a horrible death, to maintain and protect that which woman holds dearer than life."[1] The words spoken by Washington, D.C.–based author, teacher, activist, and scholar Anna Julia Cooper on May 18, 1893 at the World's Fair: Columbian Exposition in Chicago, Illinois, centered on the lives of black women. Her speech, as well as those of five other emergent and prominent African American women leaders, Fannie Barrier Williams, Frances E. W. Harper, Fanny Jackson Coppin, Sarah J. Early, and Hallie Q. Brown, forcefully and powerfully inserted the voices, standpoints, and experiences of African American women into a space committed to celebrating the triumphs of white men in the United States. From May 1 to October 30, 1893, the grand spectacle of the World's Fair formally commemorated the four-hundredth anniversary of Christopher Columbus's arrival to the New World in 1492. Although the dedication ceremonies took place on October 21, 1892, the fairgrounds did not open to the public until May 1 of the following year. Pivoting around and propelling the ideas of American industrial optimism and American exceptionalism, the unprecedented World's Fair welcomed more than twenty-seven million people who would marvel at a wide range of exhibitions trumpeting innovation and progress. The global scope of the fair, which included representations of nearly fifty peoples and cultures, however, did not overpower the broader message of white male supremacy in the United States.[2]

The fair symbolized both the city's ascendance from the literal and figurative ashes of the Great Chicago Fire and the nation's emergence as a "reconstructed" global power. Despite being only twenty-eight years past the Civil War and sixteen years past the formal end of Reconstruction, the exposition anchored this new moment in U.S. history in the discovery of the New World by Europe, and indirectly, though perhaps intentionally, in the subsequent annihilation and marginalization of the First Nation and Indigenous peoples of the Americas and the enslavement of African people. Cooper, in speaking for "colored women from the South," commenced her address by highlighting that "millions of blacks in this country have watered the soil with blood and tears, and it is there too that the colored woman of America has made her characteristic history, and there her destiny is evolving."[3] Her words provided a black-women-centered counternarrative to the "discovery" narrative promoted by the fair through Cooper's centering the enslavement of black people as foundational to the nation's history. Cooper also skillfully wove in the brevity of thirty years in marking the progress of a formerly enslaved people. More critical, however, was that Cooper pushed against a linear narrative of progress of African Americans by emphasizing that "since emancipation the movement has been at times confused and stormy, so that we could not always tell whether we were going forward or groping in a circle."[4] The combination of an abrupt end to Reconstruction in 1877, over a decade of post-Reconstruction efforts by African American communities to re-imagine their futures without concerted federal investment, and the earliest iterations of Jim Crow in state constitutions in the 1890s grounded Cooper's statement about the uncertainty and precariousness of progress for African Americans thirty years post-Emancipation.[5] The political fire and exigency of her words departed from the fair's overarching, celebratory cultural tone.

Only a year prior to the World's Fair, Anna Julia Cooper published the germinal black protofeminist text, *A Voice from the South: From a Woman from the South*. Her book, which lauded self-determination through social uplift and education for African American women, concretized in print a growing political sensibility among many black women. Cooper's words at the Exposition naturally overlapped and connected with those of the other African American women speakers. Her speech echoed some of the core arguments of her book and further heralded both the triumphs of and dynamic possibilities for African American women. Cooper's book and her speech at the fair further solidified her status as one of the most recognized and respected voices illuminating the lived experiences of African American women.[6] An educator and administrator at the prestigious African American M Street High School in Washington, D.C., and an author and speaker, Cooper had both local and national stature. By the time Cooper established herself as a fixture in the African American public sphere in the nation's capital, Washington thrived as an intellectual, cultural, and social center for black people in the United States. Black Washington cultivated Cooper's growth as a thinker, educator, administrator, and activist. Her words at the World's Fair and in her book built upon the unique cultivation as a black Washington woman and an emergent New Negro woman.

At the core of New Negro womanhood was a fundamental transformation in how African American women viewed themselves as participants and authorial figures in the modern world. The activities of clubwomen, black suffragists, teachers in newly established "Colored"[7] schools, beauticians, and domestics, from the late nineteenth century until the mid-twentieth century, composed the New Negro womanhood experience. Clubwomen advocated for the advancement of African American women in a post-Emancipation/Progressive Era context. Black suffragists demanded universal suffrage and emphasized the importance of the franchise for African American women at the turn of the twentieth century. African American teachers educated a new generation of African Americans, and particularly African American women, in a range of professions. Beauticians were among the most successful entrepreneurs and innovators during this era. Domestics and sharecroppers were the backbone of poor and working-class black communities. Although not enslaved, the conditions and hardships black domestics often endured in the homes of white families resembled those of the recent era of chattel slavery.[8] As African American women grappled with post-Reconstruction and Jim Crow realities, they began to articulate new ideas about race, class, gender, and sexuality. These evolving articulations, particularly in black urban centers like Washington, challenged the status of African American women in public life.

The tensions surrounding black women's participation in the World's Fair paralleled local struggles of African American women in Washington to become fuller participants in black public life. Before these six women were added to the program, black leaders throughout the United States protested their exclusion from the fair's planning.[9] Ida B. Wells, Frederick Douglass, educator Irvine Garland Penn, and lawyer and newspaper publisher Ferdinand L. Barnett directly addressed the lack of a substantial African American presence at the fair in "The Reason Why the Colored American Is Not at the Columbian Exposition." Wells was the primary author of the scathing document. She eloquently and passionately states in the volume's preface:

> The exhibit of the progress made by a race in 25 years of freedom as against 250 years of slavery, would have been the greatest tribute to the greatness and progressiveness of American institutions which could have been shown the world. The colored people of this great Republic number eight millions—more than one-tenth the whole population of the United States. They were among the earliest settlers of this continent, landing at Jamestown, Virginia in 1619 in a slave ship, before the Puritans, who landed at Plymouth in 1620. They have contributed a large share to American prosperity and civilization. The labor of one-half of this country has always been, and is still being done by them. The first crédit this country had in its commerce with foreign nations was created by productions resulting from their labor. The wealth created by their industry has afforded to the white people of this country the leisure essential to their great progress in education, art, science, industry and invention.
>
> Those visitors to the World's Columbian Exposition who know these facts, especially foreigners will naturally ask: Why are not the colored people, who constitute so large an element of the American population, and who have contributed so large a share to American greatness, more visibly present and better represented in this World's Exposition? Why are they not taking part in this glorious celebration of the four-hundredth anniversary of the discovery of their country? Are they so dull and stupid as to feel no interest in this great event? It is to answer these questions and supply as far as possible our lack of representation at the Exposition that the Afro-American has published this volume.[10]

The volume detailed both the limited representation of the "Colored" experience in the United States and the lack of African American attendees. The six African American women speakers forcefully counteracted the scarce visibility of African Americans and African American culture at the fair by refusing the erasure of black women's voices, experiences, and history. Cooper, Williams, Harper, Coppin, Early, and Brown spoke as part of the World's Congress of Representative Women, one of the many forums of the World's Fair. Held May 15 through May 22, 1893, in the World's Congress Auxiliary Building at the fairgrounds, the congress organized eighty-one meetings and attracted more than 150,000 people. Of the five hundred women who spoke, representing twenty-seven different countries, only six of the featured speakers were African American women. The words these women spoke at the World's Fair thereby stood as representative of an "African American women's standpoint" and carried tremendous significance. Their speeches, I argue, were points of origin for New Negro womanhood. In front of a predominantly white audience and with the world listening, the words and presence of these African American women signaled a new era of black women's voices audaciously demanding to be heard and valued on their own terms. The discourse of New Negro womanhood preemptively responded to the growing popularity of Jim Crow being etched into state constitutions as well as the rise of the white-woman-centered "Women's Era." Cooper's words in particular resonated as those spoken by someone with experiences as a black woman in Washington and as a black woman with access to a national audience. Her local experiences, derived from living and working in a U.S. black cultural and political center, positioned Cooper as a dynamic interlocutor of African American women's experiences.

The appointment of Fannie Barrier Williams to a position in which she gathered exhibits for the women's hall provided black women, although on very limited and restrictive terms, an opportunity to take part in a monumental moment in U.S. history. Each of the women who spoke at the fair used her speech to directly address the lives and aspirations of black women. A burgeoning consciousness manifested in the words Cooper, Williams, Coppin, Early, Harper, and Brown delivered at the Columbia Exposition. During the speech titled "The Intellectual Progress of Colored Women in the United States since the Emancipation Proclamation," which brought Williams to greater national prominence, she proclaimed,

> Less than thirty years ago the term progress as applied to colored women of African descent in the United States would have been an anomaly. The recognition of that term today as appropriate is a fact full of interesting significance. That the discussion of progressive womanhood in this great assemblage of the representative women of the world is considered incomplete without some account of the colored women's status is a most noteworthy evidence that we have not failed to impress ourselves on the higher side of American life.[11]

Williams also heralded possibility for African American women. Delivering her words to an audience of primarily white women, she affirmed, "The exceptional career of our women will yet stamp itself indelibly upon the thought of this country."[12] Williams set a tone for a distinct African American women's standpoint at this highly publicized and massively attended event. She, like her African American women counterparts, was direct, unapologetic, and critical.

Thematically similar, though more geographically rooted in the South, Coppin, Early, and Brown decried the pervasive racism, sexism, and poverty African American women faced. Jackson told the audience at the World's Congress of Representative Women that "there is a time coming when prejudices, discriminations, proscriptions, and persecutions on account of what is accidental will all pass away."[13] Jackson's words resounded as a clear critique of the "accidental" fiction of race. An optimistic tone pervaded the words of each of the featured African American women speakers. Despite their initial exclusion from the official program, they seized the opportunity to speak for and on behalf of black women and offered ideas rooted in history, hope, and ideas about self-determination. More specifically, their words foreshadowed a growing number of African Americans desiring new constructs for identifying their experiences. Nowhere was the desire more palpable than among black women in the nation's capital at the turn of twentieth century.

The marginalization of African Americans, and more specifically African American women at the Columbian Exposition, reflected the continued inferior political, social, economic, and cultural status that blacks in the United States occupied. On the World's Fair stage, these women confronted the hypocrisy of the narrative of national progress in the face on inertia of issues regarding racial and gender inequality. Similar to the nation's capital, the World's Fair boasted unprecedented but nevertheless limited possibilities for African American women to take center stage. Although Washington was an African American urban center, black women living there confronted the harsh and pervasive realities of Jim Crow racism, intra- and interracial sexism, and institutional patriarchy. These realities often led to a silencing of the women living in and migrating to the nation's capital in search of new opportunities.

From the Nation's Capital to the World

During the late nineteenth and early twentieth centuries, millions of African Americans moved to cities such as New York, Chicago, Baltimore, Philadelphia, and Washington in search of opportunities and to escape the harsh realities of southern racism.[14] Black migration to Washington between 1860 and 1900, however, had more profound demographic implications than it did in other urban areas during the same period. Ultimately, between 1860 and 1930 the population of black women in the District of Columbia increased by more than 800 percent. The federal census of 1860 reported that 8,402 black women lived in Washington; in 1890, the total was 41,581; by 1930, there were 69,843 black women living there.[15] By 1910, Washington had a total black population of 94,000. Whereas Harlem attracted tens of thousands of African Americans in the interwar years, Washington throughout the early to mid-twentieth century continued to have the greatest concentration of African Americans in any of the large U.S. metropolitan areas.[16]

The Great Migration is significant in terms of understanding the explosion of black communities in urban cities, more specifically in urban cities of the North. Although migration to Washington during the late nineteenth and early twentieth centuries played a significant role in Washington's becoming a New Negro city, the district also had a thriving black community prior to this mass migration. On July 3, 1926, the *Baltimore African American* published a piece titled "Most Negroes Per Sq Mile in D.C."[17] Kelly Miller, a leading black intellectual and Washington resident, pondered if Washington was the "Negro's Heaven," in the December 1926 issue of the National Urban League's *Opportunity: A Journey of Negro Life*.[18] Beyond acknowledging the growing and substantial population of African Americans in Washington, Miller's question about D.C.'s status as a Negro heaven identified the city as a contender for the "black capital" of the United States.

For African American women migrating from the South during the late nineteenth and early twentieth centuries as well as for women of multi-generation Washington lineage, the prospect of moving from enslaved or freedwoman to Colored to New Negro attracted them to the nation's capital.[19] Washington, as a black intellectual and cultural capital since the mid-nineteenth century, offered a space where African American women could imagine the possibilities of being a New Negro woman. Although racial segregation, violence, and discrimination thrived in Washington, the allure of the promise of a better life in D.C. led to the emergence of a diverse African American community. Black Washington became a New Negro city.

Cooper traveled from her home in Washington, D.C., to speak at the World's Fair. Although a prominent figure in Washington, as a teacher and recently published author, Cooper was one of many African American women residing in Washington challenging racial and gender oppression. This book does not focus on Washington because it was the only city where these seismic shifts occurred in how African American women struggled for self-determination; *Colored No More* homes in on the nation's capital because it is a ripe and understudied site for exploring the voices of African American women during the New Negro era. With its sizable and rapidly growing population of African Americans, and particularly African American women, the political, intellectual, and cultural currents circulating nationally and transnationally regarding African American women's "place" in the world inscribed the lives of African American women in Washington. The city offered unique possibilities. It boasted a substantial pre–Great Migration black population and was home to some of the preeminent black institutions in the United States, including M Street High School and Howard University.

The specific experiences of Washington's New Negro women resonate with those of New Negro women in Chicago, New York, Philadelphia, Baltimore, and other major cities impacted by the influx of African American women in the late-nineteenth and early twentieth century. The specific experiences of Washington's New Negro women also encompass unique, place-based realities that intersect with and diverge from those of New Negro women in other urban centers.

As the nation's capital, Washington literally and symbolically played a central role in African Americans' and women's activism in the early twentieth century. From marches for women's suffrage, such as the one held in downtown Washington in March 1913, to the founding of Howard University as an open-admissions university catering to recently freed persons, Washington thrived as a hotbed for national activism for marginalized communities. The stature of Washington as a national city coupled with the city's local politics, dynamics, and communities established a space for African American women to negotiate Jim Crow realities and to shape liberatory discourses rooted in the distinctive experiences of African American women.

Re(Imagining) the New Negro

Demarcating the commencement of the New Negro era, particularly for African American women within the 1890s as opposed to the interwar era, renders visible new possibilities for examining the lives of and ideas espoused by African American women. Although Henry Louis Gates Jr. chronicled a variety of meanings and usages of New Negro in "The Trope of a New Negro and the Reconstruction of the Image of the Black," a masculine-centered historiography continues to pervade how many scholars discuss New Negroes.[20] Proclaiming oneself a New Negro was, as Gates explains, "a bold and audacious act of language, signifying the will to power, to dare to recreate a race by renaming it, despite the dubiousness of the venture."[21] For African American women, New Negro also signified a desire to newly imagine black womanhood. African American women, because of laws and prevailing social norms and expectations, could not always fully exercise control over their lives and bodies in even the very limited ways in which African American men could. Nevertheless, both individually and collectively, African American women during the late nineteenth and early twentieth centuries sought to more fully articulate their political, consumptive, social, sexual, economic, and professional desires. New Negro womanhood was a discursive, imagined, and lived space for African American female claimants of a new horizon for which African American women could strive. This emergent ethos had local, national, and transnational implications for shifting ideas about African American women's place in a rapidly changing world.

These women moved into a wider array of economic, political, social, and cultural possibilities available in the public sphere, while redefining their "roles" in private and domestic spheres. African American women etched out the parameters of individual and collective aspirations and desires within a modern world in which they were treated as third-class citizens. New Negro womanhood was not a monolithic experience but rather a multifaceted and fluid space in which women could explore the possibilities and limitations of U.S. social, political, cultural, and economic life in the late nineteenth and early twentieth centuries. African American women could move in and out of this porously (un)bounded space as they shaped their political, social, and cultural identities.

New Negro womanhood was a mosaic, authorial, and constitutive individual and collective identity inhabited by African American women seeking to transform themselves and their communities through demanding autonomy and equality for African American women. Composed of race women, blues women, playwrights, domestics, teachers, mothers, sex workers, policy workers, beauticians, fortune-tellers, suffragists, same-gender couples, artists, activists, and innovators, "New Negro women," as a collective political/social/cultural identifier, encapsulated a wide range of African American women's experiences. A desire for freedom and equality rooted in the specific realities of African American women connected this continuum of experiences. As African Americans and as women, New Negro women invested in upending racial, gender, and class inequality. Modes of expression and opportunities for activism varied among these women, but an underlying vision of equality framed the lives of New Negro women.

My definition of New Negro womanhood derives from discourses created by and about African American women as well as their lived experiences during the late nineteenth and early twentieth centuries. I want to offer new ways to think about what constituted the discourse of New Negro womanhood. As early as the late nineteenth century, in spaces such as higher education, beauty shops, writing salons, and consumer culture, African American women began carving out the terrain upon which a New Negro woman could thrive. The vestiges of slavery, the contemporaneous strictures of Jim Crow, and the continual relegation of women to inferior statuses inscribed the context in which New Negro womanhood evolved. New Negro women strove to understand, and in some cases to establish, on their own terms, their "place" in the world. Their approaches included radical, progressive, gradualist, and conservative political standpoints. Each standpoint addressed (although to differing extents) who the New Negro woman was and what she could be. Resisting definitions constructed by others resulted in a flourishing of African American women's activities, subcultures, organizations, and institutions. African American women in this era created a space for demanding the right to self-articulate and for imagining a world that viewed black women as full and equal participants.

The range of African American women's experiences and perspectives during this era refuted any notion of a monolithic, singular "black woman's experience." New Negro womanhood connected women singing and enjoying songs about polyamory, same-gender desire, or sexual (dis)satisfaction (such as Ma Rainey's "Bo-Weevil Blues") with women trumpeting the high moral capacity of African American women.[22] The connections, while not necessarily explicit, signaled a diverse collection of women-centered investments in individual and collective freedom. Within a New Negro women's ethos, freedom from ideas about the inherent hypersexuality of black women as well as freedom from sexual norms and conventions intertwined. These seemingly disparate iterations of African American womanhood similarly indicate a consciousness-in-progress among African American women. Demanding sexual freedom as well as freedom from damaging stereotypes required an interest in both the idea and the actualization of a New Negro woman.

Identifying as New Negro women signaled a desire to move from the third-class status of Colored woman. Despite the move from enslaved or freedwoman to Colored citizen, Colored encapsulated a dehumanized and inferior political and social status. Colored largely remained an identifier for a disenfranchised population of people within the United States. This disenfranchisement was further complicated by contemporaneous gender norms and conventions, which situated women, regardless of race and often class, as second-class citizens as well. Consequently, African American women occupied a political/social identity that excluded them from both white and male privilege. Class privilege also evaded most African American women in the late nineteenth and early twentieth centuries. African American women in same-gender loving relationships could not claim a space within intraracial or interracial heteropatriarchal privilege. Even in Washington, a city with a comparatively sizable population of black people in same-gender relationships and expressing same-sex desire, black women were "held to a higher standard of propriety and had even less freedom and mobility . . . to act on their sexual feelings."[23] Upward mobility to equal citizenship for African

American women, therefore, encompassed challenging racial, gender, class, and sexuality status quos. The intersection of these challenges was at the core of New Negro womanhood and is the focus of *Colored No More*.

Complicating and Gendering "New Negro"

New Negro, as an identifier for both individuals and an epoch, continues to resonate as a racial concept. Without question, race, racism, and struggles for racial equality play a significant role in the New Negro era, and consequently race (questions) should pervade historical accounts of the lived experiences of African Americans in the late nineteenth and early twentieth centuries. Recent interventions into New Negro studies, however, demand that gender and sexuality as analytical frameworks play more integral roles in studies of the New Negro era. Moving beyond chronicling the contributions of women to the "New Negro movement," scholars such as Davarian Baldwin, Erin Chapman, Cherene Sherrard-Johnson, Koritha Mitchell, and Tiffany Gill implicitly and explicitly push historical and historiographical framings of the New Negro era to gender our understandings of the lives of African Americans during the Jim Crow era.[24] These scholars push the subfield of New Negro studies to reconsider the African American experience in the late nineteenth and early twentieth centuries.

Colored, as a distinct racial designation that became synonymous with Jim Crow–era racial segregation and antiblack racial subjugation, also requires a historiographical remapping. The experience of being Colored encompassed gender, class, regional, and class-based particularities. African Americans in the late nineteenth and twentieth centuries experienced antiblackness, racial terror, and racial subjugation in gender-specific ways. Although women were victims of lynching and other forms of nonsexual violence, the predominating historical narrative of racial violence from this era pivots around the lynching of black men. Crystal Feimster's work is a notable exception to this framing, as she excavates the history of lynching black women.[25] Feimster centers black women not only as antilynching activists or as the mothers/wives/sisters of lynched black men and boys, but as victims of antiblack racial terrorizing. Nearly two hundred documented lynchings of black women occurred during Jim Crow. The lynched, brutalized, and publicly violated black male body remains the primary historical signifier of this era of U.S. racial terror. While I do not seek to diminish the significance of this signifier, its preeminence as the singular signifier re-inscribes a historical narrative in which we discuss black women as secondary or "less violated" victims of antiblack racial terror.

Black men, women, and gender-nonconforming people cohabited the spaces of antiblack racial terror.

The scant though gradually growing visibility of the battered, brutalized, raped, and assailed black female body in our collective historical memory propels a primarily masculinist, historical narrative of African American lived experiences in the Jim Crow era. Masculinist framings of antiblackness during Jim Crow also contribute to contemporary discussions about antiblack racial violence. Comparisons made between the lynching of black men and boys during Jim Crow and the killing of unarmed black men and boys by police such as Tamir Rice, Michael Brown, and Eric Garner rely on a historical narrative of black men and boys as the primary victims of racial violence.[26] Thinking about African American women and girls as victims and violable subjects during the New Negro era allows for us to understand how and why gender mattered and continues to matter in the operations and praxes of antiblackness. This intervention does not stop at "we must remember black women and girls as victims too" but shifts our lenses to consider critically the relationship between gender and antiblackness.

Moving beyond a "women were there too" approach to redressing the erasure and/or limited visibility of black women in New Negro studies, I reframe "colored" as a historically specific, racialized *and* gendered identity. I seek to create a new entry point for examining the lives of African American women in the New Negro Era. In *Prove It on Me: New Negroes, Sex, and Popular Culture in the 1920s*, Erin Chapman asserts that "there was no concerted New Negro feminism advocating a woman-centered racial advancement effort or openly confronting the intra-racial masculinism and patriarchy."[27] Chapman highlights the "dissatisfaction" of some New Negro women with the idealization of race motherhood and the limited representations of black womanhood in public cultural spheres. I do not dispute this well-articulated argument about the non-existence of a "concerted New Negro feminism"; however, several of the women in *Colored No More* do explicitly address African American masculinism and heteropatriarchy in black communities. Furthermore, my interest as a feminist historian in New Negro women does not stem from a desire to identify or claim these women as black feminists per se. I unearth New Negro women-centered spaces, discourses, and sensibilities that directly and indirectly challenged the prioritizing of black men as the primary categorical signifier of the Colored experience and to reconceptualize New Negro as it pertains to African American women's lives. Exploring both the communities and cultural spaces New Negro women created as well as the intra- and interracial gender ideologies that shaped these spaces and their lived experiences allows for new understandings of what it meant to be Colored.

Shifting Colored from solely a racial construct to a distinct gender marker also renders legible the particular ways in which Jim Crow–era racial identifications relied heavily on hypergendered proscriptives and figurations for African Americans. The Jim Crow racial status quo produced a new set of challenges for African Americans seeking to articulate post-Emancipation personhood. Consequently, the establishment of what constituted African American womanhood and manhood, respectively, propelled intraracial discourses and projects of racial identity, articulation, and expressivity. Gender norms and conventions within and outside of African American communities played an integral role in the formation of a turn-of-the-century Colored imaginary. The evolving emphasis on race manhood and race womanhood as conduits to racial progress under this era of white-supremacist racial terror inscribed African American racial articulations' grounding in emergent gender-performance expectations. To combat dehumanization, dispossession, and erasure, African Americans used gender performance as a site of meaning making. "Gender—ideas about manhood and womanhood," Martha Jones explains "was at the core of this public culture from its first moments and would continue to shape its contours and possibilities for decades to come."[28] The lived experience of Colored in the United States was inextricably connected to late-nineteenth and early-twentieth-century ideas about (un) acceptable, expected, and aspirational gender performances.

This book also interrogates and challenges the temporal, and ultimately historiographical, framing of the New Negro era. Typically demarcated as an interwar movement and era, the historicizing of the New Negro era pivots around a masculinist understanding of historical experiences. When Fannie Barrier Williams delivered her career-defining address at the World's Fair in 1893, she demanded recognition of the plight and intellectual and moral capacities of African American women and for African American women's rights. "The colored women," Williams affirmed, "as well as all women, will realize that the inalienable right to life, liberty, and the pursuit of happiness is a maxim that will become more blessed in its significance when the hand of woman shall take it from its sepulture in books and make it the gospel of every-day life and the unerring guide in the relations of all men, women, and children."[29] Her words at the exposition, in conjunction with those of Cooper, Coppin, Early, Harper, and Brown, shed light on an emerging New Negro women-centered ethos. Although these women were more explicitly identified as "New Women of Color" in the late nineteenth century, the rhetoric, activism, and political standpoints of activists such as Williams and Cooper indicated a distinct historical moment for African American women. The era of the New Negro woman commenced not with the conclusion of World War I but much earlier, as African American women encountered the harsh realities of Jim Crow, the failed promise of a "Reconstructed" nation, and both intra- and interracial sexism, which prominently manifested in the lack of suffrage for all women and pervasive gender norms and expectations that dictated "appropriate" activities for women in the late nineteenth century. African American women sat at the intersection of what Jones identified as "disappointments of the nadir and the optimism of the woman's era."[30] This combination of optimism and disappointment produced a fertile ground for African American women imagining New Negro womanhood.

Moving from Colored to New Negro woman as a signifier unveiled a resistance to a singular and solely raced-based understanding of identity and inequality. Notably, prior to this historical era African American women such as Maria Stewart and Phyllis Wheatley demanded recognition of their double/multiple identities as blacks and as women; nevertheless, the New Negro era encompassed a surge of African American women pushing back against racism, sexism, and other forms of oppression. The emphasis on simultaneity of oppression became increasingly salient in the lives of New Negro women. The strictures of Colored as a racialized-gendered-class and sociopolitical identifier for African American women often relegated these women to the margins. Consequently, African American women sought to redefine Colored through participation in and creation of arenas that affirmed their voices, perspectives, and humanity. The nation's capital served as a primary battleground for this multifaceted redefinition of African American womanhood.

Building upon Jones's groundbreaking work on public culture and "the woman question," I explore the lives of African American women in Washington to uncover how these women shaped public discourses on what it meant to be a New Negro woman in one of the fastest-growing African American urban centers. Competing pressures to establish race- and/or gender-based solidarity compelled many African American women to envision a space that recognized the wholeness of their humanity. African American women seeking to upend both racial and gender inequalities existed at a point of convergence between women's movements and African American freedom struggles. The saliency of racism, sexism, and heteropatriarchy for African American women resulted in these women attempting to carve out a space for resistance that accounted for combatting multiple oppressive forces. Jane

Crow, as a conceptual framework for understanding systemic sexism and patriarchy, was not formally identified until 1965 by activist, attorney, and legal scholar Pauli Murray; however, its existence predated its accurate naming and precise description.[31] Furthermore, the term perfectly identified a set of gender-based realities African American women confronted. New Negro womanhood, therefore, also developed into a resistive standpoint that could embrace the complexity of African American women's experiences and shed light on the third-class citizenship afforded to them in the United States.

I center the "woman question" in my attempt to parse the meaning of New Negro for African American women in Washington. I concur with Paul Gilroy's assertion that "the cultures of diaspora blacks can be profitably interpreted as expressions of and commentaries upon ambivalences generated by modernity and their locations within it."[32] Within the space of New Negro womanhood, African American women struggled against interracial and intraracial political and cultural currents to claim a distinct voice and place within the modern world. This struggle occurred in numerous spaces and evolved in the wake of the failures of Reconstruction, the codification of Jim Crow, systemic sexism, rapid industrialization, urbanization, and Progressive Era and woman's era ideals.

African American women in Washington configured spaces explicitly to critique the inequalities African American women faced in the late nineteenth and early twentieth centuries. "African American politics," Patricia Hill Collins explains, "have been profoundly influenced by a Black gender ideology that ranks race and gender."[33] Black women could not escape this black gender ideology during the New Negro era. Both proactively and in response, some African American women strategically manipulated and occasionally challenged outright the existing gender ideologies that privileged racial inequality as the most significant form of oppression.[34] The intraracial contestation of African American gender ideology by African American women is key to understanding New Negro womanhood.

The failure of Reconstruction as a long-term solution for the tremendous legacy of slavery and for the lack of citizenship rights for all blacks contributed to New Negro womanhood's emergence. In addition to struggles against white supremacy and societal sexism and patriarchy, many African American women remained cynical about the promises of either racial advancement or women's rights movements for African American women. The sentiments Anna Julia Cooper shared at the World's Fair and in *A Voice from the South* echoed this collective cynicism. Aligning with either or both movements occurred, but not without vehement critiques and intragroup debates about the role of African American women in African American and women's freedom and equality struggles, respectively. Leaders and organizations focused upon African American racial advancement or women's rights often failed to acknowledge that African American women faced a particular set of social, political, and cultural realities. The African American women who spoke at the Columbian Exposition, like many black women throughout the New Negro era, illuminated specific realities for African American women. One of the most glaring examples of this unique position was the fight for suffrage.[35] Although the Fifteenth Amendment secured the right to vote for African American men, state and local governments enacted poll taxes, literacy tests, grandfathering clauses and other legal obstacles that re-disenfranchised black men. Furthermore, violence, terror, and intimidation also prevented African American men from exercising their right to vote. Women, regardless of race, had no legal standing at the national level to vote. The decision to enfranchise black men and not women, specifically white women, had profound effects on interracial cooperation between African American and white women's activists. The interplay of the passage of the Fifteenth Amendment, the re-disenfranchisement of black men, and the lack of support from many white women suffragists for universal suffrage situated African American women at a crossroads where some part of their identity remained unrecognized and devalued. The many roles of African American women in combatting Jim Crow are well documented, particularly within extant histories of the New Negro era. The framing of the New Negro activism and discourse, however, almost always begins in the interwar period, several years after what I identify as the formative years of New Negro womanhood. When women become central to our historical narratives of the Jim Crow era, herstories emerge that produce new questions and insights about the meanings of and struggles for freedom, liberation, and equality.

Turn-of-the-Century African American Womanhood

Notwithstanding the diversity of African American women's activities from the turn of the twentieth century to the Great Depression, politics of respectability, as the framework through which to understand black women's participation in intellectual, cultural, social, and political strivings outside of their homes, remain central to how scholars examine African American women's history in the late nineteenth and early twentieth centuries.[36] A significant body of the scholarship within African American women's studies focuses on what Evelyn Brooks Higginbottham identifies (citing Darlene

Clark Hine also) as "black women's adherence to Victorian ideology, as well as their self-representation as 'super moral'" in an effort to understand how black women navigated public spaces made dangerous by the conventions of white supremacy.[37] Paula Giddings, Deborah Gray White, Evelyn Brooks Higginbotham, Rosalyn Terborg-Penn, Gerda Lerner and several other scholars of black women echo Hine's assertion that the politics of black respectability "was perceived as crucial not only to the protection and upward mobility of black women but also to the attainment of respect, justice, and opportunity for all black Americans."[38] These politics, as defined by historian Joyce Ann Hanson, relied on "confidence in women's higher moral capacity, the power of educational advancement, Christian responsibility, and community activism."[39] The performance of black feminine propriety was a central tenet of the politics of respectability in the Jim Crow era.

While much of the scholarship emphasizes the productive and empowering aspects of the politics of respectability, scholars such as Tera Hunter, Victoria Wolcott, Angela Davis, and Glenda Gilmore centralize black respectability politics by exploring the experiences of women remaking or rejecting these politics. Respectability politics are integral to examining black women's experiences during the New Negro era. My conceptualization of New Negro women presents women who overtly rejected adherence to Victorian ideology, who viewed these respectability politics as elitist, and who strategically invested in black respectability politics to articulate modern political and aesthetic identities. *Colored No More* turns a critical lens to Washington women who questioned the utility of respectability politics for black women as well as black women in Washington who invested in hyperperformances of feminine propriety to render themselves politically significant and visible. From hairstyles to careers, New Negro women demanded respect for their individual voices, aspirations, and bodies on a spectrum of terms, although not in identical ways.

Urbanization, industrialization, and the rise of mass media ushered in a new era in which African American women could challenge their relegation to third-class citizenship in the United States. Foregrounding possibility, African American women's capacity for thriving in this "new world," and a particular set of African American women-centered concerns, New Negro women demanded not only to be seen and heard but also to be incorporated and integrated into the processes, markets, institutions, and discourses propelling the political and cultural currents at the heart of remaking the United States. Refusing to serve as bystanders or subjects/objects acted upon by these major political, social, economic, and cultural shifts, African American

Figure 1. U Street, 1920. General Photograph Collection of the Historical Society of Washington, D.C.

women asserted their right to create and contribute to modernizing projects, particularly those that emphasized equality as a central tenet of a modern democracy. The obstacles for these women were numerous, yet the women confronted them in spite of the realities of segregation, discrimination, racial and gender stereotypes, patriarchy, sexism, and restrictive gender and sexual mores. These realities also cemented their status as New Negro women. A collective confrontation of multiple status quo flourished in Washington.

The Nation's Capital: A City of New Negro Women

This book examines the evolution of New Negro womanhood in the nation's capital through connecting various iterations of African American women challenging white supremacy, intraracial sexism, and heteropatriarchy. New Negro womanhood manifested in the philosophical writings of women such as Lucy Diggs Slowe, who challenged gender inequality in higher education and gender/sexual norms in her personal life. It also existed among African American women who created and purchased racially marked and gendered products specifically targeting black women. From these differing yet interconnected African American women's spaces comes a black-women-centered discourse of struggles for freedom and equality during New Negro era.

Varying strains of New Negro womanhood collided in Washington. Understanding how the nation's capital developed into an intellectual and cultural capital for African Americans requires an unearthing of the voices of and contemporaneous discourses about the city's African American women community during the late nineteenth and early twentieth centuries. Cutting across class, neighborhood, organizational affiliation, and other distinctions among Washington's African American women, New Negro womanhood as a conceptual framework renders visible how seemingly disparate communities of women connected with one another. Undercurrents of self-actualization, autonomy, urbanity, and modernity conjoin communities of African American women in Washington; they also allow distinctions, diverse perspectives, and competing ideals to thrive. Although no singular community of African American women existed, a shared history and a collective sense of disenfranchisement inextricably bound together Washington's African American women.

In her book *Women and the Work of Benevolence: Morality, Politics, and Class in the Nineteenth Century United States* Lori Ginzberg discusses the shifting political contexts and meanings of women's reform activism in the nineteenth century. Her work illuminates how white women's reform activists reimagined and reconfigured womanhood through their benevolence-based activism. For African American women in Washington, several possibilities existed for these women to redefine their roles in society. Differing horizons existed for upper-middle-class white women reform activists and for African American women in Washington. The thread of possibility and the desire for social change connected these women within a broader context of activism. Furthermore, equality as a goal, although with starkly divergent meanings among these women, also propelled activism.

The unique character of Washington as a "City of New Negro Women" derived from the political, cultural, and social strivings of its constituents. More specifically, by focusing on a specific and understudied African American community with a substantial population of black women, I uncover a distinct, New Negro–era, gender discourse. Through using gender as a primary analytical lens for engaging the voices of African American women in Washington during the early twentieth century, I present New Negro and Colored as both racialized and gendered monikers. Building upon Evelyn Brooks Higginbotham's examination of the gendered nature of race, I use Colored as a racial/gender identifier that accounts for how both the racial and gender identities of black women affected how they experienced and navigated the New Negro era.[40] Class and sexuality also played integral roles in how black women moved through the New Negro era. Similar to Cooper's *A Voice from the South*, this book magnifies the voices of African American women in Jim Crow–era Washington, D.C. Understanding Colored and New

Negro as gender and racial categories allows for particular similarities and differences between black women's and black men's lives to become more visible. New Negro women emerged as interlocutors of discourses about the modern world and challenged their invisibility and marginalization on a daily basis. These challenges ranged in their execution, but they do overlap through individual and collective desires for greater freedom and possibility for black women.

I use higher education, black beauty culture, women's suffrage activism, and literary activism in Washington to examine how black women grappled with and configured ideas about African American womanhood. Each of these areas provided a distinct context in which African American women in Washington transgressed boundaries of both racial and gender hierarchies and aspired to greater visibility, mobility, and legibility. On a Saturday in Washington during the early twentieth century, a black middle-class woman could have a hair appointment at a local black-owned salon, meet with other black suffragists about drafting an editorial piece for a black newspaper that connected women's enfranchisement with racial advancement, and attend a black-female-authored play performed at M Street High School by students of the Department of Dramatic Arts at Howard University. These women moved across arenas of public life and crafted self-articulations of African American womanhood anchored in contesting the oppressive status of Colored.

New Negro womanhood sought to undo intraracial policing of women's lives and a racial caste system that afforded black people second-class citizenship. From both inter- and intraracial standpoints, participatory belonging was at stake. Securing particular rights for black women that accounted for their marginalization in both racial justice and gender justice movements became a more pressing concern for many African American women during the New Negro era. Their lived experiences, activism, and standpoints provided unique and wide-ranging responses to the Negro and woman questions. They raised their voices.

Although largely grounded in the lived experiences of African American women in Washington at the turn of the century, this book also uncovers the discourses of New Negro womanhood in which African American women engaged: advertisements, publications, plays, poetry, editorials, and other printed ephemera that captured an emergent sense of possibility for black women living in the nation's capital. Focusing on how black women self-documented and how others documented them provides an entry point for understanding the various and complex ways New Negro womanhood evolved in a rapidly changing urban center. Notwithstanding the reality of a paucity of scholarship on African American women in Washington, this is not a traditional historical examination of the lives of African American women. Through careful analyses of competing, complementary, and complex discourses and narratives authored by and or tailored to African American women, I assert that New Negro womanhood functioned both as a lived reality and as a meaningful space of racialized and gendered articulation. African American women sought a new, distinct vocabulary for living in the world as Colored.

The analysis of plays, poetry, journal articles, editorials, and other printed media offers rich insight into New Negro womanhood as an imagined and aspirational space. Emphasizing these narratives as sites of inquiry does not discount the importance of the quotidian and material experiences of African American women in Washington. My intentional investigation of the discursive sheds light on New Negro womanhood as representationally significant. Ideas about the New Negro woman in Washington circulated at one of the nation's most lauded black universities, in Washington's black press, in the scholarly writings of African American women intellectuals, and in the literary works of numerous Washington-based African American women. These ideas contributed to how African American women thought about Colored as a static, sociohistorical referential, which signified a particular disenfranchised and disempowered status. For these women, representing Colored meant something beyond depicting a Jim Crow category. New Negro women, through narratives and discourse, pushed an understanding of *Colored* that centered African American women's distinct experiences with the ubiquitous realities of racial subjugation and gender subordination.

Chapter 1, "Climbing the Hilltop," explores New Negro womanhood at one of the nation's leading black institutions, Howard University, through the experience of education and women's activist Lucy Diggs Slowe. By the first decade of the twentieth century, Howard University had emerged as the premier institution for higher learning for African Americans. I chronicle the experiences of Slowe at Howard during the early twentieth century to highlight extant intraracial gender ideologies and conventions as well as Jim Crow racial politics. Although women could attend and work at Howard, African American gender ideology and restrictive gender policies often limited African American women's opportunities as students, faculty, and staff. Slowe was arguably the most vocal advocate for African American women at Howard during her tenure in the 1920s and 1930s. She demanded that African American women be prepared for the "modern world" and that they be full and equal participants in public culture. Her thirty-plus-years' affiliation with Howard as both student and administrator makes her an ideal subject with which to map the emergence of New Negro womanhood discourse at this prestigious university.

The chapter presents Howard as an elite and exclusive site for New Negro womanhood while simultaneously asserting the symbolic significance of Howard University for African American women living in and moving to Washington as well as for black people across the nation. Although most African American women in Washington could not and did not attend or work at Howard, this institution was foundational to a sense of possibility that drove intellectual and cultural strivings of African American women in New Negro–era Washington. The chapter uses Slowe's story to unveil how ingrained African American gender ideology was at an institution lauded for its progressive politics, its nurturing of black intellectuals, and its involvement in the black cultural explosion of the early twentieth century. Furthermore, Howard was indicative of black institutional cultures rooted in conservative gender ideologies.

Chapter 2 takes a slightly different approach to the discourse of New Negro womanhood. Using black beauty culture in Washington, and specifically the advertisements that emerged out of this aesthetic-based, race enterprise, I show how African American women's beauty culture touted aesthetics as a way to reinvent African American womanhood and to publicly present African American women as new, urbane, and modern. African American beauty culture provides a space for considering the interplay of black womanhood, technology, consumerism, entrepreneurship, and prevailing aesthetic ideologies that embodied distinct racial, gender, and class implications. As a product of urbanity as well as an enterprise and a discourse, black beauty culture was deeply entrenched in politics of appearance and bodily adornment.[41] These politics also influenced other aspects of New Negro women's lives and intersected with political and cultural agendas of the New Negro movement. African American beauty culture thrived as a site of reimagining for New Negro women. African American women could partake in numerous roles within this culture, including producer, consumer, and manufacturer. Questions of autonomy and authorship affected how black women in Washington engaged bodily aesthetics and the attendant economic, cultural, and political discourses during the New Negro era. In a significant way, these aesthetics informed and intertwined with one of the most pressing political issues for African American women during the late nineteenth and early twentieth centuries: suffrage.

African American women's suffrage activism took on new forms in the first few decades of the twentieth century. For New Negro women, this shift in strategy pivoted around using the politics of appearance and adornment and of black respectability to perform a political identity that represented the black suffragist as a modern woman. In chapter 3, I trace the history of black women's suffrage activism in Washington up to the National Suffrage March of 1913. I contrast the more theatrical and eccentric approach of white suffragists during this national demonstration with black suffragists' performance of respectability politics through their "refined," "polished," and "urbane" styling. I explicitly connect the discourses derived from black beauty culture to show how African American women reconfigured their political identities. Politics of appearance and bodily adornment inscribed the political culture of New Negro suffragists. Their usage and performance of feminine propriety and "quietness" were powerful tools of resistance to prevailing racial and gender stereotypes of black women being unfeminine or libidinous. Their engagement with bodily aesthetics as a political battleground for enfranchisement introduced a new era of African American women's political activism.

In chapter 4, I explore how African American women playwrights in Washington created a community for black women to express their perspectives on pressing political issues and historical topics through the arts. In the 1920s, African American writer Georgia Douglass Johnson invited writers to her home on Saturday evenings to encourage the development of a cohesive and supportive community of black writers. The S Street Salon was a viable space for African American women writers to think about their poems, plays, short stories, and novels. Many of the New Negro–era literary works produced by African American women participants of the S Street Salon tackled politically significant and contentious issues such as racial and sexual violence and women's reproductive rights. I further de-center New York, therefore, as the premier urban center in which New Negro culture thrived. The S Street Salon was one of the most significant intellectual, political, and cultural communities of the New Negro era. This community incubated the expressivity of an elite, artisan class of African American women. The women of the S Street Salon inserted their stories and their voices into black public culture through creating an African American women-centered counterpublic. On Saturday nights this community gathered to support, critique, and interact with each other in an informal space of creativity and expressivity. Although black men participated, this gathering often provided a place for black women seeking to find a voice through the dramatic arts and other creative, literary outlets.

Their voices contributed to a distinct but diversified discourse on New Negro womanhood.

Chapter 5 centers black women in Washington during the New Negro era within the contexts of African American freedom struggles and feminist activism. By shifting the temporal framing of the New Negro era from the interwar era to the late nineteenth century, African American women become more visible and legible as New Negroes. The arenas black women created during this period continue to shape the lives of black women in the United States. Washington remains an important city for African American women seeking new opportunities. Despite recent gentrification of Washington's historical black neighborhoods, the legacy of Washington's New Negro women is ever present, from a statue erected to honor a black Greek-letter organization for women founded at Howard University in 1913, Delta Sigma Theta Sorority, to an elementary school named after Lucy Diggs Slowe. The stories of African American women in Washington during this era remain largely unknown, but *Colored No More* attempts to uncover some of their voices to help reconceptualize New Negro womanhood.

In the face of the continued pernicious effects of Jim Crow racism and perpetual and institutional sexism, African American women in Washington made significant strides toward a more equal urban center. Although some progress proved ephemeral, the long-lasting effects of these movements for equality and justice included an unwavering sensibility of determination among African American women. Witnessing the possibility of social and political change empowered African American women of D.C. to struggle for the kind of city, nation, and world they envisioned. Black women were among the most marginalized and isolated from dominant institutions and occupied the lowest tier in the city's gendered, racial, and class hierarchy. The marginalization black women confronted in Washington mirrored that of black women throughout the United States during the New Negro era. The distinct political, social, economic, and cultural opportunities extant in D.C., however, established Washington as a unique urban landscape that facilitated the actualization of New Negro womanhood in both theory and praxis. The voices of and stories about these women offer unique insight into how African American women responded to and created meaningful shifts in the U.S. cultural imaginary. New Negro women in Washington offered new meanings of freedom and equality that acknowledged the fullness of black women's humanity.

1

Climbing the Hilltop

New Negro Womanhood at Howard University

> Regardless of the wish of many parents that their daughters become adjuncts of "man," modern life forces them to be individuals in much the same sense as men are individuals.
>
> —Lucy Diggs Slowe, "The Higher Education of Negro Women," 1933

For African American women in the late nineteenth and early twentieth centuries, moving from Colored to New Negro woman pivoted around questions and concerns about the role of African American women in a rapidly changing "modern world." Industrialization coupled with the urbanization of a sizable part of the African American population in the United States contributed to the emergence of new ideas about racial progress and advancement. African American institutions, organizations, and clubs established during Reconstruction, the post-Reconstruction era, and first decades of Jim Crow provided structural entities through which African Americans imagined and advocated for their rights as full and equal participants in U.S. democracy. African American women, in particular, created specific spaces in which they could push back against racism and sexism. In addition to African American women-specific spaces, these women made space within African American, primarily black-male-centered institutions to rail against white supremacy and antiblack racism as well as intraracial sexism and heteropatriarchal and masculinist gender politics. Nowhere was this simultaneous fight against both intra- and interracial oppression more evident in the era of the New Negro woman than at prestigious Howard University, the premier institution of higher learning for African Americans.

Lucy Diggs Slowe became the first official dean of women at Howard University in Washington, D.C., in 1922. Prior to Slowe's appointment, Howard

University, J. Stanley Durkee, president of Howard at the time, officially approved the establishment of the new administrative position. From 1920 to June 1922, Helen Tuck had served as acting dean of women at the university. The role and responsibilities of the position, however, were not solidified until the appointment of Slowe. The job mirrored that of the dean of men position that President Durkee approved a year earlier. Before accepting this position, Slowe met with and wrote a detailed letter to Durkee to discuss her expectations regarding the offer to serve the university in such capacity. In a letter dated May 31, 1922, Slowe requested a salary of $3,200, a professorship in English through the School of Education, and a full-time office assistant.[1] She also stated that "all policies pertaining to the women of the University shall emanate from my office with the approval of the President."[2] This particular point of negotiation specifically unveiled Slowe's desire to become a primary figure in the shaping of women's experiences at Howard. Before accepting the position of dean, Slowe understood the vitality of expansive administrative latitude in her ability to prepare women students for modern life. This letter of negotiation established a foundation upon which a culture of contestation and transformation at Howard evolved.

This chapter explores the challenges, setbacks, and achievements of Dean Slowe during her storied fifteen-year career at Howard and her life in Washington. I situate her tremendous career within the formative years of a distinctive New Negro women's institutional subculture at this university. Raymond Wolter's *The New Negro on Campus: Black College Rebellions of the 1920s* identifies historically black colleges and universities as sites where ideas about the New Negro flourished.[3] Wolter's masculinist framing of the New Negro, however, does not account for the gender-specific experiences of African American women at Howard. The battleground for black women such as Slowe at Howard differed from that of her African American male counterparts. Exploring Slowe's life and words unveils another way to think about the New Negro on U.S. college campuses. Since the turn of the twenty-first century, scholars such as Carol L. L. Miller, Annie S. Pruitt Logan, and Linda Perkins have recovered the remarkable story of Slowe.[4] Logan and Miller's comprehensive biography, *Faithful to the Task at Hand: The Life of Lucy Diggs Slowe*, fully delves into her life. This chapter's primary focus on Slowe's tenure as dean of women, however, explicitly identifies Slowe as a New Negro woman and as a person who, as a dean, cultivated an institutional subculture anchored in a discourse of New Negro womanhood.

Slowe's writing discussed the necessity of preparing African American women for the modern world and imparted this vision to Howard's women students. Slowe conceived of the "modern world" as a place where all people, regardless of race or gender, strove for professional achievement and personal fulfillment. She confronted gender norms and conventions that produced an intraracial hierarchy, particularly in her last decade as dean of women at Howard under the presidency of the university's first black president, Mordecai Johnson. Slowe challenged and reshaped the institutional culture of the nation's leading institution of higher learning for black students. Under the leadership of Slowe, Howard University became a unique space for New Negro women's voices to arise. Her personal life, specifically her intimate partnership with acclaimed Washington writer Mary Burrill, also contributed to how Slowe defied contemporaneous gender and sexual norms at Howard and in black Washington. Slowe and Burrill were well known in black Washington, notably among both D.C.'s black artistic and elite communities.[5] Their relationship, however widely known it may have been among their peers in the nation's capital, rejected general intra- and interracial gender and sexual norms about appropriate intimate relationships. Sharing a home and their lives together pitted Slowe and Burrill against heteropatriarchal expectations for African American women of their stature. Through her work as an administrator at Howard, as a national education activist, and as a writer focused on African American women, Slowe distinctively strove to debunk and reshape prevailing African American gender ideology. Her intimate relationship with an African American woman refused a heteronormative scripting for her intimate life. Slowe's personal life and professional career fashioned a terrain in which new ideas about possibilities for African American women's lives could thrive.

The Hilltop: A Brief History of Howard University

Howard emerged as a preeminent coeducational institution for African Americans in the late nineteenth century.[6] Colleges and universities such as Harvard University and Oberlin College admitted and educated a handful of African Americans in the late nineteenth and early twentieth centuries. The number of college-educated black men greatly surpassed that of black women throughout much of the nineteenth century and well into the twentieth.[7] Notwithstanding the gender disparities, black women attending colleges and universities often became leaders and pioneers on their respective campuses. Nowhere was this more evident than at Howard University. Understanding the founding and core principles of Howard University provides insight into how this historically black institution became a unique site for New Negro womanhood standpoints to evolve among African American female students, faculty, and staff.

The abolition of slavery in the District of Columbia and later throughout the South resulted in a large influx of freedpeople into the nation's capital. This population surge created an educational "problem." Debates about how and if the nation should educate millions of recently emancipated people proliferated.[8] In response, philanthropists and freedmen's aid organizations founded schools that focused primarily on elementary studies, to serve African Americans of all ages.[9] The founding of such schools for African Americans contributed to the expansion of educational attainment for blacks.[10] Opponents of establishing schools for African Americans warned of the potential political, cultural, and social consequences that could result from educating a substantial number of African Americans. The efforts of proponents for educating African Americans led to the founding of Howard University on March 2, 1867. By design, Howard extended the education students received at the elementary/secondary schools and trained African Americans for leadership and for careers that were predominantly, if not exclusively, pursued by whites.

Before officially becoming Howard University, the institution decided to have an open admissions policy.[11] The university garnered the distinction of being a pioneer in higher education because of its lack of restrictions based on race, sex, creed, or color. This pioneering outcome did not occur without lengthy debate. Undated and sparse minutes from meetings of charter committee members reveal a lengthy discussion regarding the admission of women to the university.[12] Although the first student body consisted of only five white women (the daughters of Howard University trustees), the university laid the groundwork for a postsecondary education accessible to the children of slave owners and the children of formerly enslaved people alike. Forty years after the enactment and approval of the university's charter by President Andrew Johnson in May 1867, Howard grew to garner widespread national attention from aspiring black youth. By the early twentieth century, this institution acquired its status as the premiere place of higher learning for African Americans.

Howard University anchored a collective sense of progress and achievement among blacks in Washington. The university was central to political, intellectual, and cultural strivings of blacks locally, nationally, and globally. Its physical location in northwest Washington in LeDroit Park and just outside of the predominantly black Shaw neighborhood, however, gave many Washingtonians a tangible symbol of black progress during the New Negro era. Within a short driving distance from Howard were the famed African American institutions, M Street High School (later renamed Dunbar High School in 1906, after the death of Paul Laurence Dunbar that year), Shaw Junior High School, and Armstrong Manual Training School. Northwest Washington, D.C., served as the educational center for black people in the nation's capital. African Americans did not concentrate in one area of the city but lived in racial enclaves throughout the city's four quadrants.[13] Northwest Washington, however, had the most locally and nationally lauded schools. The convergence of the intellectual capital in one area of the city mirrored the unique concentration of cultural capital in the U Street corridor, located just blocks from Howard. The area thrived as a creative, artistic, and leisure epicenter for black people throughout the city, but especially for black residents of the northwest-quadrant neighborhoods.[14]

Enrolling in, graduating from, and working at Howard University (in an instructional or administrative capacity), the leading postsecondary institution for higher learning for Africans Americans, conferred a distinct status. Attending college was a privilege for any person in the United States during the late nineteenth and early twentieth centuries; it was far rarer for an African American, particularly an African American woman. For example, in 1908, the year Lucy Diggs Slowe graduated from Howard, and forty academic years after the school's chartering, only nineteen African American students graduated, eleven men and eight women.[15] One of the founders of Howard University noted that an institution such as this

> was demanded by the necessities of the great educational movement which was inaugurated among the freed people at the close of the late war. When primary, secondary and grammar schools were being opened throughout the South, for the benefit of a class hitherto wholly deprived of educational advantages, it became evident that institutions of a higher grade were needed for the training of the teachers and ministers who were to labor in this field. It was with this view of supplying this need that Howard University was founded.[16]

The early to mid-twentieth century was a substantial growth period for Howard University: the school experienced physical expansion, a student body on the rise, increased financial investment from the federal government and private donors, and an intellectual diversification of the curriculum.[17] The heightened prestige of the faculty, staff, and administration also contributed to the university's prominence among blacks throughout the United States. Zora Neale Hurston, Thurgood Marshall, Alain Locke, Carter G. Woodson, E. Franklin Frazier, Kelly Miller, Sterling Brown, Patricia Roberts Harris, and James Farmer Sr. were among those who called Howard home at some point in their exemplary careers as leaders, writers, intellectuals, activists, innovators, and pioneers.

The Hilltop, an affectionate nickname given to Howard by those familiar with the institution, offered a space in which black women could excel in previously unimaginable ways. Yet like many other institutions within African American communities during the early to mid-twentieth century, Howard University had an explicit gender structure that perpetuated gender inequities that marginalized African American women. Although I focus primarily on how African American men's and women's experiences differed at Howard University, similar gender ideologies regarding the role of women in modern life often existed at predominantly white colleges and universities as well.[18] In many ways, campus policies regarding women reflected broader social expectations and mores within both black communities and white communities. Pushing back against intra- and interracial gender ideologies that limited women's full participation in spheres outside of the home was an integral part of black women embracing a New Negro womanhood ethos.

Slowe, during her tenure as dean of women at Howard, stated, "Frequently, Negro college women come from homes where conservatism in reference to women's place in the world of the most extreme sort exists."[19] Many women came to Howard expecting to become servants of their communities, primarily as educators, wives, and mothers. These professional and personal paths reflected an adherence to a conservatism that relegated black women to particular positions within the modern world. Climbing the Hilltop for New Negro women required combating the prevalence of gender inequities and of narrowed expectations for postgraduate achievement at Howard and, more broadly, in their respective communities. The expectations Howard women confronted were indicative of a national and institutionally specific collegiate culture that perceived women through a lens that did not fully recognize them as equal participants in the modern world. Slowe explicitly challenged the status quo upon her arrival as dean of women at Howard and sought to create an institutional space for African American women to reconsider what it meant to thrive as a black woman in the early twentieth century. The institutional culture Slowe strove to configure posited black women as vital to the progress of blacks in the United States and to the actualization of an inclusive democracy.

The Hilltop: The Early 1900s

In November 1912, W. E. B. Du Bois informed students at Howard that "changed economic conditions" demanded a "change in the role of women," and that "women were entitled to a career the same as men."[20] Although Slowe graduated from Howard in 1908 and did not return to Howard until ten years after Du Bois spoke about the changing role of women in the modern world, the seeds for the growth of a black-women-centered institutional subculture existed as early as the first decade of the twentieth century. Slowe's belief in the necessity of leadership among black women firmly situated her as a proponent of new ideas about black womanhood and as an activist committed to black women's empowerment through leadership opportunities. More specifically, as black women became more visible as leaders in their communities, Slowe believed that issues confronting black women on college campuses, and in the black public sphere more broadly, could acquire greater visibility and significance on political agendas of African Americans. For Slowe and an increasing number of black women students at Howard University, respectability was not solely about temperance, primness, or feminine propriety. Through her works as dean and in her writing about black women in higher education, Slowe sought to reconceptualize African American gender ideology to encompass respect for and appreciation of black women's intellectual and leadership capacities and the affording of equal opportunities in development and training.

When Slowe became dean of women at Howard in 1922, three Greek-letter sororities had been founded on Howard's campus: Alpha Kappa Alpha Sorority Inc., Delta Sigma Theta Sorority Inc., and Zeta Phi Beta Sorority Inc. Each of these organizations placed a priority on sisterhood, scholarship, and leadership among black women. Slowe, a member and leader of several organizations as a student at Howard, recognized the hunger for leadership opportunities and intellectual, social, and cultural stimulation outside of the classroom among African American women students. Of particular importance to the surge of women seeking leadership roles was the issue of women's suffrage, and in particular voting rights for African American women. The sororities would come to play an instrumental role in this effort.

By the 1910s, the women's suffrage movement was at its height in terms of organization and support from women of diverse backgrounds. Leaders of the women's suffrage movement, which included African American women from Howard University, looked toward the presidential election of 1913 to articulate a clear and cogent declaration for women's enfranchisement. The first public act of the newly founded Delta Sigma Theta Sorority was the March 13, 1913, women's suffrage march held in Washington, D.C. Paula Giddings asserts that "Washington, D.C., became not only a center of Black intellectual and social development, but of feminist activity as well."[21] African American women at Howard perceived their academic and extracurricular accomplishments as necessary within this historical moment when new ideologies about women and African Americans formed. The women's suffrage movement and the presence of other forms of women's activism in the nation's capital ignited a passion among many Howard women between 1900 and 1920. The inability to secure universal suffrage in 1920 when white women attained the right to vote incited black women at Howard, including Slowe, to continue fighting for voting rights.

The zeal among black women students Slowe witnessed in the 1920s stemmed from the emergence of new opportunities for women and from the convergence of political and cultural currents such as a black radicalism, pan-Africanism, black and interracial labor movements, black internationalism, American militarism and imperialism, and jazz and early blues culture. Slowe arrived at Howard just as these multiple currents began to shape the culture and consciousness of those on the Hilltop. By the late nineteenth century, the leavening influences of Progressive Era rhetoric promoted the progress of blacks and black women in particular.[22] This "progressive" tone continued into the first decade of the twentieth century, particularly with regard to the formal education of African Americans. By the end of 1910, 4,238 blacks in the United States had received a bachelor's degree.[23] In 1910 there were twenty-five women in Howard's graduating class. Although small in number, the slight but powerful presence of African American women at the university inevitably shifted the institutional culture.

The founding of the National Association for the Advancement of Colored People in 1910 and the establishment of a Howard University chapter of the NAACP in the same year, coupled with lectures from African American intellectuals and leaders such as Du Bois, created an environment in which students grappled with burgeoning ideas about race and democracy. The relatively small group of women at Howard during the 1900s and the 1910s also encountered "race women" such as Mary Church Terrell and Nannie Helen Burroughs, who fought against racial injustice and discrimination while simultaneously examining issues like women's suffrage. The issue of women's enfranchisement, and subsequently, other issues that distinctly affected the lives of black women became the source of a budding consciousness among Howard's female population during the first thirty years of the twentieth century. This historical moment also produced a context in which someone like Slowe could emerge as a pioneer and a leader.

Lucy Diggs Slowe: The Story of a Defiant Pioneer

The journey to become a trailblazer and one of the foremost advocates for black women at colleges and universities commenced for Slowe before she arrived at Howard as a student and, eventually, as a dean and professor. After graduating second in her class from Colored High School in Baltimore, Slowe enrolled at Howard University on an academic scholarship. She became the first female graduate of her high school to enroll at Howard University and was the first student from her school, male or female, to receive an academic scholarship to Howard University. Upon her arrival on the Hilltop, Slowe involved herself in nearly every aspect of the university, from musicals to athletics. She served as president of the women's tennis team, sang in the university choir, and was a founding member and first president of Alpha Kappa Alpha Sorority Inc., the oldest Greek-letter organization established by and for black college women, founded at Howard in 1908. Respected and lauded by the university's faculty, Slowe was chosen by administrators to chaperone other Howard women on off-campus shopping trips—a responsibility bestowed only upon select individuals whom the university deemed of sufficiently high moral character. During the early to mid-twentieth century, women students could not leave the campus without university-sanctioned supervision. The policy reflected a widespread belief that the city was a dangerous place for a woman traveling alone. It restricted women's mobility and demanded the policing of women's bodies in the public sphere in a way that their male counterparts did not incur. Slowe appreciated the university's praise of her "moral character" during her time as a student; however, during her eventual tenure as an administrator at Howard, she openly criticized "the assignment of chaperons to women students as paternalistic and demeaning."[24]

After graduating from Howard in 1908 as class valedictorian, Slowe accepted a position teaching English at Douglass High School in Baltimore.

Many unmarried, college-educated black women pursued teaching as a career during this era.[25] In October 1915, Slowe received a master's degree from Columbia University's Graduate School of Arts and Science. With her degrees from Howard and Columbia, Slowe began a teaching stint at one of the three black high schools in Washington, Armstrong Manual Training School. She eventually became "lady principal" at Armstrong. During her time at Armstrong, her title "lady principal" became "dean of girls." This title change represented a shift in her role from that of a matron to that of a student-services administrator. Slowe was one of the main organizers of the first African American junior high schools in the Washington area, Shaw Junior High School. In addition to organizing Shaw, which would later become one of the most well-respected and widely recognized black educational institutions in the United States, Slowe served as the school's principal until 1922. Each of Slowe's jobs in the nation's capital further integrated her into Washington's black community, and more specifically into the middle class and elite black circles in the city. Her familiarity with the politics, ideologies, values, tensions, and debates within the black Washington community also strengthened with her continued commitment to black educational institutions.

Beyond Slowe's academic and professional achievements within the field of higher education, she enjoyed and excelled at many other activities. In 1917 she became the first African American woman to win a national title in any sport, at the American Tennis Association's (ATA) national tournament in Baltimore. Prior to the ATA's founding, African Americans in the urban upper South and New England competed in invitational and interstate tournaments but could not aspire to the prestige that accompanied a national title. Her victory at the 1917 tournament remains a too-often-unheralded moment in U.S. sports history.[26] Slowe also sang in local choirs to fulfill her interest in vocal performance. She invested in being well rounded. This proved foundational in her mentoring and nurturing of the multiple talents her African American women students embodied.

Her accomplishments as an administrator at leading institutions in Washington, particularly as one who worked with women, made her a highly attractive candidate for the newly created position of dean of women at Howard. Slowe had a stellar reputation in black Washington. President Durkee saw the impending resignation of Helen Tuck as an opportunity to recruit Slowe to the rapidly growing institution. After her appointment, Slowe studied the responsibilities, practices, and procedures of women deans at other universities, regardless of the racial demographics of these institutions. Her personal papers reveal that she "was guided in the establishment of the office of the Dean of Women at Howard University by Dr. Romiett Stevens at Columbia University, who gave the first course for Deans of women in the United States."[27] Her relationships with white women in higher-education activism and in administration proved useful at critical junctures in her career as a dean.[28] Slowe's connection to a larger body of women committed to higher education for women provided opportunities for her to fight on behalf of the black women at Howard as well as black women at colleges and universities across the United States.

In 1923 Slowe became president of the National Association of College Women (NACW), an organization for African American women alumnae of accredited colleges and universities.[29] Founded in 1910 as The College Alumnae Club by ten black college graduates in Washington, D.C., the local organization served the growing number of college graduates in the greater Washington area. Under the leadership of Slowe, the organization moved toward becoming a national entity. The NACW restricted its membership to women who had graduated from accredited colleges and universities.[30] In the broadest sense, Slowe viewed the NACW as a way to promote racial and gender equality and to spark about important conversations about how dismantle racism and racial tensions. "If there are to be peace and harmony among the races in the United States," Slowe said, "the trained men and women of both races must take the lead in bringing this about."[31] Slowe further elaborated that "the colleges of the land ought to open and keep open eternally their doors to men and women of good character and mental capacity regardless of race, in order that there may be a common meeting ground where each race can learn and appreciate that which is fine and worthy of the other."[32] Wrapped in a discourse of respectability, Slowe's words asserted the importance of interracial dialogue in which men and women, blacks and whites, fully and equally participated in steering the course of addressing and resolving racial tensions. Terms such as "good character" echoed black racial/gender discourses about who could and should "represent the race."

Composed of a small group of intellectually elite black women, the NACW directly responded to a growing number of black women on college campuses and actualized a black-women-centered iteration of what Du Bois identified as the "Talented Tenth."[33] The organization aligned itself with an elitist, class politics and emphasized "stringent" academic standards. Not entirely made up of comparatively wealthy black people, the black elite community in

Washington encompassed some black professionals who worked at the city's prominent institutions. Although Slowe worked on a predominantly black campus, she trumpeted the importance of promoting interracial conversations about race and of celebrating higher education as a means of recognizing the humanity of all people regardless of race. Slowe's commitment to interracial dialogue, however, did not dissuade her from speaking out against antiblack racism and its deleterious effects on black women specifically. Her insistence that black women have a seat at the table for discussions on race stemmed from her prioritized interest in black women.

As an organization specifically committed to the strivings of black women in higher education, the NACW promoted the growth of the number of black women on college campuses and sought to support black women students, faculty, staff, and administrators at all institutions educating African American women beyond the high school level. This support included raising the standards in colleges for black women, developing and providing resources for black women faculty and administrators, and securing scholarships and other forms of financial support for African American women. The NACW viewed the appointment of women deans at African American colleges and universities as essential to black women thriving in higher education. Slowe exemplified what NACW envisioned as the ideal women's dean—an education professional, not a matron or caretaker. Through the NACW and her role as dean of women at Howard, Slowe sought to refashion the role of women deans from policing black women's activities on college campuses to developing the intellectual, social, and cultural capacities of black college women students.

Slowe began her tenure as dean of women with a main goal of increasing possibilities for her African American women students. Although Slowe proudly served as teacher for more than a decade before becoming an administrator, she expressed concern regarding the large number of college-educated African American women becoming teachers; she did not discourage them from pursuing a career in education, but she vociferously advocated for the diversification of career aspirations among African American women college students. For Slowe, to equip black women for the demands of the twentieth century meant exposing African American women to disciplines such as psychology, economics, and sociology, which could lead black women down new paths of employment and intellectual development. "The curriculum which is pursued by students in college must," Slowe asserted, "take account of the fact that they will, upon leaving college, enter a world torn by the most profound upheaval in history. The women students, particularly, must be prepared to should the responsibility first of all for making a living because they are definitely committed in the modern world to developing their own individual talents and of being responsible for their own lives."[34] Slowe's perspective on the modern world connected to her understanding of the political, social, and cultural realities that inscribed the lives of black women in the early twentieth century. Describing the specificity of the historical moment in which she worked at Howard, Slowe explains that "living as we do in an industrial democracy, the college woman has a right to expect also some guidance toward the choice of her life's work."[35] Framing a black woman's "life's work" as something other being a wife and mother challenged predominating views about the trajectory of college-educated black women's lives. Slowe understood her role as dean of women as one of guidance for women students. She openly criticized Howard and other predominantly black colleges and universities for not addressing the new needs of women. In a piece titled "The Colored Girl Enters College: What Shall She Expect?" in the *Opportunity Journal of Negro Life*, Slowe argued:

> One of the most serious defects in the Negro college is the slowness with which it has recognized this need. . . . This guidance is even more important for Negro women than it is for white women because the former have to be guided not only with reference to their aptitude, but because of racial identity, also, with reference to possible opportunities for work. Negro women cannot assume that because they are prepared efficiently as individuals they will receive the same consideration as others when they apply for work. In every Negro college a woman has a right to expect a well-established guidance office where she can secure dependable information on the work.[36]

Slowe forcefully and adeptly recognized the unique challenges black women faced during the New Negro era and demonstratively spoke out about the importance of African American women equipping themselves to enter the modern world as workers in any and all fields of endeavor.

In addition to attempting to expand career possibilities for her black women students, Slowe contested an institutional policy that dictated that once married, African American women should resign from their careers and relinquish their professional aspirations. This ideology was deeply ingrained in the university's policies. In 1913 Howard University's board of directors voted that "any female teacher who thereafter married while teaching at the University would be considered as having resigned her position."[37] While this policy at Howard and in African America more broadly did not deter black women from participating in the African American public sphere through social, civic, and, in some cases, political arenas, it effectively rendered some

African American women dependent on men (primarily African American men) and marriage for financial sufficiency in the modern world. Through her mentoring of students and through her work with the NACW, Slowe opposed an institutionalized gender structure that prevented African American women from attaining full autonomy.

In 1923, when addressing the NACW, Slowe stated, "If a college accepts women students and employs women faculty, it should give them the same status as it gives male students and male teachers respectively."[38] Concerning African American women faculty, equal pay became a prominent issue for Slowe and the NACW. "So far as women members of college faculties are concerned," Slowe contended, "they should have the same opportunities for advancement that male members have and should receive equal pay for equal services rendered."[39] For women to achieve equal status with African American male students at Howard, Slowe declared the necessity of a women's campus. Most colleges, regardless of racial composition, required that women live off campus during this era. Leading women authorities on student personnel, largely white women until Slowe's ascendance, believed that residential housing for women functioned as sites for the development of women students and their leadership abilities.[40] Slowe further elaborated on this idea by emphasizing that "adequate housing should be made available for . . . women students for their physical and social development, as well as for the training of their minds."[41] Although hesitant during the first few years of Slowe's tenure, Howard's administration recognized the growing need for female housing and campus life. Slowe argument that "proper housing is one of the most potent influences in the education of college students." "Dormitories designed and furnished in accordance with decent standards of living, and presided over by members of the faculty trained in their supervision," she explained, "can be and should be valuable adjuncts to the academic life of a student," an assertion that resonated with many of Howard's administrators, including president Mordecai Johnson.[42] In 1931 Slowe's tireless efforts resulted in the establishment of a "female" campus. Three dormitories for women comprised the women's campus that resulted from Slowe's efforts. On the day the women's campus officially open, Slowe stated:

> The great purpose of this educational institution—the awakening of a new spirit of mind, a new mode of thought, a new standard of life, a new vision of light—can be achieved only by putting in place in the life of each student the corner stone of unselfishness, generosity, of truthfulness, courage, righteousness, and high endeavor. It is for us, the faculty, to lay our spiritual and

> intellectual corner stone in the lives of the students of Howard University as artistically, as durably, as this stone is laid today. To that great task we take joy in addressing ourselves.[43]

Slowe took great pride in establishing the women's campus at her alma mater. Through these residence halls, Slowe and faculty and staff who supported the agenda of preparing African American women college students for the modern world cultivated an environment in which women students engaged in cultural, social, and political activities. Only a year after the formal founding of the "female" campus, Slowe's efforts were heralded by the African American press in Washington. The *Washington Afro-American* published an article titled "Howard Women Run Themselves in New Dorms," which highlighted the self-governance of the dormitories, the social and cultural activities led by black women students, and the rigor of the intellectual discussions occurring in women's residences.[44] The women's campus provided tangible evidence of African American women's capacity to participate fully in all public arenas.

Furthering her investment in African American women's possibilities, Slowe emphasized the detrimental effects of differing expectations for male and female students at Howard University. Slowe wondered, "Have those who formulate policies of institutions of higher learning where Negro women study surveyed our changed modern life and consciously attempted to prepare Negro college women for intelligent participation and leadership in it?"[45] Dean Slowe recognized a hunger for leadership opportunities and intellectual, social, and cultural stimulation outside of the classroom among African American women students. "Whether or not Negro college women will be able to take their places as leaders in their communities depends, to a large extent," Slowe articulated, "upon the opportunities offered them for exercising initiative, independence, and self-direction while in college."[46]

What Slowe came to realize more insightfully throughout her tenure as dean was that "the university, tolerant of radical ideas when it came to race, was regressive when it came to the social freedoms of its female students or even the rights of its women on the faculty." Her experience as an undergraduate introduced her to the restrictions and gendered expectations Howard imposed on women. As a dean, she faced strong opposition and numerous policies that attempted to maintain a racialized gender hierarchy. In response to Howard's stated and unstated gender structure that policed African American women's participation in all facets of modern life, Slowe continued to demand the fuller participation for African American women in public arenas.

Figure 2. Lucy Diggs Slowe, 1930. Courtesy of the Moorland-Spingarn Research Center, Howard University Archives Howard University, Washington D.C.

Figure 3. Lucy Diggs Slowe on tennis court (undated). Courtesy of the Moorland-Spingarn Research Center, Howard University Archives Howard University, Washington D.C.

Figure 4. Lucy Diggs Slowe and Howard students, 1931. Courtesy of the Moorland-Spingarn Research Center, Howard University Archives Howard University, Washington D.C.

Figure 5. Lucy Diggs Slowe and Mary P. Burrill (undated). Courtesy of the Moorland-Spingarn Research Center, Howard University Archives Howard University, Washington D.C.

The Mordecai Johnson Years: Setbacks and Challenges for New Negro Womanhood

Opposition to debunking Howard University's institutionalized gender ideologies reached its peak during the tenure of the school's first African American president, Mordecai Johnson. He arrived in 1926, only four years after Slowe's appointment as dean of women and at the height of New Negro era intellectual and cultural currents converging on the Hilltop.

A graduate of the all-male Morehouse College and an ordained Southern Baptist minister, Mordecai Johnson arrived at Howard University with a vision for the future of the nationally renowned institution of higher learning in the nation's capital. Many would come to describe him as "controlling" as a president, which placed black women in particular in a unique position of being controlled. His religious background influenced his views on education and his thoughts pertaining to "appropriate" behavior and career paths for African American women. Despite the tremendous work of black women pushing for more gender-progressive theology, particularly within the black Baptist denomination, Johnson maintained a conservative understanding of black women's roles on college campuses and, more broadly, in public life.[47] Hiring African American women as faculty at Howard was the extent of Johnson's engagement with women's concerns about equality in higher education. At the time Johnson assumed leadership of Howard University, Slowe had made numerous efforts to provide African American women students with unparalleled opportunities for leadership, social and cultural exploration, and career-oriented education. Slowe explicitly critiqued African American churches and social conservatism, to which many black families adhered. She publicly acknowledged,

> Much of the religious philosophy upon which Negro women have been nurtured has tended toward suppressing in them their own powers. Many of them have been brought up on the antiquated philosophy of Saint Paul in reference to women's place in the scheme of things, and all too frequently have been influenced by the philosophy of patient waiting, rather than the philosophy of developing their talents to their fullest extent. . . . Under these conditions, it is inevitable therefore, that the psychology of most of the women who come to college is the psychology of accepting what is taught without much question; the psychology of inaction rather than that of active curiosity.[48]

Johnson, a Baptist minister, embraced the religious philosophy that Slowe denounced.[49] Because of their substantially differing viewpoints regarding the roles of African American women in the modern world, Slowe and Johnson and his all-male administration maintained a contentious relationship that lasted until Slowe's untimely death in 1937. His rigid position on "the woman question" mirrored that of many black men's attempts through both secular and religious institutions to control, limit, and dictate the behaviors of black women in public life.

Throughout his presidency, Johnson's administration rescinded many of the new opportunities Slowe established for African American women students. Under Johnson, Slowe lost her position as a member of the president's council of deans and her management role in the women's residence halls.[50] Johnson demanded that Slowe move to Howard's campus to supervise the African American women on campus. This shifted Slowe's role as a manager and a leader of women on campus to that of a "matron." When Slowe received her initial offer to serve as dean of women, she requested that she not be required to live on campus.[51] This request stemmed from a belief that her role as an administrator would in fact shift to that of a matron for Howard's female students. On most college and university campuses during this era, women administrators did function in a matronly capacity. Slowe strongly opposed the matron role as both demeaning and regressive; it undermined the general thrust of much of her work at Howard, which strove to dismantle policies based on the assumption that African American women required more supervision and restrictions and less leadership development than their male counterparts. Additionally, Slowe shared a house and her life with a woman, Mary Burrill. The implications of two unrelated, single, adult women living together contradicted the university's values surrounding "appropriate" gender and sexual roles and relations. Although, as Genny Beemyn argues, Slowe and Burrill perhaps benefited from the "ambiguity of two unmarried women living together."[52]

Slowe and Burrill met when they both worked as teachers, Slowe in Baltimore and Burrill in Washington at Dunbar High School (formerly M Street High School). When Slowe took a job at Armstrong Manual Training Academy in Washington, the relationship between the two women intensified. Although they were referred to as "housemates" in official records after they moved in together at 1758 T Street NW and then to 1744 K Street NW, their relationship was intimate and known to their peers.[53] They lived together until Slowe's death from kidney disease in 1937 at 1256 Kearny Street in the Brookland neighborhood in northeast DC. In numerous personal letters to Slowe, friends and associates asked for Slowe to give their regards to Burrill. Among personal letters Slowe received, a particular note from Mary McLeod

Bethune ended with "love to Mary Burrill."[54] A letter dated June 6, 1936, from Charlotte Hawkins Brown, founder of the Palmer Institute in North Carolina and the first African American woman named to the national board of the YWCA, asked Slowe to give her regards to Burrill.[55] Other letters from African American women to Slowe about Burrill included one from Mrs. J. C. Napier and Ella Murphy.[56] Barring "proof" of sexual contact, which "relies on a heterosexist definition of sex," it is important to note the intimate homosocial world Slowe and Burrill inhabited.[57] They shared a life together and without question forged a loving relationship in spite of prevailing heteronormative and patriarchal expectations for women to marry and not engage in "suspect" relationships with other women. Letters Burrill received upon Slowe's death further reveal the closeness of their relationship. Mollie T. Barrien wrote a note in an effort to console Burrill by reminding her that Slowe and Burrill would be "reunited in heaven, never to be separated again."[58] The registrar of Howard referred an obituary writer to Burrill, stating that "she has been a longtime friend and companion of Miss Slowe and I am sure that there is no one who knew her life better than she."[59] There is no formal documentation to prove her relationship with Burrill contributed to her increasingly antagonistic relationship with Howard's administration—and yet their nontraditional relationship, coupled with Slowe's demands for equal opportunities for African American women in higher education, pitted her against Howard's all-male administration's prevailing gender ideology and, specifically, the conservative Baptist ideology Mordecai Johnson espoused as the university's leader.[60]

The university's attempt to shift Slowe's role from that of administrator to matron exacerbated existing tensions between Slowe and Howard's leadership, who in 1933 dismantled women's program, which included career guidance for female students as well as female leadership programs. While the trustees and the administration proffered the decision as one of economic necessity, Slowe firmly believed that the dissolution of the women's program signaled a devaluation of equal opportunities for women in higher education, and she responded with ferocity: "When the trustees, in the interest of the economy, wiped out of the women's department every person except for two . . . they destroyed, in one day, practically everything that I had built up over a period of eleven years."[61] The frustration Slowe expressed stemmed also from the fact that only the dean of women was required to live on Howard's campus; the dean of men was permitted to reside in his own home in Washington. The implications of necessitating supervision for female students and faculty and staff and *not* male students and faculty and staff were particularly hurtful to African American women at Howard who could interpret these policies as a reflection on their character and potential. This requirement also appeared to reflect the administration's continued discomfort with Slowe and Burrill's relationship.

Her confrontation with gender inequity for African America women students and faculty, however, extended beyond educational issues. Slowe sought also to redefine relationships between men and women in higher education in an attempt to curb the exploitation of African American women in collegiate and professional spheres. She was focused on the daily treatment of women on college campuses and in the black public sphere more generally. Her concern for African American women's experiences at Howard became glaringly evident in her handling of a complaint made by women students at Howard about a male professor in 1927. This complaint sparked a chain of events that highlighted the lack of power women students, faculty, and staff possessed at the university. The stark contrast between Howard's racial progressivism and its adherence to traditional gender roles, expectations, and relations provided women at Howard with a seemingly insurmountable obstacle in achieving fuller equality during the New Negro era.

Slowe received an initial complaint about Professor Clarence Harvey Mills from a parent in 1927. The letter accused Professor Mills of using "improper and sometimes vulgar language in his classroom with women students present."[62] Seeking to "avoid a public controversy, Slowe arranged to speak privately with Mills about the allegations."[63] Slowe noted that Mills responded positively to their meeting and actually thanked Slowe for bringing it to his attention without involving the administration. The following day, however, Slowe received a letter from Mills, which she described as "vile." This letter accused the female student of hypocrisy, of spending time in brothels, and of pretending to be offended by the vulgar language Mills allegedly used in the classroom. His written reaction to the accusations attacked not just the character of his accusers, but also Slowe, in her position as dean. Of Slowe, Mills wrote, "You forget that you are merely the Dean of Women and not the custodian of morals of the male teachers of Howard University."[64] He suggested also that if Slowe had the same responsibilities as her male counterparts, she would not be a receptacle for "ridiculous" complaints lodged against respected male faculty members. After receiving this letter, Slowe shared what transpired from the initial complaint to this point with Dudley Weldon Woodard, professor of mathematics and dean of the School of Liberal Arts, and president Mordecai Johnson.

Woodard and Johnson agreed that both the parent's complaint and Mills's fiery letter to Slowe warranted serious actions. During a meeting with Mills, it was decided that Mills would be dismissed at the end of the term, that no public discussion would accompany the administration's decision, and that Mills must apologize to Dean Slowe for his scathing remarks about her. Inevitably, however, Mills finished the entire year at Howard and was granted a leave of absence with partial salary during the next academic year. During his leave of absence, Mills finished his doctoral degree at the University of Chicago and continued a career in education unmarred by his alleged behavior toward Howard women. Mills's eventual departure from Howard was more voluntary than punitive. Slowe's relationship with Howard's male administrators, particularly President Johnson, further deteriorated because of her insistence on Professor Mills's termination and of her advocacy against Howard women being subjected to gender-based harassment.

The consequences Slowe endured did not deter her from remaining outspoken about a campus culture that silenced the voices of women and condoned an intraracial gender hierarchy at the student and faculty and staff levels. Her 1927 "Memorandum on the Mills Case" conveyed a profound sense of disappointment and frustration with Howard University and its attitudes and policies toward African American women. This memorandum affirmed her commitment to ensuring that Howard's administration evaluated the experiences of women at the university. In addition to drafting one of the first known memos about the sexual harassment of African American women in the academy, Slowe used this memo to critique gender inequity more broadly at Howard. She explained:

> From the time this case happened down to the present, I have not had the cordial support of the President. When the time came to raise salaries, he raised mine \$200 and raised other Deans with qualifications no better than mine in amounts ranging from \$850-\$1150. He, without, explanation, exclused [*sic*] me from his conferences with the Academic Deans, although prior to 1930, the Dean of Men and the Dean of Women had sat with the Board of Deans. He has never sympathetically studied the real work of the Dean of Women, and still seems to have a wrong conception of her function sponsored by the Department of the Dean of Women, and cannot have first hand knowledge of her work. I have tried in every way to correct this but can get no co-operation from the President.[65]

Slowe utilized the Mills case and its aftermath to highlight her struggles as a dean and the resistance she encountered in her efforts to achieve gender equity for Howard women. Sexual harassment, the university's prioritizing of black male leadership, the paternalistic and patriarchal perspectives and policies of Howard's predominantly male administration, and the lack of suitable and intellectually, culturally, and socially stimulating living conditions for women students became visible through Slowe's response to the Mills case. The setbacks only further encouraged Slowe to continue to push for gender equity and to address women's exclusion from leadership and women's underrepresentation in the student population and the faculty.

Conclusion

Slowe openly criticized black men and women who placed any limitations on what black women could achieve and or aspire to in areas outside the home. She fought for and with black women to secure not just a place but an equal place in American higher education. Her politics reflected a different consciousness that specifically addressed the needs and burgeoning aspirations of black women using education as a means for greater visibility in the public sphere. As president of the National Association of College Women, Slowe achieved national attention for her commitment to black women's education in all U.S. institutions. Slowe articulated how injustices against black women signaled a broader injustice to humankind. Although she was not the first to connect the inequalities faced by African Americans to a broader understanding of inequality, she was among the first to associate the educational achievements of college-educated black women to a fuller realization of American democracy.

The broadened "justice" lens Slowe engaged added a distinctly New Negro woman's component to her activism. Slowe embodied a commitment to eradicating racial and gender oppression and almost exclusively focused on the plight of African American women. During her tenure as a member and leader of the NACW, the organization formulated its purpose and publicly circulated it. "The organization has devoted itself," she wrote, "to the study of living conditions for women and college students and to the raising of educational standards in colleges, with special emphasis upon the introduction into the curricula of courses to meet the needs of modern life."[66] Recognizing the potential for black women to become leaders in all fields of human endeavor, Slowe used her position at Howard as a dean in conjunction with her professional organizations to forward an agenda that honored black women's distinct potential. Slowe viewed Howard University as an institution that could lead the way in harnessing the gifts of African American women and training them for a range of careers.

During her illustrious career, Slowe also did not espouse rhetoric commonly associated with "racial uplift," a position that distinguished her from notable Washington, D.C.–based contemporaries such as Mary Church

Terrell and Nannie Helen Burroughs. Her primary focus was exposing and erasing the limitations black women confronted in pursuit of education and careers outside the home. Additionally, religion did not play an integral role in her educational philosophy, although it played an important role in her life. In her personal life, Slowe rejected gender and sexual mores and expectations by engaging in a romantic and intimate relationship with a woman. Professionally, she pushed back against a New Negro ethos that emphasized black masculinism by openly contesting gender structures that limited the strivings and possibilities of African American women.

Slowe unapologetically positioned herself as an advocate for educational equality for black women. Her politics reflected a different consciousness that specifically addressed the needs and burgeoning aspirations of black women using education as a means for greater visibility in the public sphere. Mordecai Johnson arrived at Howard at an exciting moment in the growth of black women students' activism.[67] Upon his arrival he enacted policies that affirmed that, "as elsewhere on black college campuses, black women were subjected to strict rules and regulations regarding their behavior and movement on and off campus."[68] Slowe guided African American female Howard students in challenging the viability of these rules and regulations and openly decried the sexism that motivated their enforcement at such a "progressive" institution. She led Howard's women in confronting sexist attitudes and practices and in demanding that the progressive vision for Howard encompass racial and gender equality. At the height of black women students' activism, Johnson and his administration attempted to debunk the substantial gains these women made toward achieving gender equity at the leading historically black university.

Slowe did not and could not speak for all black women at the university. Howard women also respected and embraced Washington race women such as Terrell and Burroughs. The standpoints of Terrell and Burroughs further illustrate the complexity and diversity of New Negro women's standpoints. Terrell vividly described the "extraordinary intellectual and political achievements of black women only two generations away from slavery."[69] Terrell emphasized issues such as black female empowerment and woman suffrage and remained committed to the goal of racial equality as paramount. An educator, writer, scholar, powerful orator, and a leader, Terrell exemplified a form of black women's leadership/activism that thrived in Washington. Turning her back on the life of leisure and "ladyhood" her family's wealth secured, Terrell chose to be a leader in the antilynching campaign, desegregation efforts, and the movement for women's rights. Her involvement with the movement for women's rights, however, did not include critiques of black religious institutions and doctrines or of prominent black male leaders in Washington such as Mordecai Johnson. Slowe willingly vocalized her contempt for Johnson's ideologies. Her dislike of Johnson and his regressive gender politics became more blatantly evident at the time of her death. Slowe explicitly asked that President Johnson have no formal role in her funeral proceedings.[70] The relationship between Slowe and Johnson magnified the difficult journey some African American women faced in contending with a rigid intraracial gender ideology in the New Negro era, specifically in the realm of education.

For many prominent African American women in Washington, education was the primary battleground for improving the status of black women in the United States. Throughout the early 1900s Burroughs established women's industrial clubs in the South. These clubs offered a range of services, including (but not limited to) short-term lodging for black women, basic domestic skills training, typing, stenography, bookkeeping, and home economics.[71] In 1907 Burroughs produced official plans for the National Trade and Professional School for Women and Girls in Washington, D.C. The school opened in 1909 with Burroughs as president and under the motto "We specialize in the wholly impossible." Focusing in on the honing of both practical and professional skills, the institution's curriculum highlighted the importance being both admirable homemakers and self-sufficient "working women." Christian womanhood was an overarching theme. In Bettye Collier-Thomas's impressive and exhaustive work, *Jesus, Jobs, and Justice: African American Women and Religion*, she details the work of Burroughs and other black women activists who used religious faith as a foundation for their political and social activism.[72] Because of the integral role both religion and education played in Burroughs's life, her school privileged them as well. The motto of the National Trade and Professional School is rather indicative of how Burroughs thought about the women she sought to educate. Burroughs's activism was inextricable from her religious beliefs and, therefore, aligned with many of the prevailing currents of race woman activism during the New Negro era. For black women in Washington and across African America, education and religion were at the core of their political, social, and cultural agendas. Many of the educated black women activists of the late nineteenth and early to mid-twentieth centuries confronted the tension of being committed to racial uplift and advocating for the imposition of certain "core values" such as feminine propriety and higher moral capacity. Howard women could draw inspiration from the New Negro standpoints of Burroughs, Terrell, Slowe, and other prominent Washington-based and nationally known black women.

Slowe represented arguably one of the most radical and gender-progressive standpoints a New Negro woman occupied.

The personal relationships Howard women formed with Slowe and other members of the women's campus staff resulted in a community of highly educated women interrogating the validity of racial-progress movements and organizations that did not critique gender inequality and the relegation of African American women to particular career paths and the domestic sphere. Slowe mentored many women, including Thelma Preyer Bando, who became a dean of women and a departmental head, and Hilda Davis, who became dean of women at Talladega College. Slowe's legacy lived on through women who forged leadership roles in higher education. She modeled new possibilities for African American women and used existing or created new platforms to promote the importance of African American women's access to higher-education opportunities. Her voice, in meetings with administrators, in academic journals, and in local publications, provided a rhetorical foundation for New Negro womanhood on college and university campuses.

Slowe confronted issues of sexual harassment, a paternalistic and socially conservative administration and board of trustees, and the national image of Howard as a progressive institution through crafting an alternative discourse for imagining possibilities for African American women. Notably, she challenged the status quo of male dominance on campus through seeking leadership positions in campus clubs, taking classes in all disciplines, and initiating programming that examined the accomplishments of African American men and women. Howard administrators, and most specifically Mordecai Johnson, rejected many of the changes Slowe sought to institutionalize and rescinded many of the advancements women made during her early years as dean of women. She occupied a contentious space in which competing ideals for black women's public behavior intersected. Lucy Diggs Slowe played an integral role in preparing Howard's New Negro women for making history as activists, professionals, intellectuals, and pioneers in numerous fields of human endeavor. She sought to transform one of the premier black institutions of the twentieth century.

African American women at Howard University in the early twentieth century were participants in and catalysts of debates about the role of black women in the modern world.[73] Black women attending institutions of higher learning were equipped with skills and bodies of knowledge that, for their mothers and most of their peers, were nearly unattainable. Consequently, a realm of possibility opened to black women who desired to pursue professional aspirations. Defiance of the status quo met with substantial backlash from Howard's administration. African American women students had an ally in Slowe. Until her death, she remained unapologetic and unwavering in her work for gender equity and a more progressive African American gender ideology. Although in an elite, exceptional, and exclusionary space, Slowe's investment in upending rigid gender expectations aligned with other African American women in Washington striving to be seen, heard, and included in New Negro discourses of freedom and equality.

2

Make Me Beautiful

Aesthetic Discourses of New Negro Womanhood

> The dressing of one's hair should be a matter of deep concern. To no other race is this more important than the Negro woman.
>
> —B. S. Lynk, *A Complete Course in Hair Straightening and Beauty Culture*, 1919

Most African American women in the nation's capital did not attend or work at Howard University. The black press in Washington, most notably in the *Washington Afro American* and the *Washington Bee*, however, often chronicled what occurred on campus. Since the early to mid-nineteenth century, Colored newspapers in Washington reported on the lives of blacks in Washington as well as national events affecting African Americans.[1] In his self-published autobiography, prominent black attorney, politician, and city judge Mifflin Wistar Gibbs heralded the black press in Washington as having "a reputation for intelligent journalism, and for energy and devotion to the cause they espouse."[2] Stories about and eventually images of Howard women circulated to the greater black Washington community as the school continued to gain prominence. The continued rise of a vibrant black press in the nation's capital permitted some cross-class engagement. Colored newspapers covered the lives of and featured the voices of the black elite, but they also provided space for the growth of African American commerce through the dedication of several pages of periodicals to advertising products and services for a growing population of African Americans in the nation's capital.[3] Access to the products and services advertised varied according to class, and yet advertisements as a distinct racial and gender discourse cut through the rigidity of social status. Advertising emerged as a primary site for "pitching" and representing African American life in Washington. During the New Negro era, many advertisements indeed captured the cultural lives of black Washingtonians.

One of the primary recurring themes evident in black Washington newspapers in the late nineteenth and early twentieth centuries was how black Washingtonians reconfigured black bodily aesthetics and cultural traditions. The newspapers captured black Washingtonians engaged in new practices and aesthetic discourses with an unprecedented sense of possibility for self-determination and autonomy. These practices and discourses revealed a concerted investment in an emergent politics of adornment. Through the altering, adorning, and maintenance of physical appearance, African Americans could literally reconstruct and refashion themselves and create new models of black aesthetic identity.[4] According to Davarian Baldwin, *re-creation* as a term during the New Negro era explained "how the industrialized leisure space of adornment was central to new and contested meanings of the modern experience."[5] Bodily aesthetic practices were integral to African Americans in shedding the vestiges of enslavement and for asserting their place within the modern world. More specifically, black women carved out new spaces in which to explore their tastes, desires, and sense of personal autonomy. Black women used bodily aesthetic innovations, discourses, and practices to grapple with and challenge prevailing ideas about race, gender, sexuality, class, and labor, and to claim a distinct space within a rapidly modernizing world. The black press in Washington captured how black women in Washington traversed the terrain of bodily aesthetics—with a striking emphasis on African American women's beauty culture.

A process of recovering and articulating a sense of self that had been previously over-determined by a national cultural imaginary that devalued black racial identities fits within a broader project of black modernity or "afro-modernity." Michael Hanchard defines afro-modernity as a process of "redemption, recovery, retribution, and revolution."[6] Paul Gilroy, building on the work of Du Bois, similarly posits black modernity as a process, while firmly situating a heightened double consciousness as central to this process.[7] Aesthetics and related discourses created by black communities during the New Negro era were integral to black modernity. Black urbanity also propelled the growth of an urban consumer culture based in bodily aesthetics. Rapidly growing mass media industries such as film, print advertising, and radio afforded blacks a space in which to partake in that process and confront existing racial, gender, and sexual ideologies.[8] African Americans in cities had comparatively greater access to these budding industries than those residing in small towns and rural communities. Nevertheless, cultures of bodily aesthetics emerged in both rural and urban spaces. African Americans in urban centers also had access to emergent technologies associated with an evolving mass-media-based consumer culture. This access shifted how black women could actualize consumer citizenship.[9] Consumption of goods and services became increasingly central to national political discourses about class, race, gender, and social status over the course of the twentieth century. The ability or lack of ability to consume interwove with ideas about the individual communities and citizenship in new and profound ways with the spread of mass media and national markets. The intentions and desires of consumers inextricably linked to racial, class, gender, and regional identities. Many black women across the United States participated in urban consumer culture as a means to recover and to restyle themselves as claimants of urbanity.[10]

During the era of New Negro women, differing ideas and practices that signaled diversification within black communities flourished. At both local and national levels, black people in the United States did not experience or create a singular idea about beauty. Multiple ideas about black beauty thrived because of the array of perspectives about being black in the modern world. Erin Chapman affirms that New Negro cultural productions were "disseminated through the powerful arbiters of white supremacist understandings and capitalist exploitation."[11] The arbiters of heteropatriarchal gender/sex regimes also affected New Negro women's cultural productions. This arbitration, however, could not fully determine how black women approached racial and gender representation through cultural mediums such as beauty culture. White supremacist understandings did not fully deter the diversification of representation of African Americans, nor did intra- and interracial gender norms and conventions. Resistance to monolithic racial and gender representations was vital to the innovators, sellers, and consumers of black beauty culture in the nation's capital.

From the arrival of black women to the United States to the early years of the national black beauty culture, the practice of hair straightening was one of many hair-styling techniques commonly associated with white female beauty standards. It is important to note that this standard was limiting not only for black women but for any woman who did not have straight hair. Notwithstanding the influence of racism and sexism, and the contributions of black men, white manufacturers of beauty products, and white cultural hegemony, African American women attempted to create a beauty culture that situated black women's bodies and voices at the forefront of discussions about competing visions for African American modernity. Spaces like the *Washington Bee* functioned as both adversarial and affirming for black women in Washington seeking to determine what constituted black beauty.

Black beauty culture was a business, a discourse, and a product of modernity. This chapter explores the connection between black women's engagement in shaping the exchange of ideas on black beauty culture and New Negro aesthetic ideologies. There were many facets of these connections, ranging from the positioning of black beauty culture as a tool for dismantling stereotypes to the development of a multidimensional consumer marketplace composed almost solely of African American women.[12] Stereotypes of black women during Jim Crow ranged greatly: they were lascivious, savage or primitive in appearance, lazy, unconcerned with their physical presentation, matronly, and vulgar.[13] Archetypes such as Mammy, Jezebel, and Sapphire affected how black women approached self-definition. Beauty culture was a vehicle through which black women could self-define and respond to these controlling images and stereotypes.

Moving from the history of the evolution of black beauty consumer culture in the late-nineteenth century to the rise of a black-women-centered beauty culture and industry in the early twentieth century, I use bodily aesthetics, visual images, and products marked for race and gender to consider the relationship between New Negro womanhood and adornment. Black beauty culture also functioned as a battleground for ideas about the intersection of the political and social agendas of the New Negro movement and the presentation and representation of black womanhood in the public sphere. One of the major currents during the New Negro era was debunking white cultural hegemony. Adornment practices, specifically the maintenance and styling of women's hair, represented a primary terrain for contesting the pervasiveness of white cultural hegemony in the lives of African American women. The rapid growth of this multi-million-dollar industry also challenged the homogeneity that existed in U.S. beauty culture. Homogeneity in this context meant that American beauty culture pivoted around bodily aesthetic valuations and traditions derived from a white cultural imaginary. The majority of products, tools, and techniques marketed to women during the late nineteenth and early twentieth centuries signaled a fairly monolithic and distinctively racialized perception of ideal, feminine beauty. Some New Negro women involved in black beauty culture sought to debunk white constructions of feminine beauty through trumpeting both the physical, natural beauty of African American women and the power of black feminine artifice (from the minimal to the excessive) that engaged a historical legacy of black women's creativity, style, and innovation.

Through the emergence of a nationalized black consumer culture and national black publications that specifically targeted African Americans, black women took a more authorial role in the portrayal of their identities. Images created by African American women circulated in the U.S. cultural market alongside derogatory and dehumanizing images that reified racial hierarchies and damaging stereotypes. The ability to create images and the establishment of outlets in which those images could circulate provided black women with a space for self-expression. Within this space, black women had options and could use aesthetics to convey their sense of modern black womanhood. The development of a parallel bodily aesthetic terrain controlled by and directed toward African American women also allowed black women to confront white cultural hegemony, black sexism, and the relegation of black women to the margins of national consumer cultures. This parallel aesthetic terrain also provided black women with a distinct space for self-care. On a quotidian level, self-care meant the ability to attend to one's physical well-being and appearance. Caring for self through beautification and adornment aligned with greater demands for restorative possibilities for black women. The black female body served as a battleground for discussions about African American politics of bodily adornment and appearance.[14]

Among the culture industries that achieved prominence in black urban communities, the beauty industry emerged as a ripe site for discussions about race, gender, skin color, class, and modernity. For African American women, ideas about New Negro womanhood predominated in this cultural space. In *Hair Raising: Beauty, Culture, and African American Women*, Noliwe Rooks discusses the importance of beauty culture for examining the politics of African American women's bodies, representation of those bodies, racial ideologies, personal freedom, creativity, autonomy, and social and economic mobility. I extend Rooks's argument to encompass how black women connected beauty culture to modernity. Although Davarian Baldwin makes a similar extended argument in his groundbreaking book *Chicago's New Negroes: Modernity, the Great Migration, and Black Urban Life*, I argue that it is a localized beauty culture in Washington that is significant for understanding how black women functioned as authorial subjects within a national, race-sex-gender enterprise.

The efficacy of self-determinative efforts by black women through beauty culture in the late nineteenth and early twentieth centuries is most visible in the local communities and markets black women created and patronized. From the black women who invented products exclusively for black women, to the black women who purchased and used these products, to those women who wrote about the physical appearance of black women, to the women who acquired financial independence and social mobility as a result of marketing and selling black beauty products, beauty culture offered black women an arena in which their needs, thoughts, desires, and tastes took center stage. Furthermore, New Negro women repurposed acts of perceived self-indulgence and superficiality into what Baldwin identifies as a "powerful black public sphere of leisure, labor, and politics."[15] The power of this public sphere in the nation's capital led to significant interest and investment from local newspapers, organizations, and political and economic leaders.

The beauty industry was not isolated from the racism and sexism that pervaded the New Negro era. In fact, white beauty ideals and trends within white beauty culture played integral roles in the developmental stages of a nationalized black beauty culture. Intraracial notions of beauty propagated by the black press also affected black beauty culture. In a piece published in the *Washington Bee* in 1910, the editorial staff, led by prominent black businessman and journalist Calvin Chase, echoed a popular sentiment among African American men and women that dominated black beauty culture discourse in its earliest stages as a national market, a cultural space, and a race enterprise:

> We say straighten your hair, ladies, beautify yourselves, make those aggravating, reclusive, elusive, shrinking kinks long flowing tresses that may be coiled or curled or puffed to suit Dame Fashion's latest millinery creations, even if it takes every ounce of hair straightening preparation that can be manufactured. . . . even God, who discriminated against our women on this hair proposition, knows that straight hair beautifies a woman. Yes, straighten your hair and do it at once.[16]

Chase, a free-born and educated native Washingtonian, founded the *Bee* in 1882. The paper's motto was "Honey for Friends, Stings for Enemies." In this particular editorial, the enemy was black women and their naturally "kinky" hair. The sentiment shared in this editorial was not an uncommon opinion during the New Negro era. Although the *Bee*'s content reflected a common rhetorical thread against racial discrimination, many divergent perspectives regarding African Americans in Washington and in the United States more broadly filled the popular newspaper's pages throughout its tenure. Black women's hair was a frequently discussed topic, and advertisements for a variety of black hair care products and processes were widespread in the *Bee*.

It is important to note that the black beauty industry is most commonly identified as a race enterprise pivoting around black women. Although this industry provided and continues to provide a distinct space for black women to contribute to black business development and entrepreneurship, scholars tend to ignore the industry's status as a *gender enterprise*, a term that refers to industries wherein gender identity propels the manufacturing, production, marketing, and consumption of the primary products. Black beauty culture in the New Negro era, therefore, was both a race and a gender enterprise, in which black women played a central and dominant role. By framing the black beauty industry as a doubly situated enterprise with class dynamics, the gendered nature of racial categories becomes more visible.[17]

Baldwin argues that "beauty culture became an important locus for the development of a contested New Negro womanhood."[18] The growing body of literature on African American women's beauty culture, including most notably the recent work of Tiffany Gill on the black beauty industry, echoes Baldwin's incisive argument.[19] Black women began shaping an alternative discourse about black beauty aesthetics that resisted adherence to prevailing ideals about beauty. For some black women, being modern meant embracing unique practices and styles derived from standards established by and for black women. Focusing on black women's beauty culture in Washington unveils how local beauty cultures incorporated black women-authored discourses about black beauty and the role black women played in diversifying the practices, products, and trends that propelled black beauty culture in the New Negro era. The local beauty culture of Washington mirrored the local beauty of cultures of other U.S. cities with rapidly growing black communities, but it also benefited from a more well-established business/entrepreneurial community that predated the Great Migration. Consequently, both localized and national discourses about black beauty influenced how black women thought about styling themselves as modern black women.

The Origins of the Modern Black Beauty Industry and Its Emergence in the Nation's Capital

The origins of the modern black beauty industry predate its emergence a national, black consumer market and commercialization. The late nineteenth and early twentieth centuries witnessed the development of products specifically for black people and the rapid growth of beauty salons and cosmetology schools in black communities. Beauty practices, intraracial and interracial ideas about the physical appearance of black women (most notably their hair texture and skin color), and an informal black beauty market have existed since the arrival of African women as chattel to the United States. A black aesthetic subculture encompassed folk traditions, intergenerational exchanges among black women, and the survival techniques black women used to maintain their appearances under the harsh conditions of enslavement.

Julia Kirk Blackwelder writes that enslaved women often "groomed their hair for health and convenience." "Braiding and head wrapping," she notes, helped the women maintain the cleanliness of their hair and kept it from being damaged while they labored.[20] Enslaved black women invested in this form of self-care as one of their outlets for recuperating their humanity. Another common practice among black women on plantations involved the use of handkerchiefs and scarves. Head wraps, made out of fabric oddments, protected black women's hair from sun damage. They also could conceal slave women's hair when they could not attend to it. The omnipresence of head rags did not deter black women from attending to their hair in a variety of ways, depending on their access to styling tools and products. Many enslaved women who worked in the homes of white masters engaged in hair styling practices that resembled those of white slave owners. Black women in slave communities shared these processes with one another. An informed and covert network of sharing among enslaved women resulted in the replication of styles by enslaved women across different roles in plantation households as well across plantations.[21]

Many free and enslaved black women put a great deal of thought and effort into hair care. Products such as kerosene, butter, goose grease, soap, cornmeal, bacon fat, lye, potatoes, and coffee became central to the cleansing, dyeing, and straightening of African American women's hair. Tools such as butter knives, strings, and eel skins assisted enslaved women in curling, wrapping, and straightening their hair. Because of the arduous and potentially dangerous nature of some straightening practices, many black women on plantations preferred other methods that did not pose the risks of chemical burns and permanent hair loss. Women who resisted hair straightening incorporated other practices that resonated in both slave and free communities. Enslaved and impoverished black women faced greater limitations in their grooming choices because they did not have access to or could not afford proper materials. Enslaved black people also struggled to attend to their general physical appearance because of the lack of time they had for personal grooming in the midst of the unrelenting and grueling forced-labor schedule imposed on them.

From its inception, African American beauty culture was simultaneously syncretic, adaptive, inventive, and semi-autonomous, combining and improvising upon African traditions brought by slaves, Anglo-American beauty styles and techniques, European ideals, and Native American practices.[22] In its infancy, black beauty culture did not fully mimic or wholly reject white beauty ideals that emerged as early as the nineteenth century. On the other hand, white manufacturers, dominant in the beauty culture industry, relied on white cultural ideals in product development and marketing throughout the nineteenth century. These manufacturers used prevailing white corporeal tastes to target black men and women who had the ability to purchase beauty products. Not yet a fully viable industry, white producers of race-specific beauty products for African Americans rarely tapped into beauty practices and techniques blacks developed during the early modern and antebellum eras.

Both enslaved and free black women confronted white cultural dominance and the associated beauty norms that degraded and dehumanized black women. White Americans and some blacks perceived the features of enslaved and free black women as physically unattractive and as indicative of the "inherent" primal, animalistic, and lascivious tendencies of peoples of African descent. White skin and other tropes of beauty associated with Anglo-Americans' appearance, such as straight hair and thin noses, proliferated as the standard for beauty in the United States. Enslaved and free black women struggled against the devaluation of their beauty, yet white cultural hegemony of the nineteenth century imparted lasting effects on African American beauty culture and class and color politics within the black community.[23]

Before emancipation, many black people in the United States associated light skin and straight hair with greater freedom and opportunity as well as with membership in an elite class among African Americans. Because a number of free black women were of both European (white) and African (black) descent, their physical features, including their hair texture and skin color, represented freedom to enslaved and impoverished African Americans. Washington was no exception. Many of the black elite in Washington, including women such as Mary Church Terrell and Anna Julia Cooper, were mixed race. While not accepted fully by whites, free black women often attained comparably more social and economic freedoms than enslaved women. Free black women were the foremothers of the "Negro Elite" class that more prominently emerged after emancipation in D.C. Many of the mixed-race black elite in Washington, with their naturally straighter hair and lighter skin, became an ideal promoted in black beauty advertisements. The physical appearance of the Negro elite became entwined with a burgeoning African American collective ethos in which the politics of appearance intersected with African American possibility and the fashioning of a New Negro identity. According to black beauty scholars Ayana Byrd and Lori Tharps, "by the time slavery was officially abolished in 1865, 'good' hair and light skin had become the official keys to membership in the Negro elite," although exceptions were made based on one's educational attainment and occupation.[24] The Negro elite of Washington created insularity through lineage, color, educational and occupational achievement, and corporeal aesthetics. Hair texture and styling and skin color mattered and contributed to the demarcation of a comparatively privileged community of black people living and working in the nation's capital.

Prior to emancipation, there was a population of more than one hundred thousand free blacks in the United States.[25] Many of the free blacks in Washington descended from interracial encounters between African slaves and American whites, though not exclusively slave owners. For many, the features of the Negro elite, and more specifically the mixed-race population, signified freedom, mobility, and greater acceptance into white, dominant institutions. Washington occupied an important space for the Negro elite across the United States during most of the antebellum period and throughout most of the early twentieth century.[26] The physical appearance of this small but powerful community also produced lasting effects on the black beauty culture, which emerged in Washington during the New Negro era.

The ideals of straight hair and light skin anchored how white manufacturers who dominated the black beauty industry throughout the nineteenth century created and marketed race- and gender-specific beauty products. This also influenced how African Americans consumed beauty products. From the 1830s onward, white-owned companies manufactured and sold haircare products that claimed to straighten black women's hair. These advertisements appeared in African American periodicals and reified "straight" hair and lighter skin as both American and modern beauty ideals. These products primarily targeted free women of color. Hair salons and a small market for haircare and skincare products for the black elite in D.C. emerged in the 1840s and 1850s. Among black Washington women of all classes, skin-lightening and hair straightening techniques continued to flourish after emancipation and well into the twentieth century.[27]

These beauty practices often reflected the aspirations of some black Washington women to adhere to prevailing beauty norms and to escape the vestiges of "physical blackness," which located them at the bottom of the American beauty hierarchy and connected them to their past as enslaved persons. Whether formerly enslaved or born free, all black women bore the political, social, economic, and cultural consequences of "physical blackness," though to varying extents, depending on skin color, hair texture, class status, educational attainment, institutional affiliation, and familial background. Whereas economic security arguably functioned as the most significant factor in policing the boundaries of Washington's Negro elite, skin color, hair texture, and adornment practices also played integral roles in determining who belonged and who did not. The relative exclusivity of this privileged, black community, which in numerous ways manifested in a burgeoning politics of appearance, created a context for aspiration, resentment, rejection, ambivalence, and admiration among those migrating to the nation's capital in search of new opportunities.

By 1910, Washington had a black population of ninety-four thousand; many had migrated to the city during the late nineteenth century in an to escape their rural or "enslaved" past and their labor identities. Some black women among them mimicked the styling choices and practices of D.C.'s "negro bluebloods" and white women. Dark skin or tightly curled or kinky hair, features commonly associated with people of African descent in the United States, were not viewed as attractive or modern within certain black elite circles in Washington, as echoed by prominent papers such as the *Washington Bee*. Accordingly, the beauty standards of light skin and straight hair became synonymous with being urbane and modern. The pervasiveness of messages and products and processes encouraging black women to straighten their hair and lighten their skin imparted lasting effects on black beauty culture and on the collective psyche of black women attempting to identify themselves as New Negro women.

This imposing and historically rooted imaginary, however, could not and did not fully dictate the choices that black women in Washington made regarding their appearance. The desire to preserve and build upon traditions that black women brought with them from Africa or that black women crafted once in the United States impelled the rise of a local African American beauty culture. This burgeoning racialized-gendered market encompassed competing ideals of beauty, both responding to and shaping the predilections of black women consumers in the early twentieth century. Of particular importance to this industry was the cultural knowledge exchanged among black women about African American beauty practices.

Enslaved and free African American women partook in an intergenerational folk culture that fashioned its own standards and authored its own bodies of knowledge. Older black women passed on traditions to younger generations and created an informal economy for beauty products, using accessible ingredients such as those derived from plants. Communities of enslaved women and of black women in cities like Washington, Baltimore, and Philadelphia discussed and exchanged tonics, styling techniques, and other haircare and skincare practices.[28] This communal exchange moved toward formalization in Washington during the early twentieth century through the black press. The formalization of previously informal dynamics contributed to a sense of racial progress that both formerly enslaved and free blacks affirmed. Where they had been excluded and or devalued before, African American women optimistically anticipated emerging markets would open doors to them and their ideas about black womanhood.

Hopes for that kind of inclusion, however, quickly dissipated after Reconstruction. Black women, who confronted both racism and sexism, faced particularly difficult circumstances. As John Burrows describes the situation, Reconstruction optimism turned into Jim Crow realism.[29] Jim Crow realism, however, encouraged innovation. Despite scarce resources and a finite consumer base, African Americans created products and services to address the specific needs and desires of a New Negro community largely ignored and offensively addressed by white entrepreneurs.[30] Pioneers such as Annie Turnbo Malone, Sarah Breedlove (more commonly known as Madame C. J. Walker), and Marjorie Stewart Joyner, along with thousands of black women beauticians, manufacturers, salon owners, and saleswomen, capitalized on this distinct historical moment and transformed a folk subculture into a race-gender enterprise that provided the aesthetic foundation for New Negro womanhood.[31] "It is important," according to Baldwin, "to bear witness to how and why working-class migrant women turned bottles of white emulation into a *black* beauty culture to 'make over' racial landscapes as agents, entrepreneurs, chemists, inventors, and political activists in their communities and throughout the world."[32] Black women of Washington capitalized on the transformative possibilities of black beauty culture and created a local culture that trumpeted the arrival of a New Negro woman who had multiple entry points into and perspectives regarding black women's adornment practices. The multiple and variegated investments in black beauty culture by black women in Washington aligned with a growing diversification of standpoints among black women during the New Negro era.

The Birth of the Black Beauty Industry in Washington

Black migrants envisioned greater opportunity and more possibilities for themselves and their families in northern cities. Educational and employment opportunities as well as established black-owned businesses that catered to African Americans drew black women migrants to Washington and encouraged a continuous migration of African Americans in general to the District of Columbia during the late nineteenth and early twentieth centuries.[33] In her examination of Washington's growing black community during this period, Sharon Harley emphasized employment opportunities as well as the "lure of the city" as driving forces for the "steady migration" of black women in particular to Washington, where, compared with those available in the southern communities from which black women migrated, a large number of professional and nonprofessional jobs for African Americans waited.[34]

Opportunities did not erase the presence of Jim Crow racism, however. The horrors of racial violence and economic oppression affected urban areas, including Washington, but many African Americans viewed the situation in northern cities as preferable to their plight in the South. Additionally, industrialization, urbanization, the expansion of the mass communications industry, and burgeoning interstate commerce at the turn of the twentieth century catalyzed unprecedented economic growth that catered to an increasing Progressive Era penchant for consumption and made cities more appealing to all Americans and recent immigrants seeking better lives. The developing black beauty industry, which connected to those larger economic changes, offered black women professional prospects and new opportunities for self-expression, self-care, and self-presentation. At the intersection of economic and employment opportunities and evolving ideas about black womanhood was the black beauty industry.

Black women migrating to urban centers seeking employment brought with them the traditions and skills they learned in their southern communities, equipped themselves with beauty techniques and practices. Prior to the institutionalization of black beauty techniques through training schools and the establishment of national standards for manufacturers of beauty products, black women could enter beauty-culture occupations with relative ease. Operating out of their homes and developing a customer base through word of mouth, a local beauty industry that served the adornment-centered, acquisitive desires of a diverse community of black women emerged in Washington. Because of the informality of this early iteration of Washington's black beauty culture, very little documentation exists to accurately account for the number of women working in the beauty industry; nevertheless, daily advertisements placed by Washington-based women in the black newspapers indicate an evolving market in which black women could sell and consume black beauty products and services. A niche market of unique tastes expanded as the black population exploded in Washington and demanded race- and gender-specific service enterprises.[35] Because of prevailing gender norms, intraracial gender hierarchies, and the lack of educational and vocational opportunities available to black women, the black beauty industry thrived as one of the few major sectors in which black women dominated and could make a living from their race-gender ventures.[36]

The leading black periodicals in D.C. captured this explosion in their frequent publication of advertisements for beauty products and services. For example, *The Colored American*, a leading periodical in Washington throughout its brief decade-long existence, contained three or more advertisements for beauty services in each issue. Advertisements for hair-straightening preparations such as Ozono, Nelson's Straightine, Ford's Hair Pomade, Hair Vim, Kink, and MeLange, for devices such as The Magic (a hair-straightening hot comb), and for skin-lightening products or bleaching agents such as Black-No-More and Black Skin Remover frequently recurred in print throughout the New Negro women's era. The Chemical Wonder Company of New York—"the best business friend colored people have"—placed large, single display ads in the black press for whole lists of the company's beauty products, including Complexion WonderCreme, the Wonder Comb, Wonder Uncurl pomade, and Wonder Hair Grow scalp fertilizer.[37] In addition to these advertisements for products promoting a particular ideal of black feminine beauty, during the 1890s and the early 1900s, typically one or two advertisements featuring beauty businesses owned and operated by local black women ran in Washington's black newspapers on an almost daily basis. The majority of the local advertisements did not promote hair straightening or skin lightening products or services: advertisements for local beauty services did not feature as prominently as the thousands of advertisements for black beauty culture products and services that ran in the *Colored American* and the *Washington Bee* from 1880–1920. Of the nearly one hundred different beauty manufacturers and businesses advertised in Washington's leading black periodicals during the New Negro era, African American women beauty culturists and businesswomen in Washington who built upon skills and traditions honed during the early and mid-nineteenth century made up a small, but noteworthy faction of the newspapers' advertisements. Far fewer advertisements targeted black men as consumers of beauty culture—although perceived preferences of African American men for particular bodily aesthetic practices of African American women affected African American women's discourse on beauty.

Primarily patronized by the city's nationally recognized black elite class, the periodicals were also read by upwardly mobile poor and working-class blacks who became sellers, entrepreneurs, customers, and business owners.[38] Black beauty culture unfolded and evolved on the pages of newspapers and journals. In these ads, however, black women were not often authors of their content and ideology. The majority of advertisements encouraged black women to look more like their white or mixed-race female counterparts. Black beauty culture manufacturers—who included white men and women, black men, and black women—promoted skin-lightening and hair-straightening techniques honed within black communities during the nineteenth century. These practices became situated within a formalized national economy that grew as a result of advertisements in African American newspapers and journals. Because of the substantial population of African Americans in Washington, beauty culture manufacturers advertised their race- and gender-specific products in black Washington newspapers throughout the New Negro era.

Many of the earliest advertisements in black periodicals in Washington reveal the centrality of particular practices to black beauty culture. The advertisements, however, obscured the fact that many in black urban elite communities rejected skin lightening and hair straightening in the nineteenth century. From a business standpoint, the African American elite had the ability to indulge in conspicuous consumption. Additionally, the black elite's perceived embrace of white beauty standards and those standards' connection to social and economic mobility structured the predominating discourse of both national and local black beauty cultures. Manufacturers and sellers placed advertisements in publications that widely circulated in black middle- and upper-class communities and built on the perception, already in circulation, that African American women desired straighter hair and lighter skin.

In an 1899 edition of the *Colored American*, an advertisement highlighted the predominant discourse that shaped national black beauty culture in its formative years. The ad for a "Black Skin Remover: A Wonderful Face Bleach" presented a product manufactured in Richmond, Virginia. Many of manufacturers of black beauty products remained in southern states throughout the Great Migration. Before the Great Migration, interstate manufacturers played a small role in black beauty culture because of the primarily localized nature of the industry; black consumers purchased and bartered for products from within their respective communities. African Americans in cities from the 1890s onward represented a significant portion of the consumer base for black beauty products. Black publications became the vehicle through which manufacturers could reach a national audience with their products. Informal exchanges of beauty products and techniques among African Americans in different regions of the United States occurred before the Great Migration, but these exchanges became formalized as African Americans populated urban areas throughout the Upper South, Northeast, and Midwest and as black publications with space for advertisers circulated more widely.

The advertisement for "Black Skin Remover" champions the product's ability to make black skin several shades whiter and mulatto skin "perfectly white." The "before" and "after" images used in the advertisement display a stark transformation of dark skin to white skin. While boasting other "positive" effects such as the removal of wrinkles and pimples, the most significant selling point of the face bleach was the equation of beauty with whiteness. Toward the end of the advertisement copy, the manufacturer notes that the product will be sent to the consumer in such a way that the contents of the package would be known only to the consumer. Despite the popularity of skin-lightening processes among African Americans, this small aside suggested the potential backlash and or shaming a consumer of skin-lightening products might endure. It also intimated that consumers of skin-lightening products desired a transformation that appeared "natural" and not achieved through use of products. The selling point of "confidentiality" also implicitly addressed concerns among blacks regarding what altering one's physical appearance meant. Baldwin rightfully asserts that "much of the black resistance to cosmetics was a reaction to their implicit suggestion that black people required physical (quasi-genetic) alterations to be moral and equal."[39] Debates about what cosmetic and physical adornment practices signified for blacks proliferated throughout the New Negro era.

Similar advertisements ran in the *Washington Bee* throughout the early twentieth century. An advertisement for a skin-bleaching product manufactured by the Chemical Wonder Company of New York ran almost weekly for the entire first decade of the century. The advertisement combined many of the ideas perpetuated in black beauty discourse about African American skin and hair. The consistent theme of these advertisements was that straight hair and light skin were the ideal for black women. Most of these advertisements also equated kinky or tightly curled hair and dark skin with being undesirable.

The seven "chemical wonders" described in the advertisement promise to make African Americans more attractive through lightening the skin and straightening the hair. Although the advertisement targeted African American women and men alike, the "benefits" for black women were greater in number. The ad for the "seven wonders" system states that women using their products would "have better positions, marry better, get along better."[40] The manufacturers of the "chemical wonders" explicitly connect their products with black women achieving a higher or "preferred" status through their physical appearance. This advertisement also implied that African American

THE COLORED AMERICAN, WASHINGTON, D. C.

GRADUATES OF PROVIDENT

Chicago's Famous Hospital Sends Forth a Bright Bevy of Carefully Trained Nurses.

The Recrudescence of Smith.

HON H C SMITH.

Afro-American Council is Non-Partisan.

Tuskegee Institute Notes.

In The Antipodes

SEND US ONE DOLLAR

THE ACME QUEEN

GUARANTEED 25 YEARS

OUR RELIABILITY IS ESTABLISHED

SEARS, ROEBUCK & CO. (Inc.) ... CHICAGO, ILL.

Tenth Cavalry Souvenir

H. V. CASHIN & CO., HUNTSVILLE, ALABAMA

Publishers of Martial and Pictorial Literature of the Negro Race

... AGAINST SICKNESS

Accident and Death In

The American Home Life Insurance Company.

OF WASHINGTON, D. C.

SECURE A POLICY WHILE IN GOOD HEALTH.

Patronize Home Industry

HOME OFFICE: 907 U STREET, NORTHWEST.

G. W. CAVE, Manager.

S. S. Shedd & Bro

Plumbing, Heating, Tinning, Electric and Gas Fixtures, Furnaces, Ranges, Latrobes.

432 Ninth Street n w

The Central Dining Room

BLACK SKIN REMOVER

A WONDERFUL FACE BLEACH.

TRUSSES, 65c, $1.25 AND UP

SEARS, ROEBUCK & Co. CHICAGO

Johnson the Hatter

816 Ninth Street Northwest.

C. A CHANEY,

Flour, Feed, Baled Hay and Straw, STORE 462 N Street Northwest

MADDEN BROS.

1841 SEVENTH STREET N. Washington, D. C.

Cascarets

CANDY CATHARTIC

REGULATE THE LIVER

SKIN SPECIALIST!

MME. G. A. FINNIE MACA

Is located at 1431 W ST., N. W.

Picture of the Baker Family

HUDSON'S VARIETY STOR[E]

China, Toys, Tinware, Glass

and House Furnishings

423 Seventh Street N. W

CREDIT

GROGAN'S MAMMOTH CREDIT HOUSE

817-819-821-823 Seventh Street N. W.

Between H and I Streets.

HAIR-HEALTH.

Doctor Hay's Hair-Health

KEEP LOOKING YOUNG.

Every Bottle Warranted

LARGE 50c. BOTTLES.

FREE SOAP Offer

TRY AT ONCE DR. HAY'S HAIR-HEALTH AND HARFINA SOAP.

W. H. BUTLER.

PAINTS OILS

GLASS, &c.,

609 C STREET, N.W.

Cooper's

The Easy Way to Cook Or Heat

Gas Appliance Exchange

1424 New York Ave.

HOOVER

811 H Street Northwest

Justh's Old Stand

619 D Street Northwest

W. M. DRURY'S RESTAURANT

Figure 6. Advertisements Section, *Colored American*, November 25, 1899. Library of Congress, Chronicling America: Historical Newspapers Collection.

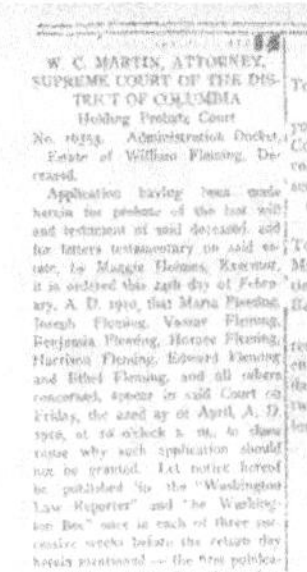

W. C. MARTIN, ATTORNEY.
SUPREME COURT OF THE DISTRICT OF COLUMBIA

SEASON OF 1910

Yours for pleasure and comfort,
Lewis Jefferson, 1910 First Street, S. W.

HE WHO HESITATES IS LOST

African Mining AND REAL ESTATE CO.

206 Broadway, New York City.

Development

SEND 10c FOR SAMPLE OF WONDER HAIR GROW

We Represent The Chemical Wonder Company of New York

M. B. BERGER & CO., 2 Rector St., New York

OLD MADE NEW.

If you want your clothing cleaned, altered or repaired, you should send a card or call at the up-to-date repair establishment. All work guaranteed or money refunded.

Mrs. D. Smith, Proprietor, 614 D street, northwest.

Christian Xander's Malaga Wines

The Family Quality House, 909 7th St.

HOLTMAN'S OLD STAND FINE BOOTS AND SHOES

491 Penn. ave., N. W.

Ford's Hair Pomade

Ford's Hair Pomade

The Ozonized Ox Marrow Co.

NOTICE TO LADIES

HAIR TONIC

EX-SENATOR PLATT

WHY EXPERIMENT?

Prof. F. N. Cristo, 713 4th St., N.E.

ROBERT ALLEN Buffet and Family Liquor Store, Phone North 2340, 1917 4th Street, N. W. Washington, D. C.

Her-Tru-Line FOR THE HAIR

Southern Medicine Company Box 754 Atlanta, Ga.

The MAGIC SHAMPOO DRIER AND HAIR STRAIGHTENER

LADIES LOOK!

Magic Shampoo Drier Co., Minneapolis, Minnesota.

MATTINGS

HOUSE & HERRMANN

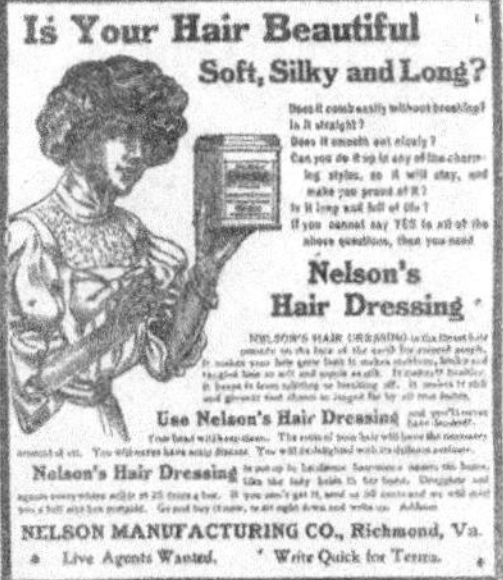

Lots For Sale

H. K. FULTON'S LOAN OFFICE, No. 314 Ninth Street N. W.

BURNSTINE LOAN OFFICE
GOLD AND SILVER WATCHES, DIAMONDS, JEWELRY, GUNS, MECHANICAL TOOLS, LADIES' AND GENTS' WEARING APPAREL.
OLD GOLD AND SILVER BOUGHT.
UNREDEEMED PLEDGES FOR SALE.
361 Pennsylvania Ave. N. W.

Figure 7. Advertisements Section, *Washington Bee*, March 12, 1910. Library of Congress, Chronicling America: Historical Newspapers Collection.

The Colored American

A National Negro Newspaper

VOL. X, NO. 31 WASHINGTON, D. C., FEBRUARY 13, 1904. PRICE, FIVE CENTS

D. E. V. Jordan. Prof. Pulliam then presented Rev. T. O. Fuller, President of Howe Institute, who had been selected to introduce the speaker of the evening.

Among other things Rev. Fuller said: "It gives me more than ordinary pleasure to greet this host of intellectual, and the unterrified of the city of Memphis, who have escaped the destructive influences of that volcanic eruption, which occurred at Mississippi's capital the other day, when Vardaman was inaugurated governor.

Since the early dawn of civilization comrades who have struggled together in trenches, on heights, in the valley and on the sea, in the defence of their country's flag and for principles which they held sacred and dear, have associated themselves in organizations for the purpose of keeping fresh in their minds the incidents and relics of the conflict. It is in keeping with this idea that the Alumni Association of Howe Institute was formed. They are a noble set and are bringing fresh honors to their Alma Mater, in the schoolroom, at the bar, at the bedside as physicians and on foreign battle fields in defence of the flag of their country. The Alumni is seeking to give inspiration to a higher culture which bespeaks an advanced civilization and they have been wise in their selection when they bring before you this evening for the inspiration of the manhood and womanhood of this race,

(Continued on Page 2).

MR. THOMAS DRURY, Rehearsing.

IN DIXIE LAND.

A Revival in Education and General Progress.

Miss Burroughs Charms a Large Memphis Audience Taking for Her Subject "Up From the Depths"—The Alumni Association of Howe Institute Honor Itself—Rev. Fuller's Eloquent Introduction of the Speaker of the Evening.

Memphis, Tenn., Special:—Miss Nannie H. Burroughs of Louisville, Kentucky, Corresponding Secretary of the Women's Auxiliary to the National Baptist Convention, delivered her famous lecture, "Up From The Depths", at Memphis, Tenn., January 25th, under the auspices of the Alumni Asociation of Howe Institute. At the hour appointed the spacious chapel of Howe Institute was crowded with a well selected audience of the best people of Memphis. Prof. W. L. Pulliam, president of the Alumni Association, rapped for order and announced an instrumental solo by Mrs. Emma B. Jones, which was most beautifully rendered. A double quartett followed. Rev. H. C. Owens of the Tabernacle Baptist Church delivered the invocation. A most excellent solo was sung by Mr.

MISS NANNIE H. BURROUGHS.
Cor. Sec. Woman's National Baptist Convention, Louisville, Ky.

Figure 8. Nannie Helen Burroughs in the *Colored American*, February 13, 1904. Library of Congress, Chronicling America: Historical Newspapers Collection.

women did or should value marriage and respectable social affiliations. The alleged benefits of black women using the Chemical Wonder Company's beauty products were relegated to the domestic and semi-private spheres of marriage and social interactions. Another striking aspect of this advertisement is its broader claim about the importance of beauty culture. The

Chemical Wonders Company claimed that "white people spend millions to beautify themselves." Immediately following this announcement, the advertisement avers "colored people should make themselves as attractive as possible." This attractiveness, the company said, could be achieved through lightening the skin and straightening the hair of African Americans. Additionally, the "seven wonders" advertisement illuminates the parallel beauty industries that thrived as well as race- and gender-specific markets that similarly heralded "beautification" as a means to social mobility and individual and collective progress. The insertion of information about white beauty culture revealed the continuing effects of white cultural hegemony on black beauty culture that lasted well into the early twentieth century.[41]

The language of these African American beauty advertisements were inextricably linked to broader discussions about disavowing the past and embracing cultural ideologies that compelled African American women to use their physical appearance as a vehicle for debunking racial and gender stereotypes. Black beauty advertisers further expanded the exchange of ideas regarding the importance of appearance to racial progress through emphasizing African American women's ability to transform themselves into respectable women by adhering to dominant cultural norms, which dictated that black women's natural, kinky hair and darker skin symbolized unruliness, primitiveness, and a lack of intelligence and refinement. Words such as "soft," "glossy," "silky," and "refined" were attached to straightened hair. Kinky hair, the hair texture commonly associated with African Americans, was depicted as "stubborn," "harsh," and "stiff."

Advertisements did not always reflect the ideology of the *Washington Bee* staff. From the paper's inception, *Bee* editor Calvin Chase "spoke out against racism and the internecine elitism of color-consciousness"[42] and against the negative impact of colorism in black Washington as well in African America more broadly. Seemingly contradictory to that position were editorials that encouraged black women to straighten their hair as a means to asserting a modern, New Negro identity. Advertisements for skin lighteners and hair-straightening products and techniques made up the majority of black beauty advertisements in the *Bee*. At least once a week, the *Bee* ran an ad for *Ford's Hair Pomade*, a product for "straightening kinky and curly hair."[43] These advertisements and this aforementioned editorial overtly contradict the *Bee*'s founding principle of debunking the "elitism of color-consciousness." By 1905 the United States Post Office barred the mail-order sale of skin lighteners such as Black-No-More that had history of causing severe skin damage. A market for these products, however, remained intact despite these legal proscriptions. Local manufacturers continued developing concoctions that promised drastic effects, products like Imperial Whitener and Mme. Turner's Mystic Face Bleach, and newspapers continued to carry advertisements for these products.

The emphasis on straight hair gradually came under fire as more black women became involved in the marketing of black beauty products in the 1900s and the early 1910s. African American women also became increasingly involved in the manufacturing of products and the founding of businesses targeting black women. In the early twentieth century, black women in Washington from all classes began fashioning an advertising discourse within the black beauty industry in which competing aesthetic ideals led to the development of a wider variety of products. As black women took a more direct role in marketing black beauty culture in the black press, they both embraced and challenged a mainstream beauty culture that promoted white aesthetic norms. In the process, they shaped an alternative black advertising subculture premised on standards and aesthetic expressions originating from traditions honed in black communities. Although competing beauty practices and aesthetic norms reflected emerging class struggles in Washington as well as political struggles surrounding the viability of feminine artifice and physical "naturalness," as vehicles for expressing modern black womanhood, hair straightening and skin lightening were not necessarily class-specific aesthetic practices nor wholly indicative of a individual black women's political standpoint.[44]

In Washington, one of the most notable proponents of a beauty culture who did not advocate white beauty standards was Nannie Helen Burroughs. Founder of the National Training School for Girls and Women, Burroughs explicitly connected the practices of skin lightening and hair straightening to white emulation. In her 1904 essay, "Not Color, but Character," Burroughs asserts, "What every woman who . . . straightens out needs, is not her appearance changed, but her mind. . . . If Negro women would use half the time they spend in trying to get white in trying to get better, the race would move forward."[45] Burroughs's comments also captured the time investment black feminine artifice required and called out black women to utilize that time for what she viewed as more important endeavors: racial uplift and intellectual growth. In *Jesus, Jobs, and Justice*, Bettye Collier-Thomas fleshes out Burroughs's ideas on African American beauty and explicitly connects these ideas to Baptist theology. Burroughs desired for black women to maintain "feminine propriety" in their bodily appearance, but she did not view black feminine artifice as the most viable means of self-presentation. Conversely, fellow Washington woman Mary Church Terrell wrote about the joy of black feminine artifice in the styling of black women's hair. Reflecting on late nineteenth century African American beauty culture, Terrell reminisced in her autobiography, "And 'way back in the 70's women had to buy a quantity of false hair to keep up with the prevailing style. There were waterfalls and curls galore hanging coquettishly under their chignons at the side of their heads."[46] Terrell did not specifically promote hair straightening but acknowledged the reality of black women delving into practices of feminine artifice to assert themselves as stylish and in vogue. Black feminine artifice, most notably hair extensions products such as weaves or hair pieces, were a part of the modern black beauty culture and continue to play an important role black women's adornment practices in the twenty-first century.

Half-Century Magazine, headed by Katherine Williams, an editor-in-chief who was an African American woman, ran editorials and stories from black women that mirrored Burroughs's position and criticized the predominance of advertisements for hair straightening and skin lightening. A particularly scathing critique titled "Betrayers of the Race" appeared in the February 1920 edition of the magazine.[47] Williams described those advocating for hair straightening and those straightening their hair as "traitors."[48] Editorials such as this served as the rhetorical foundation for the anti-hair-straightening and skin-bleaching "movement" in cities that led to the formation of anti-hair-wrapping clubs.[49] In the March 3, 1915, edition of the *Washington Bee*, a brief mention of a Washington anti-hair-wrapping club meeting is made. Responding to black beauty industry advertisements and a national black discourse that identified straight hair as an African American feminine ideal, these black women's clubs gave voice to those opposing hair straightening as a means for racial advancement and cultural progress.

These clubs rallied around hair wrapping in particular because the practice encouraged African American women to eradicate the natural kinkiness of their hair through the potentially dangerous process of wrapping the hair in heated fabric with an ample amount of oil. This method caused burns and, in many, hair damage. Many black women also used hair wrapping on their children, because they believed that the process would result in the permanent straightening of their children's hair. The practice also had the effect of ingraining in future generations of African Americans the desirability of straight hair. Anti-hair-wrapping clubs emerged in Washington and openly challenged newspapers such as the *Washington Bee* through disparaging articles connecting hair straightening to white emulation in black-women-authored publications such as *Half-Century Magazine*. Black women opposing the discourse forwarded by the majority of advertisements in African

American newspapers used these same publications to configure an alternate advertising discourse that trumpeted the health of African American women's skin and hair and that promoted black women as entrepreneurs, innovators, and teachers. What became apparent by the late 1900s were differing perspectives among New Negro women about whether artifice and adornment, physical naturalness, or a hybrid of both would come to represent modern black womanhood.[50] Washington women waged battles on the pages of local newspapers, and although significantly outspent by manufacturers peddling products associated with white emulation, local Washington black beauty culturists offered new possibilities of thinking about naturalness and race-/culture-based gendered adornment practices and processes.

New Negro Women and Advertising Discourses in Washington

Advertisements crafted by black women built upon the New Negro ethos of racial progress, racial pride, and gender identity of the early twentieth century. Early manifestations of this alternative black beauty discourse emerged in the last few years of the nineteenth century. In Washington, New Negro women carved out an advertising subculture within black beauty culture that championed racially distinct adornment practices, techniques, and styles of African American women. Although these practices were integral to black beauty culture prior to the 1890s, this alternative discourse formalized through advertisements in black periodicals. Increasingly, advertisements for products/processes for skin lightening and hair straightening ran alongside ads African American women placed to promote their own products, techniques, and services. This competing, black-women-centered and black-women-authored discourse had its roots in the informal and generational exchanges among African American women.

An 1899 advertisement in the *Colored American* targeted black women as potential customers for skin care, not skin-lightening products. This short ad championed the local hair and skincare services of Madame G. A. Finnie Mack.[51] A "Skin Specialist" based in the predominantly black U Street Corridor neighborhood, at 1431 West Street NW, Washington, D.C., Madame Mack guaranteed to treat and cure "all Skin troubles," within reasonable terms. In this ad, black beautification became synonymous with the health and well-being of the skin and hair. Madame Mack did not mention hair-straightening or skin-lightening products, but she spoke vaguely about skin treatments that beautified and hair treatments that cultivated hair growth. Despite many of the skin-lightening and hair-straightening advertisements in black newspapers affirming that their products addressed the health of

THE COLORED AMERICAN. 5

Afro-American Council

Continued from page 1.

[illegible] of the teachers of the [illegible] and Albert S. White. [illegible] McGhee and W. A. Pledger, [illegible] Atlanta, Ga., responded to the [illegible] Bishop A. Walters, founder [illegible] Afro-American Council, told [illegible] was organized five years ago, [illegible] that it was the burning of [illegible] which led him to appeal to [illegible] to call the meeting in [illegible]. The Council took a recess [illegible]

[illegible] session opened with a [illegible] Rev. John H. Frank, D. D., [illegible] street Baptist church, [illegible] was followed by the report of [illegible] Committee on Credentials.

[illegible] WAS FIXED.

[illegible] was caused by Frederick L. McGhee, of St. Paul, who [illegible] that the Constitution had [illegible] tampered with, and the election [illegible] be held at once, was fixed [illegible] Tuesday afternoon. He de[illegible] an explanation.

EDITOR T. THOS FORTUNE, President of the National Afro-American Council.

[illegible] will read the Constitution [illegible] on the question raised.

[illegible] Cyrus Field Adams read, [illegible] from the far West was [illegible] satisfied, and he was ruled off [illegible] by President Fortune, who at [illegible] proceeded to read his annual ad[illegible] the Council, which was the [illegible] of the afternoon.

T. Thos. Fortune, in discussing the [illegible] the Council, said, in part:

The report of the financial secretary, Frederick L. McGhee, was read.

MR. WILLIAM H. LEWIS.

[illegible] complaints were made on the [illegible] of the affairs of the Council [illegible] the secretary, which will, per[illegible] mean a fight in the Council, to[illegible] when it comes to electing officers [illegible] the next twelve months.

President Fortune announced as the [illegible] to draft resolutions and address [illegible] the country, the Rev. I. B. [illegible] D. D., of Louisiana; W. H. Steward, Kentucky; Bishop C. H. Phillips, Tennessee; M. M. Lewey, H. T. Johnson, New Jersey; R. H. Jefferson, Maryland; A. D. Griffin, Oregon; Jas. H. Guy, Virginia and W. H. Lewis, Massachusetts.

Auditing Committee—Emmett J. Scott, Alabama; Cecelia V. Rodney, Missouri; Dr. E. B. Jefferson, Texas; Mary Detheridge, Kentucky; W. L. Cohen, Louisiana.

Fully 1,500 persons attended the meeting of the Council Wednesday night, at Quinn Chapel, during which addresses were made by representative colored men on the race question. T. Thomas Fortune presided.

Dr. Booker T. Washington, the apostle of industrial education, was the center of attraction at Macauley's Theater Thursday night and over 3,000 colored and white citizens were present.

Mr. Washington made a characteristically sensible speech. Others who spoke were T. T. Fortune, Dr. H. T. Johnson, Bishop Walters and W. H. Lewis, whose appointment as District Attorney of Massachusetts attracted so much attention recently.

The full list of officers is as follows: T. Thomas Fortune, New York, president; W. A. Pledger, Georgia, William H. Steward, Kentucky, J. Q. Adams, Minnesota, J. H. Guy, Kansas, G. Hunt, New York, Col. James Lewis, Louisiana, R. J. Griffin, Oregon, Mrs. R. J. Jeffrey, New York, W. H. Lewis, Massachusetts, vice presidents; Cyrus Field Adams, secretary; F. L. McGhee, Minnesota, financial secretary; Mrs.

MR. EMMETT J. SCOTT, Tuskegee, Ala.

Fannie Barrier Williams, Illinois, corresponding secretary; L. G. Jordan, Kentucky, chaplain; John W. Thompson, New York, treasurer; executive board, E. J. Scott, Alabama; Mary Dethridge, Ky.; C. F. Adams, Illinois; A. K. Manning, Indiana; James H. Guy, Kansas; W. H. Steward, Kentucky; W. L. Cohen, Louisiana; W. M. Trotter, Massachusetts; Mary E. McCoy, Michigan; W. T. Francis, Minnesota; Cecil Rodney, Missouri; H. T. Johnson, New Jersey; J. J. Adams, New York; Bishop J. W. Hood, North Carolina; M. C. B. Mason, D. D., Ohio; L. G. Jordan, Pennsylvania; J.C. Napier, Tennessee; Chas. Stewart, Maryland; M.M. Lewey, Florida.

ADDRESS TO THE AMERICAN PEOPLE.

Believing confidently as we do that a vast majority of the people of this country favor that spirit of freedom and exact justice to all which not only gave birth to the nation, but has led it more than once to espouse the cause of the oppressed, and insist that every man shall be permitted to adjust the standard of his own worth, and thus settle for himself the place he will occupy in life, we, the representatives of 10,000,000 American citizens of African descent, do thus the more readily present our case before the great bar of public opinion, as hereinbefore set forth:

First—That we would call attention to the readiness with which we have at all times responded to our country's call, and fought patriotically and bravely to sustain the nation's honor and the country's flag.

Second—Our presence in this country, and the place we occupy therein, were not of our own choosing; we came in possession of this heritage as the result of an unusually and remarkably strange chain of circumstances. As we now look back over the past, it

FANNIE BARRIER WILLIAMS.

appears that our interests were guided by a divine hand, and that the outcome is the culmination of the divine purpose. This being true, our future is secure, and this country will in the years to come, as in the years that are past, profit by our presence.

We recognize with pleasure the friendly relation that has all along existed between the best people of the white race and our own, and we sincerely desire that nothing may be permitted to intervene to mar this relation. Still we are confident that no one who notes carefully the signs of the times can fail to discover that there are influences at work in nearly every part of the land to accomplish this very end. Who can fail to see that just at this time, and more so than for a number of years past, the Negro is being held up to public gaze as the most objectionable and undesirable citizen that treads American soil? The ignorant, vicious criminal classes are pointed to as the types and products of the race, rather than those who are the output of the Negro's best endeavors for race development and uplift. We declare this standard of measurement to be unfair to any people, and believe that fair-minded citizens of the entire country will agree with us in this view. These do not indicate our capacity, either for present or future citizenship. It

MR. JOHN W. THOMPSON, Treasurer, Rochester, N. Y.

would be as fair to judge the white race of this country by those of their number who have assassinated Presidents or been guilty of treason or have betrayed and murdered innocent women. Judge us as you judge the mechanic; judge us as you judge the scholar; judge us as you judge yourselves, not by the worst, but by the GAL 19.
best products time and opportunity have enabled us to send forth to take their place among their fellows. It is manifestly unjust to seek to impress the country that because the Negro was once a slave he is not and never can be a man; because there are Negroes who commit crimes, therefore, the Negro is a criminal race.

FEWER MOB VICTIMS.

As to mob violence it is gratifying to note that for the past year or two the number of victims show a decided decrease, and while all these were not members of our race the vast majority were. But notwithstanding this fact, we should not feel called upon to discuss the matter at all at this time were it not that though the number of victims is decreasing the variety of provocations which lead up to this act of violence is growing more and more numerous. It is not an unusual thing to read these days of Negroes being lynched for impudence, refusing to obey, striking a white man, etc. Now, we submit that lynching for any cause is destructive of law., is demoralizing. But to subject persons accused of or even guilty of such trivial offenses as we have indicated to unlawful punishment and death is to make the Negro the marked man of the nation; for him to suffer violence for such causes will eventually involve many of our best people. Even as it is in some sections of the country it means death for a Negro to attempt to protect the females of his family. We ask in all sincerity, is this American? Is it right? Such conditions indicate clearly a tendency to anarchy, and anarchy for the Negro will terminate for anarchy for all men. Law sustains our splendid civilization, and the absence of it means its destruction. Lawlessness begets its kind and its increase can bring no good to any one.

But again, the number of those of our race who are now accused of the nameless crime against women is so small as compared with the whole number lynched that it is scarcely nec-

Continued on page 9.

DRESS MAKING ACADEMY

The de Lam Orton Famous French Perfection Tailor System. Mme. J. A. Smallwood, sole agent, 1513 Madison street, northwest.

Morning class from 9 a. m. to 1 p. m. Afternoon class 2 to 5 p. m. daily. Evenings from 7:30 to 10 o'clock. Mondays, Wednesdays, and Fridays, dressmakers and ladies who wish to do their own dress-making.

WANTED.—To learn the wonderful De Lam Orton French Perfection Tailor System. Seamless Basques without one inch of visible seam, in lining or goods, not even on the shoulder. Successful dressmaking requires as much earnest progressive study as successful work in any profession. No detail is too small to be looked after. We teach you to make dresses with or without seam and guarantee perfect fits, and complete your course with a diploma.

If you have a spare room that you would like to rent to desirable parties, advertise them in The Colored American.

SUMMER RESORTS.

FOR RENT—Summer of 1903 Lincoln Hall Harper's Ferry, W. Va. For particulars address N. C. Brackett.

Please Help Me Find My Brother

Sauah Joyce was sold in Mecklenburg, Virginia several years before the civil war, to Connigan a Negro trader. His mother, Willie, was a slave on the Joyce plantation. He had one sister Betty, who is very anxious to find him. Any information will be gladly received.

Mrs Betty Reynolds
44 Parker street, Atlanta Ga.

WANTED

For the Famous Troubadours Company,

Three Chorus Girls, with strong Soprano voices. Must be good looking, good dressers on and off the Stage. State salary expected; we pay railroad and Hotel expenses. The season of 1903-04, beginning Sept., 15th. Address all communications to E. W. Dale, Cape May City, N. J.

BOARDING

By The Week or Month.
Apply to—
MRS. M. J. BUNDY,
941 T St., N. W.

Figure 9. Fannie Barrier Williams in the *Colored American*, July 11, 1903. Library of Congress, Chronicling America: Historical Newspapers Collection.

African American women's hair and skin, their primary focus was championing lighter skin and straighter hair. Local beauty culturists such as Madame Mack placed their advertisements for black beauty products and services in a burgeoning discourse about black women's health and its connection to her overall appearance. On average, one to two advertisements for local beauty specialists appeared in the *Washington Bee* on a daily basis. Although not as prevalent when compared with advertisements by major manufacturers of black beauty products, black women in Washington used local periodicals to claim a distinct space for an evolving black beauty subculture in which black women's self-care and culturally rooted adornment took precedent.

By the 1910s, advertisements designed by African American women surfaced in local black periodicals in cities with substantial African American populations. These ads did not conform to the standard tropes of black beauty marketing that prevailed in the nineteenth century and the first decade of the twentieth. Responding to the rapidly growing population of African American women and the increasingly diverse tastes of these women, a locally based black beauty industry evolved. In neighborhoods such as Georgetown, Anacostia, LeDroit Park, and Howard University/Shaw, African Americans could patronize black-owned salons that catered to black women. Advertisements for black women beauty culturists, black-owned salons, products manufactured by black women, and home-based businesses shared space in local black periodicals with ads for established beauty products for hair straightening and skin lightening. In Washington papers such as the *Bee*, these advertisements captured the ethos of a black women's subculture within African American beauty culture.

The March 12, 1910, edition of the *Bee*, for example, contained many advertisements for black beauty products. The most visible advertisements include those for Ford's Hair Pomade (a hair-softening product), The Magic hot comb, and Her-True-Line (a hair-growth and hair-straightening product).[52] Each of these highlights hair straightening and softening. They use words such as harsh, kinky, and unmanageable to describe the natural texture of African American hair as undesirable. Advertisements for these brands ran throughout the tenure of the leading African American newspaper in Washington. What is less noticeable on this page of ads, however, is a small ad with no images located directly below the Ford's Hair Pomade advertisement. The advertisement is offered as a "Notice to Ladies."[53]

The contents of the "Notice to Ladies" advertisement unveil several of the key facets of the New Negro aesthetic subculture that developed during the first and second decades of the twentieth century in Washington. The first information provided in the "Notice to Ladies" is the address, 935 R Street NW, Washington, presumably the home of the manufacturer and seller, Mrs. A. J. Smith. Mrs. Smith resided in the Shaw neighborhood of Washington, a well-known racial enclave for blacks in the nation's capital. Shaw residents and black Washingtonians from other neighborhoods patronized many of the black-owned businesses in this nationally known African American neighborhood. Immediately following the address, the ad provides information about what constitutes unhealthy and undesirable hair for African American women. Kinkiness and manageability were not among Mrs. Smith's concerns. Instead, she sought to address hair thinning, hair loss, dryness, lifelessness, and itchy scalp. In response to these conditions, Mrs. Smith offered a hair tonic with an assurance of giving new life to the hair, a clean scalp, and a guarantee that her product met safety standards under the law.

The ad concludes with an offer of a free clipping and "singeing" for all patrons of her salons and her address. Singeing was a process used by black women beauty culturists to stimulate hair growth. This simple and comparatively uncreative and visually bland ad nevertheless indicated a gradual shift in how black women in Washington could market and advertise products and services offered by women in the African American beauty industry. Black women began using the knowledge and skills they honed in their communities prior to their migration to cities to create a formalized space within black beauty culture. This space did not solely champion beauty practices that heralded light skin and straight hair as preferable for black women.

The launching of a local industry based on salons (both inside and outside the home) and black beauty product manufacturers and suppliers crafted an alternative space to "provide a beauty regime for African American women that would allow them to fashion and meet their own ideals as well as create opportunities for themselves."[54] The local beauty industry in Washington, although predominated by ads promoting hair straightening and skin lightening, found space in the pages of black newspapers to target African American women not invested in rendering the kinky or curly straight or lightening their brown skin. Shifting the focus from "white emulation" or becoming more "urban" and "modern," advertisements such as Mrs. Smith's and the gradual spread of black-women-owned salons that emphasized the importance of healthy and styled black hair, African American women in Washington configured a space in the New Negro movement that emphasized bodily aesthetic values defined by, for, and about black women. From the perspective we gain from black Washington newspapers, it appears that the gradual spread of local beauty salons commenced in the early twentieth century. Formal records for most of these businesses do not exist, but the increased frequency of advertisements in black newspapers signals a growth in their presence and viability. Beginning in the first decade of the twentieth century, almost one beauty culture advertisement per week featured a local black woman trumpeting her beauty products or services for black women.

The recurrence of advertisements like Mrs. Smith's gave voice to black women who owned small businesses and who did not have access to the financial capital of national manufacturers.

The black press in Washington also highlighted the emergence of black women as entrepreneurs and business owners. Of particular note, black beauty schools received considerable ad space in Washington's black publications. Advertisements for Southern Beauty Culture School ran from the fall of 1909 through the Summer of 1910 in the *Bee*.[55] The June 4, 1910, edition of the *Bee* featured a comparatively large advertisement for Southern Beauty Culture School.[56] The ad served as a notice of relocation, a declaration of its commitment to "colored young women," and a heralding of their national reputation and impact as evident through their alumni. Located in the U Street Corridor neighborhood at 1410 Fourteenth Street NW, the Southern Beauty Culture School sought to educate African American women in Washington in a range of black beauty practices and to prepare these women for opening their own salons, developing new products, and inventing new techniques for styling and attending to African American women's hair. As Tiffany Gill explains, "Beauty college was . . . cheaper than teacher's colleges and nursing schools," other professions in which black women thrived, and was accessible to women beyond the burgeoning middle class.[57] The relative accessibility of beauty colleges for black women contributed to the rapid growth of black women beauty culturists throughout the New Negro era.

The only boldfaced typography in the advertisement features the name of the school and its president, Mrs. Lucie R. Pollard. The significance of a black woman being president of such a business was not lost on African American women in Washington. Mrs. Pollard and others who founded and presided over black beauty businesses in D.C. were lauded by many New Negro women as symbols of progress and the promise of greater possibility for African American women in cities. Mrs. Pollard's advertisement does not discuss hair straightening or skin lightening, but it implicitly addressed the connection between her business and a New Negro agenda, with its offer to train black women to participate in the modern world as businesswomen and consumers of beauty. Additionally, black beauty schools functioned as sites for black women to invest in their communities and as spaces to assist recent black women migrants to urban centers such as Washington in, as Gill asserts, "getting acclimated to urban life."[58] Her school represented a vision of New Negro womanhood and the means by which it could be attained. After black women in Washington began to market their services, products, and businesses more frequently, discussions about black beauty culture in the nation's capital expanded to encompass new trends in black beauty culture advertising.

VOL. 7. NO. 47. WASHINGTON, D. C., SATURDAY, FEBRUARY 17, 1900. PRICE FIVE CENTS

WOMAN'S CASE IN EQUITY

Gracefully and Forcefully Presented by Mrs. Mary Church Terrell Before the Brainiest of Equal Suffragists in America—The Premier Representative of our Womanhood Makes the Hit of the Convention.

The equal suffragists have come and gone. Those who followed their proceedings and digested their arguments will all agree that the cause they advocate with so much earnestness and intelligence is today better understood than ever before, and has been made to command a more and more serious degree of consideration. Woman suffrage, once a subject for ridicule, has ceased to be a joke. It is one of the grave problems of the hour. The wonderful advancement of the feminine sex in business, in the professions, in the industries, and in the world of finance, is giving her an importance in the affairs of life which the sensible man must recognize, and subscribe to a change of laws and customs to accord with the higher conditions that have come about in consequence of woman's broadening influence.

All of the week's sessions were instructive and interesting. Well informed and witty women, thoroughly alive to everything, not only where the advancement of women is concerned, but in all things and events which are under discussion throughout the whole world, addressed the meetings when they were thrown open for that purpose, and delivered their opinions with great force of logic and intelligence. There is nothing about the woman suffragist today to remind one of the agitator of a quarter of a century ago. The unsightly attired, short skirted, short haired woman, who, for so many years, was the butt of the satirist and the cartoonist, has been shoved off of the board, and in her place stands the cultured, womanly woman of the twentieth century. In her dress she keeps pace with fashion. She is in many instances a mother, and she boasts of it and the home which she ennobles.

Many of the nation's brightest women took part in the gathering, headed by the veteran Susan B Anthony, but no one made a better impression for wisdom, happiness of expression and power of oratory than did our own Mrs Mary Church Terrell, president of the National Association of Colored Women. As was noted in a former issue

MRS. MARY CHURCH TERRELL,

President of the National Association of Colored Women. Her Address on "Woman Suffrage" the Hit of the Recent Gathering of America's Brainiest Women.

of this paper Mrs. Terrell was announced to speak on "The Justice of Woman Suffrage," the piece de resistance of the whole convention. We said Mrs. Terrell would meet the highest expectations in handling this trying topic—and she more than did so. Her effort was a masterpiece of argument, scholarly and logically put, and was delivered with that ease and grace of bearing, that ineffable charm and magnetism of manner, and dignity and force that are characteristic of all Mrs. Terrell does or says. She was herself—at her best—that's all, and to state that her presentation was "Terrellesque" will convey a perfectly clear idea of its excellence to all who know the leader of Afro-American womanhood. The race may well feel proud of such a splendid representation. By Mrs. Terrell's appearance at this convention both the cause of women in general and the Negro in particular has been incalculably benefited.

We cannot give the entire address, but Mrs. Terrell said in part:

(Continued on Fourth page)

A Banquet in Honor of Abraham Lincolns Birthday.

Baltimore, Md., Special—On last Monday night at the McKinley Club on Druid Hill avenue, a banquet was tendered in honor of Abraham Lincoln's birthday. After a very fine dinner was served, the table being laden with all the delicaces of the season, Hon. Warner T. McGuinn was made toastmaster of the evening. The gathering was largely attended by many of the prominent citizens of the city.

Dr. J. Marcus Cargill responded to the toast, "Abraham Lincoln," Mr. J E. G. Webb, "The Political Outlook of the Negro," Hon. George B. Mills, "Organization," J. Henry Bayton, "The Field of Journalism," Mr. Lewis Tunsell "The Hustler," Samuel C. Brown, "The Qualities of a Man" and Mr. Alex. McDaniel, "The Good Work of Abraham Lincoln." The evening was one of great interest, many fine speeches were made. The annual banquet committee was appointed as follows:

Dr J. M. Cargill, Messrs. Geo. Mills, J. E. G. Webb and W. T. McGuinn. The inclemency of the weather did not at all prevent a goodly number being present, and all seemed to have enjoyed the celebration of the noted and worthy chieftain's birthday, in the personation of Abraham Lincoln.

POLITICS IN CONNECTICUT.

The Patriarchie Meeting in June—Death of a Prominet Woman Social Horoscope—News Notes

New Haven, Conn., Special—All colored men who are interested in the political welfare of the race in New Haven should be up and doing. There should be more interest along that line now than ever. There is something in store for the colored man if he will only get out and hustle for himself. We have a great many men who will "blow" around and say what ought to be done, but are never ready to assist. There is also a class of men who go into politics looking only for their own interest and when they find they cannot win out they will try to kill the progress of every other colored man. This spirit must die before the Negro can prosper in New England. The Negro must learn to talk his business with his friends and keep it from the white man the white man is looking for himself everytime, and when he asks any favors of the Negro, the return is always made with a promise. But, ah, the Negro of today has seen the folly and has decided to demand such rights as belong to the Negro, simply by casting an honest ballot next spring.

The Goffe street branch of the Y. M. C. A. is the only colored Y. M. C. A. in New England today and it is very painful to say that there are nearly six thousand Negroes in this city and this association has such small attendance. The young men in New Haven should feel it a duty to support this organization.

The annual Field day and Convention of the New England and New York Patriarchie Union which was to convene in New Haven on the first day of June 1900. All Patriarchie under the jurisdiction of this Union will govern themselves accordingly. For further information address A. Lee Epps, No. 78 Webster street, New Haven, Conn.

Mrs. Josephine Mitchell, of Milford, after returning from church Sunday evening, February 4, met with a very sad death. Early Monday morning she was found in the well by her husband. It proved to be an accidental death from the verdict rendered by the coroner's inquest. Mrs. Mitchell was born in Norfolk, Va., 50 years ago and has lived North for 25 years or more.

(Continued on Fifth Page.)

Figure 10. Mary Church Terrell in the *Colored American*, February 17, 1900. The Library of Congress, Chronicling America: Historical Newspapers Collection.

Beauty culture provoked contentious discussions throughout the 1920s. Prominent African American intellectuals, activists, artists, and writers such as W. E. B. Du Bois, Alain Locke, Mary Church Terrell, Zora Neale Hurston, and Marcus Garvey debated the meaning of hair straightening and skin lightening and what role these practices played. Well-known figures in the national African American community and in local black communities recognized the importance of the politics of appearance in the political and social struggles of the decade, which included Pan-Africanism, Garveyism, Racial Intergrationism, Black Separatism, and Black Cultural Nationalism. Several of these New Negro movements decried the use of hair straighteners and skin lighteners as self-hatred and underdeveloped racial consciousness. Tiffany Gill's *Beauty Shop Politics: African American Women's Activism in the Beauty Industry* skillfully and thoroughly explores the contentious debates about black beauty culture waged on the pages of black newspapers in the early to mid-twentieth century.[59] Throughout the 1920s, Garvey's Universal Negro Improvement Association's *Negro World* published numerous pieces about the beauty and innate value of black women. In August 1925, *Negro World* pondered in a headline, "Are We Proud of Our Black Skins and Curly Hair?" and concluded that black people, but particularly black women, did not value their "natural beauty."[60] The piece lamented, "instead of being proud of their black skins and curly hair, they despise them."[61] On July 10, 1926, *Negro World* featured a piece titled "I Am a Negro—and Beautiful." Similar to Washington's leading newspapers in the late nineteenth and early twentieth centuries, the message of "natural black beauty" promoted in *Negro World* circulated side by side with advertisements for hair straightening, skin bleaching, and other products and processes associated with excessive artifice, and in some cases, white emulation, such as Madam Rhoda's Twelve Minute Hair Straightener.[62]

The Messenger, billed as the "Only Radical Negro Magazine in America," often provided a space for backlash to the prevalence of black beauty culture advertisements championing white emulation as well as advertisements for black beauty culture. Co-founded in New York City in August 1917 by A. Phillip Randolph and Chandler Owen, *The Messenger* provided a space for black people, and in some cases black women, to counter the pervasiveness of beauty products and processes that explicitly and implicitly devalued "physical blackness." In the March 1924 issue of *The Messenger*, Chandler Owen sharply criticized *Negro World*'s dependence on advertisements championing hair straightening and white emulation in his biting piece, "Good Looks Supremacy: A Perspicacious Perusal of the Potencies of Pulchritude by a

Noted Authority."[63] Notably, *The Messenger* ran beauty ads as well, but Owen attempted to show how *Negro World* specifically undermined its own message of race pride by running ads for skin lightening and hair straightening. The local black beauty culture honed by black women in urban centers like Washington preceded the national political and cultural currents of 1920s that lauded black women's beauty in its natural state. The periodicals more commonly associated with the New Negro era, and the Harlem Renaissance more specifically, took their cues from the beauty subculture that New Negro women of the early twentieth century created, fostered, and patronized. The black press in Washington was a unique, public space for black women to contest the primacy of advertisements and discourses promoting bodily adornment practices rooted in devaluations of black beauty.

In the face of political and social movements that framed hair straightening and skin lightening as attempts at white emulation, many black women throughout the United States continued to straighten their hair in an effort to articulate a modern sense of self as consumers, not simply as emulators or perpetuators of a white, feminine ideal. Some black women used hair straightening processes to achieve styles honed within black women communities. In *Hair Raising*, Rooks provides a point of departure for exploring the new meanings black women attached to hair straightening outside of white emulation and aspirations for social and economic mobility.[64] Similar to how people contemporarily consume images of "celebrities" and well-known figures, black women in Washington often modeled their hair styles after prominent African American women.[65] The straightening of hair often led to the temporary lengthening of the hair, which allowed black women to delve into an array of styles that became popularized through the circulation of images in the black press. Arguably, the most photographed black women in African American periodicals in Washington during the early twentieth century had neatly coiffed "up-dos." Whether tightly pulled back into a bun or loosely swept up into a multitextured pinup, hairstyles of black women photographed in the black press drew attention to the women's faces. Black women engaged in a variety of up-dos that were specific to black beauty culture and did not parallel styling choices in dominant beauty culture.[66] For black women in D.C. seeking to style themselves according to the latest trends, hair straightening was one of several options available to achieve styles popularized through local and national black media outlets.

In Washington, well-known and oft-photographed women such as Mary Church Terrell provided a template for black beauty. Images of her circulated in the *Bee*, the *Washington Afro-American*, and the *Colored American* throughout much of the early twentieth century. Terrell was a "political celebrity" in black communities throughout the United States, particularly among African American women in Washington. Many black women aspired to imitate and riff upon the hairstyles of prominent figures. Even well-known Washington women such as Nannie Helen Burroughs were photographed with hairstyles that for many black women could not be achieved without temporarily lengthening the hair. Images of Burroughs and other well-known black women associated with her Washington school display the pervasiveness of "up-dos" among black women during this era as well. Despite her adamant stance against black women's investment in hair straightening practices, photographs of Burroughs in black newspapers in Washington offered black women a hairstyle that for some would require hair straightening. Although not necessarily contradicting her position on hair straightening, it is worth noting that Burroughs and her NTS associates chose hairstyles that resonated with African American hair-styling trends and often relied on hair straightening to achieve.

Despite arguments about being modern consumers and the reality that hair straightening provided some black women with race-specific styling options, the movement against hair straightening gained considerable traction in numerous black urban communities.[67] Advertisements for skin-lightening products and processes continued to flourish throughout the New Negro era, and yet a rapidly growing number of African Americans opposed skin lightening, and the use of these products declined throughout the early to mid-twentieth century.[68] Although the anti-wrapping sentiment became more prominent during the 1920s, it was black women in cities such as Washington who pioneered divergent discourses that focused on black women's beauty that both engaged and rejected hair straightening techniques and practices. The health and styling of African American women's hair became central in localized black beauty industries during the New Negro era.

Conclusion

The New Negro experience in Washington black beauty culture was not monolithic. Bodily/beauty aesthetics were intensely political. African American women maintained a wide array of perspectives on the appropriate means and ends for presenting and representing themselves and for self-care. While no aesthetics "core principle" existed per se, the understanding of appearance as meaningful underpinned New Negro womanhood. Examining the black beauty industry in Washington during the late nineteenth and early twentieth centuries reveals ideas about racial pride, racial separatism, assimilation, integration, and intraracial gender, class, and color politics that propelled the New Negro movement. The bodies and representations of the bodies of black women in Washington were a terrain in which the sociocultural dynamics and competing notions of a New Negro women's ethos magnified. Black beauty culture during this era had far-reaching implications and effects for black women's culture and, more broadly, American culture.

Through beauty culture, African American women both upended and accepted white constructions of feminine beauty, created a multimillion dollar industry in which women made up the majority of proprietors and consumers, constructed a space for self-care through adornment and artifice, and situated themselves at the center of a public discourse of political, economic, social, and cultural significance. Many communities of women, including African American women, experienced black beauty culture as a means to political, social, economic, and cultural freedom. Additionally, beauty culture provided a space in which black women could connect with other black women through the experience of "fashioning self." Many black women in Washington entered into the beauty industry with the hope of transforming themselves and the collective image of African Americans. Imagining new ways of living in the urban, modern world, New Negro women in Washington refused to surrender control of their bodies and images of their bodies to a white cultural imaginary, intraracial gender and class politics, and an increasingly service-based urban economy that ignored the predilections of African American women.

Black women manufacturers, intellectuals, sellers, advertisers, and consumers configured an arena for self-determination. Myths, stereotypes, and derogatory images of black women continued to circulate during the early twentieth century. African American women in Washington found a way, through the black press, to challenge beliefs and products that devalued black womanhood. Politics of respectability, black Victorian femininity, "New Woman" ideology, race enterprise, popular culture, and ideas about individual and collective subjectivity and autonomy intersected in New Negro women's beauty culture. In Washington, black beauty culture functioned as one of the few domains in which contestation and transformation prospered. Some African American women in Washington used the hairstyles of well-recognized black women as inspiration for their styling preferences. Increasingly, black beauty culture discourse became less overtly reliant on the preferences and ideals articulated by dominant beauty culture and more focused on self-care, black feminine artifice, and adornment. African American women could not fully usurp dominant culture's images of black women but did create alternative aesthetic discourses for New Negro women to participate in that reflected race-, culture-, and gender-specific penchants and ideals.

As an industry predominated by women, beauty culture functioned primarily as a gender-specific site for self-definition, self-actualization, and contestation. Competing politics of appearance inscribed the New Negro women's era and tapped into contemporaneous discussions about what it meant to be Colored or Negro. Beauty culture also revealed the gendered nature of these monikers typically used to identify a person's race. Both "Colored" and "Negro" resonated in particular ways within the black beauty industry and more specifically among African American women. To dismiss the investment black women made in beauty culture during the New Negro era risks erasing a distinct history of black women's creativity, innovation, and desire. Beyond the multimillion-dollar industry black women's beauty culture became, this industry also flourished as a unique site of pleasure, ingenuity, and agency for African American women. "[From] a business enterprise based on something as seemingly frivolous as hairstyling," as Tiffany Gill explicates, "there emerged a platform through which black women could escape economic limitations imposed by racism and its enduring legacies and, in turn, build enduring institutions that challenged not only the social discourse of their respective communities but also the larger political arena."[69] Although this industry could perpetuate narrow, restrictive, racist, and hegemonic beauty ideals for women, black women invested in beauty culture as a conduit toward modern womanhood.

Some African American women rejected historically rooted and deeply entrenched racialized gender stereotypes about black women and created subcultures within the broader beauty industry that catered to an emergent sense of possibility for fashioning the New Negro woman. "Black working-class women," Davarian Baldwin explains "inserted their own visions and desires into beauty culture to enact a gendered politics of black re-creation."[70] The beauty culture created by local beauty culturists and manufacturers in Washington opened the door to a New Negro women's politics, which began to emerge toward the end of the nineteenth century. When Mary Church Terrell noted the practice of black women using "false hair" to achieve the latest, "in vogue" styles in her 1940 autobiography, she offered a different temporal lens through which to consider when New Negro womanhood, and more specifically New Negro women's beauty culture, emerged. Black women in growing urban centers such as Washington began crafting a black-women-centered public sphere in which their voices, images, tastes, and perspectives thrived almost immediately after Emancipation.[71]

Despite the continued devaluation and dehumanization of black women, the beauty culture created by black women in Washington served as a powerful and multifaceted site for black women demanding autonomy and the right to self-determination. While not inextricable from or unaffected by the imperious power of a racist, classist, and sexist U.S. cultural imaginary rooted in white cultural hegemony, heteropatriarchy, and global white supremacy, black beauty culture from the late nineteenth century to the early twentieth century offered a dynamic and unique space for resistance, innovation, self-care, and creativity. Bodily adornment for New Negro women of Washington was not simply a mundane practice aimed at combatting myths of inferiority and ugliness, it signaled the importance of self-care within a society that repeatedly denied the humanity of black women. Black beauty culture was political discourse pivoting around the physical presence of black women's bodies; it thrived because of black women's investment in authoring new realities and visions of self.

3

Performing and Politicizing "Ladyhood"

Black Washington Women and New Negro Suffrage Activism

The politics of appearance and bodily adornment flourishing among African American women in Washington in the late nineteenth and early twentieth centuries greatly contributed to the evolution of black women's political activism in the Jim Crow era. Suffrage activism was one the major hotbeds for established and new African American women activists.[1] In the context of Jim Crow and women's continued disenfranchisement, African American women began to re-imagine and implement new strategies anchored in strategic performances of black femininity in public acts of protest.[2] The black press in Washington acknowledged this new chapter of African American women's suffrage activism. On February 17, 1900, the *Colored American* published a column titled "Women's Case in Equity." With a triumphant tone the writer remarked,

> There is nothing about the woman suffragist today to remind one of the agitator of a quarter of a century ago. The mannishly attired, short skirted, short-haired woman, who, for so many years, was the butt of the satirist and the cartoonist, has been shoved off the board and in her place stands the cultured, womanly woman of the twentieth century. In her dress she keeps pace with fashion.[3]

The description connected the masculine physical appearance of the "agitator of a quarter of a century ago" with her political efficacy and viability. Agitator, in this article, reads as more derisive and undesirable, and, arguably, as masculine. According to the newspaper, the self-presentation of earlier activists marginalized them. Even the reference to short skirts suggested a lack of feminine propriety and a childish demeanor. Throughout the nineteenth century, women wore long skirts; young boys and girls wore short skirts. Perceived as comical, unattractive, and unfashionable, suffrage activism of African American women was something the *Colored American* seemingly devalued the until the arrival of the "cultured, womanly woman of the twentieth century." This cultured woman did not have short hair, and she kept abreast of fashion's trends. The seriousness of African American women's political voices was linked to a politics of appearance and bodily aesthetics even by those in support of universal suffrage.

In this chapter, I examine the interplay of politics of appearance and bodily aesthetics to New Negro–era suffrage discourse and activism. The nation's capital played a particularly integral role in the national movement while also serving as a battleground for localized efforts for enfranchisement. Black women in Washington participated in suffrage organizations and clubs and protest activities, including elite and well-known Washington women such as Mary Church Terrell and Anna Julia Cooper.[4] Both Terrell and Cooper in their respective autobiographies gave voice to the necessity of equal rights for black women—specifically the right to vote. The voices of African American suffragists in Washington reached a fevered pitch during the early twentieth century, and yet this voice took shape in the performance of strategic quiet, feminine propriety, feminine artifice. and resistive equanimity.

The road to passing a constitutional amendment that secured the right to vote literally and figuratively ended in Washington. Only in the capital city would a constitutional amendment be ratified. Black women's suffrage activism did not have a singular approach.[5] Kate Masur maintains that black women valued the vote as a vehicle through which they could claim a space within public debates on their own terms.[6] Other scholars, notably Elsa Barkley Brown, emphasize that many freedwomen tended to view the enfranchisement of black men as a means of achieving communal goals.[7] In her "To Catch the Vision of Freedom: Reconstructing Southern Black Women's Political History, 1865–1880," Brown posits that the concept of family and community bound African Americans together in the postslavery world, not the pursuit of full personhood or citizenship as defined by the Constitution.

The notion of "shared responsibility" for communities and families extended to how these women viewed the enfranchisement of black men. Enfranchising black men thereby enfranchised the families and communities from which these black men came. Furthermore, the notion of freedom that thrived among these particular communities of African American women was that of a "collective freedom." Brown argues,

> Their sense of community, related to the collective character of their notion of freedom, had foundation in their understanding that freedom, in reality, would accrue to each of them individually only when it was acquired by all of them collectively. It was this very sense of community rather than citizenship, of peoplehood rather than personhood, that was the basis for their activities.[8]

Combating racist "New Women" and sexist "New Negro" men, New Negro women created political agendas and developed performative strategies to address their status as third-class citizens.

Existing scholarship on black women's participation in the women's suffrage movement emphasizes the complexity of the relationships between black and white women suffragists.[9] Much of the scholarship also addresses the issue of suffrage from an intraracial perspective and details how black male political activists either supported or fought against women's suffrage.[10] Scholarship of black women's post-Reconstruction activism also details black women's engagement with the politics of respectability. Black women in Washington strategically invested in these politics for a New Negro womanhood vision that demanded respect for black women as political actors and full citizens. Several factors influenced the development of a new black women's political culture: the passage of the Fifteenth Amendment, which affected interracial and intraracial cooperation in the suffrage movement, the disenfranchisement of black men through state-authored legislation, the formation and re-energizing of local black women's organizations, and the configuration of political agendas that encompassed aestheticized approaches to African American women's suffrage activism. The combination of these factors sparked a new wave of suffrage activism among African American women.[11] Two of the periods often discussed in relation to post-Emancipation black women's suffrage activism are 1870 to 1896 and 1896 to 1935. These years are central to my temporal conceptualization of the New Negro era, as I demarcate the commencement of the era of the New Negro woman in 1893. This demarcation thereby engulfs the last few years of the first major period of post-Emancipation black women's suffrage activism. The interplay between black women's political aspirations during the early twentieth century in conjunction with African American women's bodily aesthetic discourses were foundational to New Negro women's political activism. Through a brief historical overview of the herstory of suffrage, with a particular focus on Washington, an examination of the fractures that occurred after the passing of the Fifteenth Amendment, and a critical consideration of how African American women in Washington configured their performative strategies for activism, using the Women's Suffrage March in Washington of 1913 as a specific site of inquiry, I rethink the disruptive possibilities of African American's women's politics of appearance and bodily aesthetics. More specifically, I show that African American women using feminine propriety were not merely adhering to existing gender norms and expectations but were remixing feminine propriety as an audacious practice for claiming space.

African American Suffrage and Suffrage Activism in the United States

As early as 1670 the North American colonies denied free black people the right to vote.[12] In the existing U.S. colonies, property was the preeminent qualification for suffrage.[13] Enslaved blacks could not vote in any colony or state. Formal legal restrictions, however, do not tell the whole story. Free black men voted in nearly every colony and state during the mid- to late eighteenth century.[14] After the American Revolution and in the early nineteenth century, state constitutions in Delaware, New Hampshire, New York, Pennsylvania, Massachusetts, and Maryland protected the voting rights of black men. Prior to the formation of the United States as a nation, the vote was not connected to citizenship or subjects; therefore, it was not expected that all subjects would vote. Neither was it expected, in the newly formed republic, that all citizens would vote. In the earliest incarnations of black voting rights in states such as North Carolina and New York, black women were excluded. Although only a small number of free black men could and did vote, free black women encountered the triple bind of inferior racial, class, and gender statuses as early as the eighteenth century.

In some cities, such as Baltimore, black voting in some elections outnumbered white voting.[15] Philadelphia attorney and legal historian John Hancock acknowledged that black and white male voters alike in numerous states ratified the proposed American Constitution. The number of eligible black voters increased when states such as Connecticut, Rhode Island, and Vermont abolished slavery in the post–Revolutionary War era. According to the state constitutions of Pennsylvania, Massachusetts, and New Hampshire, free black men in these early states also had the right to hold office. By 1820, the period of postrevolutionary abolition ended and even those areas that abolished slavery began to restrict the rights of free blacks. White women and property-less white men were denied many legal rights, including the right to vote. Whiteness, however, guaranteed greater legal protections.[16] Although abolition became the leading political cause among free blacks during first half of the nineteenth century, many African American political activists embraced a broader political agenda that included universal suffrage. The political agendas of free blacks of the late eighteenth and early nineteenth centuries conveyed both the immorality of slavery and political aspirations for equality.

Historian Leon Litwack explains that demands for suffrage were often encompassed in the rhetoric of black abolitionists and that suffrage was thought of broadly and not in gender-specific ways.[17] In the city of Washington and the Territory of Columbia, many free blacks participated in local and national efforts for abolition and universal suffrage. This small but powerful community employed gender-neutral suffrage rhetoric in their struggles for political equality in the early nineteenth century. The 1800 U.S. Census reports that the total population of enslaved and free people of color in Washington was 4,037; 3,244 were identified as slaves and 793 as free blacks.[18] The Georgetown area in Northwest Washington had a significant population of black people, including 1,449 black slaves and 227 free blacks in 1800.[19] The population of enslaved blacks increased until the abolition of slavery in Washington and Georgetown in 1862. The free black population grew more gradually but encountered a notable surge immediately following the Civil War. Free blacks in Washington and the Territory of Columbia fighting for equal suffrage during the antebellum era produced a political landscape in which racial equality was defined more broadly.

The fight for universal suffrage among African Americans in Washington during this period was also largely led by religious institutions. As some of the few black institutions, early black churches became central to African American political activism in Washington. The Mount Zion United Methodist Church and the African Church were cornerstones in this political effort.[20] Congregants adamantly opposed slavery and advocated for universal suffrage and other rights from the pulpit and the pews.[21] Women were among the leaders in these fledgling congregations. As early as 1814 the leadership and congregants of the Mount Zion Methodist Church aligned themselves with progressive political agendas and attempted to address the religious, educational, and social needs of Washington's enslaved and free black communities.

The first Anti-Slavery Convention of American Women took place on May 9, 1837. This interracial gathering of women developed a far-reaching, progressive agenda: redefine women's roles both inside and outside the domestic sphere, to abolish slavery, and to end racial discrimination in non-slaveholding states.[22] The resolution they drafted proposed:

> That this convention do firmly believe that the existence of an unnatural prejudice against our colored population, is one of the chief pillars of American slavery—therefore, that the more we mingle with our oppressed brethren and sisters, the more deeply are we convinced of the sinfulness of that anti-Christian prejudice which is crushing them to the earth in our nominally Free States.[23]

The women at this convention denounced both slavery and racial inequality in non-slaveholding states. This denouncement was similar to that made by congregants and leaders of Mount Zion Methodist Church in Washington. While local institutions such as Mount Zion provided the foundation for local, universal suffrage activism, this convention initiated a national, interracial suffrage movement.

This interracial, mixed-gender movement cohered, though not without disagreements and differing approaches. The greatest test to this movement came after Emancipation and with the ratification of the Fifteenth Amendment, which granted African American men the right to vote. Tensions spilled over in the debates leading up the amendment's ratification and culminated with powerfully divergent standpoints on the meaning of enfranchising African American men. Nearly three years before the ratification in 1870, women's rights activist and racial equality advocate Sojourner Truth proclaimed, "There is a great stir about colored men getting their rights, but not a word about the colored women; and if colored men get their rights, and not colored women theirs, there will be a bad time about it. So I am keeping the thing going while things are stirring; because if we wait till it is still, it will take a great while to get it going again."[24] Alliances between black and white suffragists changed substantially during the late nineteenth century. Schisms along racial and gender lines created a context in which a new but continually evolving black women's political culture emerged.[25] African American women fighting for the vote faced the difficult conundrum of supporting universal suffrage or the more politically expedient and more probable enfranchisement of black men. Universal suffrage was the only path to black women's enfranchisement, but the chance of it becoming a reality in the late nineteenth century did not measure favorably against an amendment securing for black men the right to vote.

In debates leading up to the ratification, some prominent white women suffragists made powerful statements against black men being enfranchised before white women. White abolitionist-feminist movement figures such as Elizabeth Cady Stanton stated at the First Annual Meeting of the American Equal Rights Association that "there is a depth of degradation known to the slave women that man can never feel. To give the ballot to the black man is no security to the woman. Saxon men have the ballot, yet look at their women, crowded into a few half-paid employments. Look at the starving, degraded class in our 10,000 dens of infamy and vice if you would know how wisely and generously man legislates for woman."[26] This particular statement indicated Stanton's belief that black men could not understand the experience of black women. She used the example of white women's oppression as being a result of only white men being able to vote in order to insist upon fighting for universal suffrage. When pushed further, however, Stanton traversed more contentious territory in her privileging of education as a determinant for suffrage. Stanton explained,

> If we are to have further class legislation, . . . the wisest order of enfranchisement was to take the educated classes first. If women are still to be represented by men, then I say let only the highest type of manhood stand at the helm of State. But if all men are to vote, black and white, lettered and unlettered, washed and unwashed, the safety of the nation as well as the interests of woman demand that we outweigh this incoming tide of ignorance, poverty and vice, with the virtue, wealth and education of the women of the country. With the black man you will have no new force in government—it is manhood still; but with the enfranchisement of woman, you have a new and essential element of life and power. Would Horace Greeley, Wendell Phillips, Gerrit Smith or Theodore Tilton be willing to stand aside and trust their individual interests, and the whole welfare of the nation to the lowest strata of manhood? If not, why ask educated women, who love their country, who desire to mould its institutions on the highest idea of justice and equality, who feel that their enfranchisement is of vital importance to this end, why ask them to stand aside while 2,000,000 ignorant men are ushered into the halls of legislation?"[27]

Calling African American men "2,000,000 ignorant men" alienated Stanton from many African American suffragists. She and Susan B. Anthony left the American Equal Rights Association in response to the group's endorsement of a suffrage amendment that enfranchised only black men. Founded in 1866 by abolitionists-feminists, the AERA's purpose was to fight for rights for both women and African Americans. Until the schism that occurred as a result of the ratification of the Fifteenth Amendment, the AERA served as a viable political vehicle for interracial cooperation and for addressing both racial and gender inequities. By 1868, however, Stanton and Anthony formed a partnership with antiblack Democrat George Train to finance their publication, *Revolution*.[28] The publication made "disparaging references . . . to black men, who frequently were depicted as being inferior and prone to commit criminal acts."[29] Stanton and Anthony's move to support "educated suffrage," coupled with the publication of such an inflammatory document, strained relationships between white women and African American suffragists.

The racist and sexist rhetoric of opposing factions situated black women in a complicated space, torn between elimination of racial restrictions on the vote and the affirmation of all women's exclusion from it. Even outspoken political activists such as Truth found it difficult to navigate this polarized, political terrain. As the contours of the new political landscape became more visible, Truth and several women from the abolitionist-feminist community attempted to sketch out a productive space within a contentious and increasingly volatile political climate.[30] In *Sojourner Truth: A Life, a Symbol*, Nell Irvin Painter discusses Truth's political shift toward "neutrality" in the aftermath of the ratification of the Fifteenth Amendment. Carol Faulkner's *Women's Radical Reconstruction* and Rosalyn Terborg-Penn's *African American Women in the Struggle for the Vote, 1850–1920* document in detail the transforming of the political climate for abolitionist-feminists as well as how black women navigated an increasingly divided suffrage-activist community during and post-Reconstruction. The shifts these scholars explore, I argue, resulted in the emergence of a New Negro suffragist. This particular era of suffrage activism by black women grew out of post-Reconstruction and Jim Crow realities.

As Darlene Clark Hine explains, many African American women "were outraged that women—of any race—should 'stand in the way' of obtaining the vote for black men."[31] Notable black women activists such as Frances Watkins Harper advocated acceptance of black men's enfranchisement and embodied the outrage Hine describes. This perspective cannot be reduced to the simplistic argument that race trumped gender for black women political activists; it also indicates a strategic intraracial alliance based on the belief that black men could better represent black women's political interests than white women. In most cases, these women also continued fighting for universal suffrage and for black women's political power in a more general sense.[32] Within the post-Reconstruction political climate, black women suffragists had to rethink how to approach the struggle for universal suffrage. An additional challenge surfaced on the agendas of African American women suffragists as Jim Crow laws and other state-authored policies and regulations re-disenfranchised black men across the nation in the late nineteenth century. With both black men and black women disenfranchised once again, black women recast their efforts for achieving racial and gender equality within the public political sphere. In 1890 the National American Woman Suffrage

Association formed out of merging of two suffrage associations, mending previous relationships between white and black suffragists and proffering an "intergrationist" approach to political activism. During this period African American women suffragists made difficult choices that imparted lasting effects on their roles and voices within the national suffrage movement.[33]

Black women built on the tradition of using the public arena and established new networks and organizations to advance their own goals and their sense of themselves as free women of color. The multidimensional terrain of African American women's political activism during this period was particularly visible in Washington. The "victory" of black male suffrage, however, was short lived there. During the 1870s, as Kate Masur's work shows, Washington underwent significant political changes that altered how and who controlled the nation's capital.[34] In 1871 the president and a popularly elected House of Delegates appointed a governor and council to govern Washington.[35] Within this new territorial government, African Americans held fewer seats in the elected, legislative body. In the first incarnation of this new governing structure, President Ulysses S. Grant appointed three black men to the council. By 1873, however, financial mismanagement, deepening economic depression, and political corruption led Congress to reorganize Washington's government. Whites from both the Democratic and Republican Parties, seeking to explain economic and political hardships in Washington, identified black suffrage and the appointed black council members as the problem. In 1874 Congress disenfranchised all Washingtonians. While whites lost control of the local government, the disenfranchisement of black Washingtonians had more far-reaching consequences.

From both local and national perspectives, the political terrain upon which black women in Washington were acting required new alliances and strategies to address their disenfranchisement. In the nation's capital, however, the context for suffrage activism greatly differed from suffrage activism in other cities and states. African American women suffragists in Washington had to combat the disenfranchisement of all Washingtonians, efforts to circumvent the Fifteenth Amendment by local and state governments outside Washington, and staunch opposition to women's suffrage. Black women suffragists in Washington vehemently fought for enfranchising D.C. residents, in addition to fighting for women's suffrage and protecting black male suffrage.[36] They also had the additional obstacle of local disenfranchisement. Consequently, black women's suffrage activism in Washington paralleled yet diverged from the national African American and women's suffrage movements of the late nineteenth and early twentieth centuries. All Washingtonians, regardless of race or gender, were disempowered to an extent at the ballot, and that changed the political calculus. Local efforts for enfranchisement extended beyond any particular group; African American women political activists concerned themselves with the struggle for suffrage and political representation for Washingtonians at the local level and for African Americans at the national level.

The influx of thousands of blacks to Washington during the Civil War and Reconstruction also altered the political terrain for African Americans in the nation's capital, particularly for black women. Allan Johnston's *Surviving Freedom: The Black Community in Washington, D.C., 1860–1880* explores the effects of Civil War and Reconstruction black migrations to Washington. Johnston, however, does not focus on the gender-specific ramifications of African American migrations to Washington during this period. Although acknowledging differences between the access black men and women had to property, his portrait of Washington primarily illuminates the struggles of black men, which becomes conflated with the struggles of black Washingtonians.[37] Greater access to educational institutions was one of the most significant changes for blacks. The establishment of schools increased the number of literate black Washingtonians, which fueled the circulation of black newspapers, political propaganda, and other activist ephemera. The circulation of such material also connected local struggles to an imagined, national racial community striving for greater equality. This connection informed black Washington women's activism in national suffrage movements. African American suffragists in Washington mobilized around a political goal that would not provide them with the right to vote because universal suffrage would not secure full representation for residents of the nation's capital. The vote was subordinated within a broader vision of full inclusion within the body politic. Black women in Washington based their activism in their unique circumstance of disenfranchisement. In the nation's capital, the face of the African American women's suffrage activism was Mary Church Terrell. Her voice and elite status placed Terrell at the center of a new wave of political activism in Washington.

New Negro Women's Suffrage Activism: Washington and Beyond

African American women in Washington capitalized on emerging Progressive Era ideals and the invention of new strategies for racial progress within African American communities. They founded organizations that attended to basic needs of African Americans as well as social issues such as temperance, the maintenance of the black family, and black female respectability. The majority of black newspapers in Washington focused on activism around issues such as lynching, economic disparities, and African American suffrage, efforts led by black men and supported by black women. The widespread, intraracial expectation for black women's involvement in social and political movements for racial equality, nevertheless, was not leadership.[38] Black women used their gender-specific organizations to promote African American political struggles for racial equality, to articulate new ideas about the future of African American women's political identities, and to situate advocacy for gender equality within a still-forming and multifaceted political consciousness.

African American women configured an intraracial, gender-specific political culture that strategically employed an array of tactics that included but was not limited to the politics of respectability, self-determination, and racial uplift. Cynthia Neverdon-Morton argues that "even though black women living in different communities realized that there were some needs unique to their areas, they also understood that certain needs were common to all communities where African Americans lived."[39] The connection between the local, national, and, in some activist circles, international political struggles of peoples of African descent informed African American women's political culture. Nearly all black women believed that they should have the right to vote. Although not all black women were suffragists, Paula Giddings explicitly states in *When and Where I Enter: The Impact of Black Women on Race and Sex in America* that "one would be hard pressed to find any Black woman who did not advocate getting the vote."[40] Black women political leaders rallied around this widely held sentiment. In Washington, African American women participated in suffrage organizations and in discourses regarding the significance of enfranchising black men and women alike despite their local predicament, which deprived them of the possibility for full representation in the body politic for distinct reasons. The specific needs of African Americans in Washington did not preclude black women from actively engaging in a political movement that would not improve their unique status as a triply disenfranchised community. Black women in Washington fought for suffrage on three fronts: as blacks, as women, and as Washingtonians.

All roads to a constitutional amendment for women's or universal suffrage led to Washington. Cognizant of this, black women suffragists in Washington perceived their role in the voting rights movement as particularly significant. African American women in the District made the most of residing in one of the most cosmopolitan southern cities. They lived in a city with a more progressive politics regarding race and gender than other cities and towns to the south. Washington also had an established black community that provided financial resources and extensive networks for black women to build on as they forged new paths in African American political activism. The localized efforts of black Washington women worked in conjunction with national organizations such as the National Association of Colored Women, the Commission on Interracial Cooperation, and the National American Woman Suffrage Association. Additionally, prominent educational institutions in Washington such as M Street High School and Howard University produced an educated, politically savvy community of black women who recognized the importance of the politics of appearance for political efficacy in the early twentieth century. Although not limited to this elite group of women, black women's suffrage activists in Washington invested in "political celebrities." How these women were styled in the images of them that circulated in black periodicals affected how receptive African Americans were to their political messages.[41] For black women political activists, their appearances often determined their political cachet and effectiveness. Skepticism, optimism, and disillusionment informed black women's political behavior as they entered into the public arena through both traditional and nontraditional political activities. Hope for fuller citizenship co-existed with what Kate Dossett identifies as ambivalence about participating in a women's movement that historically and continuously relegated black women to the margins.[42]

Black women's refusal to remain on the political periphery was particularly evident in Washington. Their political activism took center stage in African American political discourse in the local black press. Both the *Colored American* and the *Washington Bee* supported universal suffrage. The editorial staff of both periodicals published these pieces while maintaining their commitment to universal suffrage. These newspapers participated in the elevation of black women activists in Washington to "political celebrities," most notably Terrell. The *Colored American* column I cited earlier in the chapter, "Woman's Case in Equity," was paired with a line drawing of Mary Church Terrell and proclaimed,

> Woman suffrage, once a subject for ridicule, has ceased to be a joke. It is one of the grave problems of the hour. The wonderful advancement of the feminine sex in business, in the professions, in the industries, and in the world of finance, is giving her an importance in the affairs of life which the sensible

> man must recognize, and subscribe to a change of laws and customs to accord with the higher conditions that have come about in consequence of woman's broadening influence.[43]

Noting the progress women had made in inserting themselves into spheres from which they were historically excluded, the *Colored American* called upon "sensible" men to respond to the increased presence and political necessity of women in the public sphere. Her 1898 address specifically tackled the racial and gender oppression black women confronted. The subheading of the article, "Gracefully and Forcefully Presented by Mary Church Terrell before the Brainiest of Equal Suffragists in America—The Premier Representative of Our Womanhood Makes the Hit of the Convention," conveyed a profound sense of pride in Terrell, specifically in her ability to engage with a group of women identified as among the "brainiest" in America.

The editorial detailed how black women were transforming political, cultural, and economic spheres. The article's also focused on a speech Terrell delivered at a meeting of National American Woman Suffrage Association, where her message echoed an earlier speech she gave at NAWSA in 1898. Invited by suffragist and NAWSA leader Susan B. Anthony, Terrell delivered "The Progress and Problems of Colored Women." Her 1898 and 1900 addresses specifically tackled the racial and gender oppression black women confronted. By 1900, Terrell was a political activist of national repute. Widely recognized by blacks and whites alike as a spokeswoman for African American and women's rights, black Washington suffragists at Howard University as well as other prominent figures such as Nannie Helen Burroughs and Anna Julia Cooper interacted and exchanged ideas with Terrell on a regular basis. Terrell was uniquely positioned and privileged to articulate a black women's political agenda that was informed significantly by African American's women's political discourse and activism in the nation's capital.

Terrell delivered "The Justice of Woman Suffrage," a keynote address for the February 1900 meeting of the NAWSA. The *Colored American* described her speech as "a masterpiece of argument, scholarly and logically put and was delivered with that ease and grace of bearing, that ineffable charm and magnetism of manner and dignity and force that are characteristic of all Mrs. Terrell does or says."[44] This glowing review mirrored the respect and admiration black women Washingtonians held for the founder and president of the National Association of Colored Women. Before presenting Terrell's own words to black Washington, the newspaper's editorial staff concluded that "by Mrs. Terrell's appearance at this convention both the cause of women in general and the Negro in particular has been incalculably benefited."[45]

Unlike her prior speech to the NAWSA in 1898, in which she addressed the plight of black women, "The Justice of Woman Suffrage" positioned Terrell as a women's activist who spoke for all women, equally and publicly affirming the importance of gender as well as racial equality.

"The Justice of Woman Suffrage" is a foundational speech for New Negro women involved in the struggle for voting rights. Excerpts from her speech accompanied the *Colored American* story about Terrell and circulated among black suffragists in Washington. Terrell's words resonated with black women in Washington who were conversing with Terrell and developing and refashioning their political rhetoric to more accurately articulate the necessity of suffrage for black women locally, nationally, and internationally. In her speech, Terrell explained:

> The founders of this republic called heaven and earth to witness that it should be a government of the people, and by the people; and yet the elective franchise is withheld from one half of the citizens, many of whom are intelligent, cultured and virtuous, while it is unstintingly bestowed upon the other, some of whom are illiterate, debauched, and vicious, because the word "people," by an unparalleled exhibition of lexicographical acrobats, has been turned and twisted to mean all who are shrewd and wise. The argument that it is unnatural for women to vote is as old as the rock ribbed and ancient hills. . . . Nothing could be more unnatural than that a good woman should shirk her duty to the state, if it were possible for her to discharge it.[46]

Terrell touched on many significant points—including the founding principles of the United States, the denial of suffrage to intelligent and virtuous citizens, and the conflation of personhood with manhood. Terrell pointed to the founding principles of the United States to legitimate universal suffrage. Positioning universal suffrage in this way aligned it with broader political trends that called upon individuals to serve the interests of the state through personal and collective responsibility. Terrell's speech exemplified what Salamishah Tillet calls "critical patriotism."[47] Tillet commences her genealogy of critical patriotism with Frederick Douglass. Similar to Douglass's, Terrell's patriotism "enables [her] to become a model citizen, one who does not repudiate but reifies, does not dismantle but reengages the meta-discourse of American democracy."[48] Terrell calls out the hypocrisy of democracy while maintaining an investment in the possibility of a liberatory and just democracy.

What is most striking about Terrell's speech is her emphasis on class as the basis for her characterization of suffrage as both a right and a privilege that should be extended to blacks and women. Her statement aligns with a political agenda influenced by politics of black respectability. In her emphasis on illiteracy and debauchery, Terrell gestured toward widely held perceptions about low-income communities. "The Justice of Woman Suffrage" suggests that individuals of "questionable" moral character should not be enfranchised, if "respectable" women and blacks remain disenfranchised. Terrell's support for respectability in defining the suffrage, the body politic, and political culture was not unique among black Washingtonians. Washington's black newspapers contributed to political discourses that demonized poor people, regardless of race. Leading publications focused primarily on black women suffragists who adhered to a burgeoning politics of respectability that emerged out of the black clubwomen's movement.

In the "Woman's Case in Equity," the *Colored American* staff made a clear distinction between suffragists of the past and the modern suffragist. Placing the image of Terrell on the front page of the paper confirmed the arrival of this modern activist, which connected women's appearance and style to the content of their politics. "Woman's Case in Equity" articulated that the perception of suffragists as women falling outside of the parameters of respectability distinguished the earlier movement from the current one. The paper's coverage of Terrell provided a modern example of the ideal black suffragist. Terrell's sketch portrays a fully covered woman with long hair pinned up into a neatly coiffed bun. The only visible skin in the image of Terrell is one side of her face in profile and the very top of her neck. The newspaper's conception of a "woman suffragist of today" also exemplified a particular vision of femininity that fit the politics of respectability. For women like Terrell embracing this performance of femininity, hyperpropriety became a vehicle through which African American women could articulate the New Negro standpoints regarding equality for black women.

The connection between effective political activism and feminine fashion reveals how prevailing racial, sexual, and gender ideologies influenced New Negro women's political culture. The heightened visibility of black women's bodies in the public arena sparked discussions about the significance of black women's physical appearance to social and political movements for equality. Black women could not escape myths about their hypersexuality, depravity, uncontrollable anger, and impropriety, and they therefore fashioned and performed a distinct form of feminine propriety while engaging in political activism.[49] While black suffragists like Terrell embraced respectability as one of many political tools, white suffragists in the early 1900s began rethinking their strategies and how to reclaim the national spotlight for their political agenda through more stylized and theatrical political demonstrations.[50] Both black and white suffragists recognized the importance of performance and bodily aesthetics to women's political activism, but how this recognition affected their political acts differed.

The Suffrage Parade held on March 3, 1913, in Washington highlighted the differences, tensions, and points of divergence for black and white women suffragists in the modern suffrage movement. African American women used this historic event to bring national attention to a burgeoning African American women's political culture that would not be silenced by white suffragists or anti-suffragists. The white women organizers of the march also had a distinct political agenda that reflected a "New Woman" ethos and an emerging political culture.[51] The clash of these racialized, political cultures had a history dating back several decades but was reignited in the planning stages of the parade. This convergence of political cultures exposed the fragility and fluidity of coalitions across the lines of race and gender that had shaped the national suffrage movement from its inception.

During the first decade of the twentieth century, the National American Woman Suffrage Association began exploring new political strategies. Despite progress at the state level, there was little movement toward a constitutional amendment. Members of NAWSA traveled annually to the nation's capital to petition for federal protection of women's suffrage. While largely symbolic, this regular political performance also reflected growing support for the movement. Each year, the number of signatories grew.[52] The act also solidified a potential political base composed primarily of women. Some African American suffragists took part in this process despite reservations about the commitment of NAWSA to a fully universal conception of suffrage that applied to women as well as blacks.[53] African American women's reservations were grounded in NAWSA's refusal to pass a resolution against Jim Crow at its 1899 convention and a consistent trend of racist argumentation at the annual conventions.[54] Despite warranted skepticism of NAWSA and its leadership, African American women in Washington continued to involve themselves in local and national actions for suffrage. A glimmer of hope in the struggle for women's voting rights appeared in 1912 with Theodore Roosevelt's Progressive Party, which pledged to secure equal suffrage for men and women. Roosevelt, however, lost the election to Woodrow Wilson, prompting renewed fervor and dedication to achieving national recognition of women's suffrage.

To garner greater attention for the suffrage cause, leaders at the 1912 NAWSA annual convention in Philadelphia decided to plan a suffrage parade on the evening prior to Wilson's presidential inauguration in March 1913.

NAWSA and suffrage leadership selected Alice Paul to organize a parade of such scale that it would attract significant press coverage. Paul was one of the most prominent figures in women's suffrage movement of the early twentieth century. Before age thirty, she had participated in the militant branch of the British suffrage movement, endured a hunger strike and being forcibly fed, had been arrested and imprisoned, and was now organizing the parade. Many historians situate Paul within a radical feminist tradition.[55] Her relationship to black suffragists and support for equal rights for African Americans, however, complicates how to historicize Paul's activism. Differing accounts exist of her attitudes and behaviors toward black suffragists prior to, during, and after the parade. During the planning stages, Paul and her organizing committee imagined a political spectacle in which costumes, floats, banners, dynamic speakers, and ornate programs would convey the importance of women's suffrage and the political power of suffragists and suffrage supporters. On Monday, March 3, 1913, clad in a white cape and astride a white horse, lawyer Inez Milholland led the great woman suffrage parade down Pennsylvania Avenue in the nation's capital. Behind her stretched a long line of marchers and participants: nine bands, four mounted brigades, three heralds, about twenty-four floats, and more than five thousand supporters.[56] The spectacular vision became a reality. The parade proved to be a historically significant event that made suffragists more visible to the national body politic.

NAWSA discussed the role of African American women prior to the event. In a letter dated January 15, 1913, Paul noted to Alice Blackwell, editor of the *Woman's Journal*, that "as far as I can see we must have a white procession, or a negro procession or no procession at all."[57] As a Quaker, Paul seemingly struggled with how to manage the staunch, racist opposition within NAWSA and in the nation's capital.[58] Notably, a specific racially charged incident occurred in D.C. months before the planned march. On December 24, 1912, Nathaniel Green, a black man, brutally attacked and raped a white woman government clerk near the Capitol.[59] The case inflamed existing racial tensions in the city, and a heightened sense of the possibility of retaliatory violence pervaded. According to a Mary Walton's *A Woman's Crusade: Alice Paul and the Battle for the Ballot*, Paul confided in Blackwell that she worried that many if not a majority of white marchers will refuse to participate if negroes in any number formed part of the parade.[60] Fearing the opposition of white southern suffragists, Alice Paul attempted to evade direction questions about black women's participation. On February 15, 1913, she received a letter from Nellie Quander, the graduate advisor of Alpha Kappa Alpha Sorority Inc. at Howard University, inquiring about participation in the suffrage parade.[61]

Paul did not respond to Quander until February 23. Paul's response included an invitation for Quander to come to her office "to decide on the best place for your section."[62] No record exists attesting to whether this meeting occurred. Prominent African American suffragists such as Ida B. Wells perceived Paul's inaction as intentional evasiveness and unequivocally denounced the possible exclusion of colored delegations. "Southern women," Wells asserted, "have tried to evade the question time and again by giving some excuse or other every time it has been brought up. If the Illinois women do not take a stand now in this great democratic parade, then the colored women are lost."[63] In her personal recollections, Paul explained that she reached a compromise with Terrell and the National Association of Colored Women in which black women suffragists would march in the rear of the procession in a separate section. From actual photographs taken at the parade, it appears that Paul's recollection is more accurate, because black women are largely invisible in images of state and occupational delegations.

The hypervisibility of white feminine spectacle as political strategy attracted most of the mainstream media attention, as coverage of the march focused almost exclusively on the theatrics white suffragists employed.[64] The *Chicago Tribune* reported on the exhaustion and unnerving of Helen Keller.[65] The *Washington Post* detailed ambulances attempting to aid injured people at the march over the course of six hours.[66] According to an article written by Mary Walton about the parade on its centennial, violence commenced almost immediately after the parade. "Men, many of them drunk, spit at the marchers and grabbed their clothing, hurled insults and lighted cigarettes, snatched banners and tried to climb floats. Police did little to keep order."[67] Despite the "chaos" and attempts thwart the parade's progress, the *New York Times* piece on the march ultimately described the pageant as "one of the most impressively beautiful spectacles ever staged in this country."[68] The reporting in major white newspapers conveyed much of what Paul and NAWSA intended—the violent responses of "ignorant men" to suffrage, bringing national awareness to this new chapter in suffrage activism.

The official order of the parade procession was detailed in the "Suffrage March Line." The first section of the procession was occupied by women from countries that enfranchised women. Following the international section were the "Pioneers" of the women's suffrage movement. Pioneers were suffragists who had participated in decades of suffrage activism. The Pioneers section was a whites-only delegation. Despite NAWSA's acknowledgment of black women's participation in the suffrage movement for several decades, black women pioneers were excluded from marching in this revered delegation of "activist" women. The occupational and state delegations marched behind the Pioneers. The final group on the Suffrage March Line consisted of male suffragists. According to a NAWSA diagram, floats and bands brought up the rear of the parade. Particular delegations of black suffragists, men and women, were absent from the processional order and did not appear on NAWSA's depiction of the Suffrage March Line. The invisibility of black suffragists on this representation of the parade processional spoke volumes about the relationship between black and white suffragists and the NAWSA vision of suffrage.

Despite attempts to limit the visibility of African American women at the parade, a few black women suffragists "snuck in" and marched with state and occupational delegations. Ida B. Wells-Barnett, a strong proponent of universal suffrage and founder of the Alpha Suffrage Club of Chicago, vehemently protested segregation in the parade. Founded in 1913 by Wells, the Alpha Suffrage Club of Chicago worked exclusively for woman's suffrage. Prior to the march, the Illinois delegation insisted that Wells march in a separate, colored delegation. Wells refused to march, if not with her state.[69] In defiance, Wells joined the Illinois Delegation during the march, literally inserting herself and, by extension, black women into white suffragists' political culture. While not obviously visible in the images, other black women

Figure 11. Women's suffrage procession, National Women's Suffrage Association, March 3, 1913. Postcard Collection, Historical Society of Washington D.C.

Figure 12. Women's suffrage procession; protestors demanding a constitutional amendment, March 3, 1913. Postcard Collection, Historical Society of Washington, D.C.

participated in the parade or looked on as spectators. Contrasting with the spectacle-like political performances of white suffragists at the parade, black women performed political respectability using bodily adornment.

The experience of the founding members of Delta Sigma Theta Sorority Inc. at the March 1913 parade exemplifies how black Washington suffragists negotiated the political terrain created by NAWSA for the parade.[70] Only two months after their formation at Howard on January 13, 1913, with the guidance of honorary member Mary Church Terrell, the sorority's founders agreed that participating in the parade would be their first public act.[71] They collectively affirmed that black women needed the right to vote for protection, equality, and advancement. Twenty-two women marched along with Terrell under a Delta Sigma Theta Sorority banner. Dressed in attire similar to that in the sketch of Terrell in the *Colored American* in February 1900, this group of black women, newspapers reported, presented images of modern suffragists who mobilized around respectable femininity to garner respect for their political activism. Subjected to racism from opponents of woman's suffrage and from parade organizers, participants, and spectators, the women of Delta Sigma Theta Sorority strategically articulated a black female presence that countered damaging racial and gender ideologies. These women could not engage in the theatrics employed by their white suffragists counterparts, yet their visibility came through their ability to epitomize black feminine propriety in how they adorned their bodies for civil disobedience.

Terrell, members of Delta Sigma Theta, and smaller, unidentified "delegations" of black marchers from Washington assembled in a racially segregated area. After congregating, these women marched toward the rear of the procession and encountered hostility from spectators and fellow parade participants alike.[72] Their relegation to the periphery of the parade caused Terrell to reevaluate her involvement with NAWSA. Several years after the parade, she "conclude[ed] that, if [Paul] and other white suffragist leaders could get the Anthony Amendment through without enfranchising African American women, they would do so."[73] This question circulated among most black suffragists, but particularly among the black Washington women who participated in the March 1913 parade. Their experiences with the white women's suffrage movement at this event further distanced African American women's political activism from that of their white women counterparts.[74] White women could transgress the boundaries of feminine propriety and public "respectability" in their political culture without contributing to racialized discourses of inherent inferiority.[75] The rigidity of interracial stereotypes about the lasciviousness and wildness of black women, coupled with historical perceptions touted in the black press of African American women suffragists as "masculine," unattractive, and unfashionable, created context in which African American women engaged politics of adornment and bodily aesthetics to claim a distinct space within New Negro activism. Black women structured a political culture that simultaneously encompassed their engagement with racial uplift and advancement. White women could not escape gender ideologies that privileged particular notions of appropriate political behavior for women. Their racial identity, however, allowed them to create exclusionary boundaries for political activism.

Notwithstanding the racism black women in Washington endured during their involvement in the parade of March 1913 and in subsequent interracial protests and organizations, Washington's African American suffragists continued to fight for suffrage, often independently from the white women's suffrage movement.[76] They also fought against racism within the white women's suffrage movement. Looking back on the parade, participant and Delta Sigma Theta founder Florence Toms noted, "We marched that day in order that women might come into their own, because we believed that women not only needed an education, but they needed a broader horizon in which they may use that education. And the right to vote would give them that privilege."[77] Toms's reflection on the event captured a widely held sentiment that propelled New Negro women's suffrage activism before, during, and after the March parade. Toms's statement also captured the New Negro women's ethos extant among Howard women in the early twentieth century. "Coming into their own" meant etching out space for black women to aspire and to achieve. Racism and sexism could not destroy black women's political culture. Black women from Howard University participating in the parade in the face of racist spectators and participants signaled an emergent audaciousness. The hostile racial climate of the nation's capital on parade day, more heightened than usual because of the rape of Adelaide Grant, proved to be a testing ground for a new generation of local African American women suffragists. Their performance of fashionable and "respectable" black femininity positioned this small group of Howard women and Terrell as the face of this new era of African American women's political activism in the nation's capital.

Conclusion

Based on their particular experiences with prevailing racial and gender ideologies as well as existing political and cultural currents, black women developed a distinct political culture. Working within the parameters of a black women's culture of respectability, these women strategically invested in a politics of appearance that connected to their public political behavior.[78] New Negro women suffragists addressed the social conditions that African Americans confronted, but they also wanted to have their own voice as African American women, within the national body politic. With greater access to mass media outlets such as newspapers and other periodicals, New Negro suffragists capitalized upon a longstanding strategy in black women's activism to situate themselves as modern activists. In the October 24, 1915, edition of the *Afro-American*, Lucy Diggs Slowe publicly commented on the connections between the National Association for the Advancement of Colored People (NAACP) and the suffrage movement. Slowe proclaimed, "[The NAACP] was in favor of universal suffrage because it could not support the one without supporting the other. It knows only too well that the voteless group in any republic is a helpless one. To a large extent the Negro in this republic is voteless, and therefore helpless."[79] Slowe, although not at Howard when she made this statement, echoed the widespread sentiment of the Howard women who marched in the suffrage parade in Washington. When she arrived at Howard in 1922 as the dean of women, Slowe walked into a campus greatly affected by the historic act of Terrell and the twenty-two founders of Delta Sigma Theta. The desire of Nellie Quander to have Howard women such as members of Alpha Kappa Alpha Sorority participate in the march, in spite of Paul's evasiveness and potential harm, mirrored a fearlessness entrenched in a strategic performance of feminine propriety.

Noting the utility of the politics of respectability as they pertained to personal aesthetics, black women marching in the March 1913 suffrage parade used aesthetic tropes of respectable femininity to insert themselves into political activism. Although their white women counterparts engaged in theatrics and other forms of pageantry to make themselves more visible in the national political arena, black women performed respectability to attain greater visibility through embodying the antithesis of myths about their character and lack of political savvy. Existing stereotypes about black women positioned their bodies, their expressive practices, and their styling choices within the realm of spectacle without having to employ theatrics. Whereas white women suffragists moved more toward the use of spectacle in the early twentieth century, African American women suffragists in Washington chose to perform ladyhood to claim a distinct space within the twentieth century women's suffrage movement.[80] White women suffragists, particularly those inspired by New Woman cultural currents, embraced the use of spectacle and theatrics to visualize a burgeoning political consciousness that began to think of ladyhood as restrictive and oppressive.[81] For white women, the Washington suffrage march represented a departure from ladyhood and a rejection of feminine propriety. Christine Stansell, in *City of Women: Sex and Class in New York, 1789–1860*, thoroughly discusses how white women mobilized around rejecting "bourgeois female decorum" using dress and manner. This new era of white women's suffrage activism tapped into this legacy of women decidedly existing outside of ladyhood. Conversely, black women lacked access to the protected status of ladyhood and its accompanying privileges. Ladyhood had racially specific meanings. For white women suffragists and women's rights activists, ladyhood signaled the policing of their bodies and the relegation of their bodies to private and semi-private spheres. African American women suffragists from Howard University in 1913, however, claimed and inhabited ladyhood. They recognized ladyhood as a powerful performative strategy that could transform public perceptions of black women's political capital. These women did not have white or male privilege. They confronted the harsh historical reality of exclusion from discourses of ladyhood. The performance and articulation of female decorum served a similar purpose to that of white women suffragists rejecting what they viewed as a protected/regulated/policed status.

The political articulations of black women such as the founding members of Delta Sigma Theta Sorority who participated in the suffrage parade also garnered the support of leading African American political outlets. African American male editors of the premier newspapers of Washington such as the *Colored American* trumpeted the arrival of a modern black political woman and presented this political ideal as a "splendid representation" of African American progress.[82] In Washington the African American media placed Terrell at the center of New Negro women's political culture. Her national and emergent international status bolstered their positioning of her as one of the most important black women political celebrities. Her words, fashion, and hairstyles coexisted as integral components to her success as a black woman political activist. In Terrell, black women in Washington had a prototype for a modern "political" woman; they, along with Slowe, recognized the importance of performing ladyhood both as a liberatory act and as a strategy for distinguishing themselves from their New Woman counterparts and for solidifying alliances with New Negro men.[83]

Whereas the black press honed in on "respectable" black political women as representatives of this new era of political activism, white press outlets such as the *New York Times*, the *Chicago Tribune*, and the *Washington Herald* reported on the pageantry and spectacular political performances of white women suffragists during large-scale protests such as the suffrage parade. The *New York Times*' description of the parade as "one of the most impressively beautiful spectacles staged in this country" failed to capture the marked exclusion of black women or the nonspectacle of the small delegation of African American women marching. The *Washington Herald*, although also reporting on injured marchers, spoke of the use of pageantry and spectacle as well. The white press viewed the theatrics of white women suffragists as attempts to reinvigorate a fledgling national movement. White newspapers acknowledged a distinct shift in the strategies of white women suffragists. Similar to the black press's coverage of women's suffrage activism of the early twentieth century, white newspapers proclaimed a new era in women's political activism.

This new era became evident through the fashion, styling, and politics of appearance women suffragists adopted. Both black and white women created political cultures in which aesthetics and representational politics were integral. For New Negro women in Washington, the ability to present themselves as cultured, fashionable, and respectable through their dress and hairstyle choices carried significant political weight. Politicizing respectability had a history in African American women's activism prior to the New Negro era but became solidified as a primary tactic during the late nineteenth and early twentieth centuries.[84] The demand for respect for women's broadened influence in the public sphere propelled black women's use of the performative feminine propriety during the New Negro era. Black clubwomen also used politics of respectability to counter prevailing racialized gender stereotypes of black women; New Negro women employed these politics to embed themselves more fully in contemporaneous political movements. Performing "ladyhood" offered an aesthetic path to becoming visible and viable within New Negro political culture. As "splendid" representations of themselves, New Negro women in Washington both contributed to an evolving political discourse and created a localized political culture authored by black women, one that connected them to a national vision of equality for African American women.

4

Saturday Night at the S Street Salon

New Negro Women Playwrights

Alongside vibrant African American women's political culture evolving in Washington, D.C., in the late nineteenth and early twentieth centuries was a rich and diverse creative and expressive culture and social scene. From nightclubs and restaurants to social events, black Washingtonians could partake in a variety of social and cultural activities.[1] The city boasted race-specific cultural and social infrastructure because of the relatively substantial population of African Americans and the historical legacy of black communities there. The number of social and cultural venues founded by and serving African Americans only increased as the black population grew.[2] This growth also sparked a further diversification of available diversions. While many black Washingtonians used their Saturday nights as a designated time for leisure and consumption, many had to work. Still, others chose to engage in social and cultural activities that involved explicit political purposes and that contributed to a New Negro political agenda. This chapter sheds light on how a small but dynamic community of black women in Washington invested in art as politic. Their work facilitated and aligned with an emergent political ethos among black women in the nation's capital.

Social and cultural activities with political purposes became central to both the political and expressive transformation in black America in the early twentieth century. The circulation of literary publications, the emphasis on the importance of developing the arts in black educational institutions such as Shaw Junior High, M Street High School, and Howard University, and the establishment of literary, musical, and other arts-based clubs contributed to a politicized, black cultural landscape in Washington. Musical societies such as the African American women's Treble Clef Club founded in 1897 and the Samuel Coleridge-Taylor Choral Society founded in 1903 by Mrs. Andrew F. Hilyer contributed to a creative milieu for blacks living in the nation's capital. Within these societies and clubs, African American women debated, for example, what music they should play and sing. Discussions about singing popular or vernacular music continued throughout the late nineteenth and early twentieth century. According to Gregoria Fraser Goins of the Treble Clef Club, members decided that "there should be no jazz in our program."[3] By 1925 however, club minutes captured a shift in the culture of the club. Meetings became an opportunity to study African American music. Participation in a program on the blues at which they performed "St. Louis Blues," "Turner Blues," and "Basement Blues," signaled a move toward a more inclusive approach in listening to and playing various genres of African American music.[4] From being anti-jazz in the 1890s to stating that "there is a blues streak in each and every one of us," we see a shift in how these women thought about the value of African American musical culture.[5] Debates about the musical identity of these clubs paralleled ongoing discussions about the nature and purpose of black artistic expression during the New Negro era.[6]

In this period, African Americans built on a legacy of using art as a vehicle for realizing change and became increasingly invested in using cultural venues to promote racial progress.[7] In Alain Locke's groundbreaking collection, *The New Negro*, Albert Barnes affirmed the greatness of Negro art because it embodied "the Negroes' individual traits and reflects their suffering, aspirations and joys during a long period of acute oppression and distress."[8] Communities in black Washington heeded the call to produce Negro art with a fervor that established the nation's capital as a cultural and political center for African Americans in the early twentieth century—prior to and during the Harlem Renaissance. African Americans artists in Washington created musicals, wrote poetry, novels, and short stories, painted and sculpted artwork, composed songs, and choreographed pieces that both illuminated and commented on political currents of the New Negro era. African American theater, in particular, became central to the politicization of art during this period.[9] Leading African American activists and intellectuals such as W. E. B. DuBois, Alain Locke, and Montgomery T. Gregory encouraged African Americans to write plays about their experiences and provided unprecedented opportunities for the performance and publication of black-authored plays.[10] More specifically, these men supported the emergence of a new cadre of black women writers who would become instrumental in the movement to politicize African American expressive and aesthetic cultures.

Black women playwrights used African American drama as a means to make visible the experiences of black women, building on a tradition already well established in poetry and fiction. New Negro women playwrights focused on black women's perspectives, struggles, and triumphs.[11] A foundational work in the genre was Pauline Elizabeth Hopkins's *Slaves' Escape; or, The Underground Railroad.* Written as a musical drama in 1879 and performed by the Hopkins Colored Troubadours at the Oakland Garden in Boston on July 5, 1880, her play depicts the importance of the Underground Railroad to runaway slaves and abolitionism. The play focuses on both men and women runaway slaves, but highlights African American women as leaders and conductors on the Underground Railroad. Hopkins's work served as a template for plays by and about black women that also dealt with historical, social, and political themes.

Black women in Washington were among the first to craft a cohesive artistic community in the New Negro era. The birth of this community paralleled the growth of black theater both locally and nationally. This growth occurred through the establishment of outlets and venues for the production and performance of African American drama. Additionally, black women playwrights in Washington could interact with, learn from, and exchange ideas with some of the most prominent figures associated with black intellectual and cultural production in this era. Gregory and Locke were particularly significant in the emergence of the black women playwrights' community of Washington in the 1910s and 1920s. Their mentorship and training catalyzed a self-sustaining and, at times, gender-specific community of black women playwrights. At the heart of this community were Howard University and M Street High School.[12]

Beyond the walls of these nationally recognized black educational institutions was the S Street Salon, a more informal but equally important space for black women playwrights in Washington. The home of writer and playwright Georgia Douglas Johnson, located at 1461 S Street NW in the U Street Corridor, the S Street Salon became the literal and figurative home for black women playwrights in the city. On many Saturday nights during the New Negro era, Johnson welcomed "the brightest local talent" into her home.[13] Black Washington women attendees included Mary Burrill, Marita Bonner, May Miller, and Angelina Weld Grimké. Although frequented by notable African American men writers like Alain Locke, Lewis Alexander, and Willis Richardson, the S Street Salon functioned as a black-women-centered site of friendship, love, and artistic nurturing.[14] Eventually, Johnson's home became an artistic hotbed for numerous writers from around the country who contributed to the New Negro movement, including Langston Hughes, Jessie Fausset, Jean Toomer, Anne Spencer, and Zora Neale Hurston.

This chapter focuses on black women in Washington who regularly participated in the S Street Salon and the body of work that resulted from these Saturday night sessions. Although black men did play an integral role in forming and shaping the contours of this black women's playwright community, the interactions among these women were profound. They influenced and inspired each other to articulate their unique experiences through theater and propelled the outburst of cultural production in the nation's capital in the form of plays.[15] I use the works of Georgia Douglas Johnson and Angelina Weld Grimké, the interactions of Grimké and Johnson and other S Street Salon frequent participants, Mary Burrill, and May Miller to examine the role of the salon in New Negro women's writing culture in Washington. The connections among these women and their shared and divergent experiences illuminate a New Negro women's discourse that evolved as a result of the specific cultural and intellectual infrastructure that existed in Washington during the early twentieth century. New Negro women playwrights at the S Street Salon used their creativity and writing prowess to comment upon issues such as lynching, women's reproductive rights, the challenges facing African American families, and the plight of black mothers. Saturday nights at the Salon were not women-only events, yet black women formed a gender-specific group within this literary and expressive community to develop the voices of African American women playwrights.

The plays of Johnson, Burrill, and Miller captured an array of black women's experiences. Specifically, their antilynching plays aligned with a distinct political consciousness. Female-authored antilynching dramas of the early twentieth century challenged racist and sexist ideologies that fueled racial violence against all African Americans.[16] "Emerging from a rigorous interpretation of their surroundings," Koritha Mitchell notes, "lynching drama indexes African Americans' recognition that the turbulent decades of the Progressive Era made embodied practice important to all U.S. citizens."[17] While Mitchell temporally frames the lynching drama within the Progressive Era, I would also argue that these dramas were indicative of a New Negro women's literary/performance culture that critically considered the "turbulence" experienced by African American women from the turn of the twentieth century through the Great Depression. Mitchell's conceptualization of the lynching drama as a site for African Americans to chronicle their stories opens a space to examine the community of African American women producing this literary genre.

Engaging political themes such as race suicide, rape, and the broader social impact of lynching, these playwrights created an alternative political space in which women became central to lynching and antilynching narratives. Because of women's exclusion from traditional political activities such as voting and holding offices, black women seeking political voices often adopted culturally expressive forms, while still demanding greater access to more traditional forms of political activism. These plays were part of an alternative, cultural discourse on lynching. Black women playwrights used antilynching dramas to broaden conversations about racial violence to include black women, black families, black communities, and white women. Mitchell rightfully posits that the lynching dramas (such as those written by many of the women who took part in the S Street Salon community) served as mechanisms for coping with the reality of lynching.[18] To Mitchell's compelling argument, I add that the community these women fostered at the S Street Salon also provided a space for New Negro women to foster community through creative survival. I explore this black-women-predominated space dedicated to the writing and production of antilynching plays to further establish Washington as a cultural center for African American women. These women played an undervalued role in what we call the New Negro or Harlem Renaissance. Their words emboldened assertions about the value of black art as politic—and, more specifically, black women's art as politically exigent.

Before Saturday Nights: Black Women Playwrights in Washington in the Early New Negro Era

Saturday nights at the S Street Salon gave black women in Washington a space in which they could think collectively about how to present and represent black experiences. The cadre of Washington women participating in this Saturday night community included Georgia Douglass Johnson, whose house was the meeting place, Angelina Grimké, Mary Burrill, May Miller, Zora Neale Hurston, Eulalie Spence, Shirley Graham (prior to her marriage to W. E. B. DuBois), and Marita Bonner. Theater historians Kathy Perkins and Judith L. Stephens have anthologized many of the works of black Washington women who attended Saturday nights at the salon.[19] While comprehensive and thorough in their presentation of the plays as literary texts, these anthologies do not delve into the historical significance of the community that produced them. Mitchell's work offers substantial contextualization; however, my explicit focus on the S Street Salon uncovers this informal space as a central institution within the emergence of New Negro culture.

The faculty at Howard University, which included Locke and Gregory as well as W. E. B. Du Bois, were instrumental in the formative stages of the African American theater movement that took place in Washington and benefited from the resources of Howard University, M Street High School, and other black organizations and institutions in the District. Du Bois organized the Krigwa Players, a small theater group based in New York City who performed race—or "propaganda"—plays in cities such as Washington, Denver, and Baltimore. In 1921 Gregory founded the Department of Dramatic Arts at Howard with the intention of launching the first National Negro Theater in the United States. One of the many initiatives of this newly organized department was the creation of the Howard Players, a small theater group who wrote, produced, and performed black-authored "folk plays" that addressed the historical and cultural experiences of African Americans. By 1922 the *Chicago Defender* acknowledged the work of Gregory and the newly established Howard Players in a piece titled "Howard Players Appear in Their Own Show."[20] Prior to the 1910s and 1920s, blacks did not have access to professional theater training through institutions, particularly not in the field of playwriting, and minstrelsy predominated as the primary theatrical form "depicting" black life.[21] The advisory board for the Department of Dramatic Arts at Howard consisted of both black and white leaders in academia and the theatrical arts. Notably, whites primarily composed the board. James Weldon Johnson was one of few African Americans to serve on the advisory committee, along with Gregory and Locke, who were the most influential African American voices in the group.

At the inception of the New Negro theater movement, there were two distinct standpoints regarding the form and content of African American plays. For Du Bois, New Negro theater must "reveal Negro life as it is . . . must be written by Negro authors who understand from birth and continual association just what it means to be a Negro today . . . must cater primarily to Negro audiences and be supported and sustained by their entertainment and approval."[22] Du Bois openly advocated for the use of Negro theater as propaganda not only for articulating black experiences but also for improving the lives of African Americans. In juxtaposition, Gregory articulated a differing standpoint within the burgeoning African American theatrical arts community. As he maintained, "the Negro has a wonderful opportunity through drama to win a better standing in the community."[23] But that would not come "through the production of plays of propaganda; that would be mistaken effort," he said. "I believe that we can win a broader recognition of our rights and responsibilities as citizens by demonstrating our abilities as artists."[24] Gregory viewed New Negro plays as a way to validate the humanity of African Americans through the display of their artistic abilities.

Whereas Du Bois focused on the content and political intentions of Negro plays, Gregory affirmed that creativity and artistic excellence, not explicit political propaganda, would help blacks secure rights and other freedoms. Although these distinct standpoints existed, many writers crafted a repertoire that reflected both perspectives on African American playwriting. Both standpoints also acknowledged the significance of New Negro theater to racial progress. African American women in Washington embraced both standpoints and incorporated propaganda and "folk culture" into their works when they became playwrights. Furthermore, their invocation of women's issues and perspectives centered black women in the conversation about both artistic expression and political propaganda. The question of what New Negro art could or should be for New Negro women did not solely pivot around race and racism and proving the worth of black artists. African American women playwrights in Washington pushed for the valuing of black women's literary contributions and the injustices black women endured.

During the New Negro era, many of the most prominent African American artists and intellectuals wrote about the "proper" use of black art. Langston Hughes's 1926 "The Negro Artist and the Racial Mountain," published in *The Nation*, and Alain Locke's "Art of Propaganda?" in the November 1928 issue of *Harlem* are two of the best-known pieces about this issue. Recent secondary literature[25] about arts and letters during the New Negro era chronicles the significance of these debates among artists and writers such as Locke, Hughes, Hurston, Toomer, Fausett, Grimké, Johnson, Burrill, and Miller, as well as Countee Cullen, Jacob Lawrence, Aaron Douglass, Claude McKay, Alice Dunbar-Nelson, and Nella Larsen. The standpoints of these artists regarding the use of art as propaganda is evident through their respective works that reveal varying facets of African American culture. New Negro women playwrights in Washington tended to produce more explicitly politicized pieces.

Although the African American theater movement and the S Street Salon came to prominence during the 1920s, the origins of a New Negro women's writing culture began in the 1910s. Prior to Du Bois's call for a "new birth" in African American theater in 1926, the NAACP chapter in Washington and members from the Howard University community spearheaded efforts to develop Negro theater in the nation's capital, outside of formal institutions, such as universities.[26] Using expressive culture to recast a political movement was not a new phenomenon for African Americans. Because of barriers preventing women's participation in formal politics, black women in particular often employed cultural expression as a vehicle to comment on historical and contemporaneous social and political issues. In 1916 activist and writer Angelina Weld Grimké wrote the first known example of a drama written in the antilynching tradition and the first twentieth-century full-length play written, performed, and produced by African Americans.

Angelina Weld Grimké, a journalist, poet, educator, and playwright, was the only child of one of the most prominent and respected African American families in the nation. Her father, Archibald Grimké, an attorney and a community activist, was the second African American to graduate from Harvard Law School. He served as president of the Washington chapter of the NAACP in 1913 and eventually became the national vice president of the NAACP. In 1919 the NAACP awarded him the prestigious Spingarn Medal for his work on racial equality.[27] In 1902 Angelina Grimké began a teaching career at Armstrong Manual Training School. After nearly fifteen years at Armstrong, she took a job at the prestigious Dunbar High School (formerly M Street High School), where she taught future New Negro writer and S Street Salon participant May Miller. Grimké primarily wrote love poems. Her diaries, love letters, and unpublished poems reveal a woman who struggled with despair, heartbreak, and desperation.[28] From lamentations about her mother, who committed suicide, to missing a white male love interest, to longing for a kiss from a female partner, Grimké's personal papers tell the story of a woman struggling to connect.[29] She survived a potentially fatal train crash in 1913, which resulted in a precarious state of health for an unknown period. She built relationships with African American women in Washington, particularly Georgia Douglas Johnson. After Grimké left Washington in 1930 for New York, she remained in close contact with Johnson. The production *Rachel*, although predating the S Street Salon community, foreshadowed the evolution of an African American women's writing culture in the nation's capital.

The play was produced by the Drama Committee of the Washington, D.C., branch of the NAACP. The Drama Committee and the NAACP presented the production at the Myrtilla Miner Normal School in Washington on March 3 and 4, 1916. The NAACP's political agenda converged the play's major themes, although dissenters within in the NAACP criticized the use of the stage as a platform for political propaganda.[30] Although the play wrestled with themes associated with the NAACP's call for race propaganda via theater, Grimké circulated a draft of the play in 1915, before the NAACP's call for such work.[31] *Rachel*, one of Grimké's many artistic endeavors, is noteworthy not only as a progenitor for a tradition but also for its particular standpoint and political underpinnings.

Set in the home of an African American family, *Rachel* focuses on a black matriarch's recollection of the lynching of her husband and son, the consequences of this lynching at the time, and her family's response to her recollection of racial violence. Grimké specifically targeted white women, hoping to reach them through the common ground of motherhood and to acquire their support in opposing lynching. "If," she argued, "white women of this country could see, feel, understand just what effect their prejudice and the prejudice of their fathers, brothers, husbands, sons were having on the souls of colored mothers everywhere . . . great power to affect public opinion would be set free and the battle would be half won."[32] In fact, lynching was among one of the most common themes black women playwrights addressed. "When Black women first picked up the pen as playwright," Kathy Perkins notes, "they chose to speak out against the atrocities of lynching."[33] Most of the black women playwrights who frequented the S Street Salon addressed lynching in their works, although varying in their approaches, content, and form.

The melodramatic, emotive, and sentimental nature of the play attempted to unveil the psychological consequences of white supremacy and racial violence on African Americans, particularly black mothers. Grimké attempted to capture how black families experienced lynching as an imminent horror that any family could undergo at any moment. The character Rachel, after hearing her mother's story of how her father and brother were lynched, laments:

> Then, everywhere, everywhere, throughout the South, there are hundreds of dark mothers who live in fear, terrible, suffocating fear, whose rest by night is broken, and whose joy by day in their babies on their hearts is three parts—pain. Oh, I know this is true—for this way I should feel, if I were little Jimmy's mother. How horrible! Why—it would be more merciful—to strangle the little things at birth. And so this nation—this white Christian nation—has deliberately set its curse upon the most beautiful—the most holy thing in life—motherhood! Why—it—makes—you doubt—God![34]

Rachel's cries distinguish lynching as a lived reality specific to the South, where the vast majority of lynchings of African Americans occurred. Lynching was not as frequent an occurrence in the nation's capital during the early twentieth century; nevertheless, many of the black women migrating to Washington from the South had experience with lynching. A notable exception to this southern exclusivity was the July 1919 race riot that occurred in Washington. One of the many cities that experienced tremendous racial violence during the summer of 1919, Washington's race riot illuminated racial tensions that pervaded interracial interactions in the federal city. The outburst of "mob violence" that commenced on July 19 also revealed the growing strength of the African American community in Washington. African Americans engaged in armed resistance and violently fought against being relegated to victimhood.[35] After the riot, racial hostility became more virulent, and African American organizations such as the NAACP became more active in addressing racial violence and other forms of racial oppression and inequality confronting African Americans both locally and nationally.

To make her appeal to white women, Grimké appropriated contemporaneous dominant gender ideology, which idealized motherhood to show how black mothers were excluded from that ideology. The dominant ideology of this era categorized women as society's moral keepers. Mothers carried the added burden of epitomizing "positive" normative values such as propriety, respectability, prudence, and temperance. Subject to cultural expectations that upheld social and ideological constraints for women regardless of race, Grimké manipulated prevailing ideology to compel white women, and white mothers specifically, to oppose lynching because of its detrimental effects on motherhood.[36] The very thought that a woman could fathom killing her children out of fear of an inability to protect her children was purposely present in her play. If mothers across racial lines could visualize the effects of lynching, Grimké felt, then white women could be inspired to mobilize against lynching—not because of its racist implications, but because of its devaluation of the idealized construction of motherhood as a gendered but protected status for all women. Grimké built upon a tradition in abolitionist literature in which black and white women framed their opposition to slavery in terms of a common motherhood.[37]

Grimké also illuminated the unique pain of black women. Using motherhood was not solely a strategy for inciting interracial cooperation for anti-lynching campaigns; *Rachel* provided a cathartic space for black women to engage their pain as mothers, daughters, aunts, and friends of black boys and men who were lynched. "Lynching plays," Mitchell explains, "were one of the resources that helped African Americans survive this period still believing in their right to full citizenship."[38] For black women playwrights in Washington, they used lynching dramas to cope, to incite, to inspire, and to mourn. Plays such as *Rachel* had political overtones, but the affective implications of these works also resonated in the intimate community these women cultivated in the nation's capital. Like the communal spaces in which the performances of many lynching dramas took place, the S Street Salon offered black women in particular a space in which to imagine their safety and a reality without racial and gender violence. Although evaluating the efficacy of a play in motivating individuals to oppose lynching is a difficult task, it is indisputable that

Grimké employed ideologically and historically specific representations of persons affected by lynching and the antilynching movement, and that she created a text in which African Americans could see themselves and their experiences within a context of racial terrorism in the United States.

Rachel's monologue also appeals to Christians. By positing Christianity as antithetical to the horror and spectacle of lynching, Grimké illustrated the glaring contradictions extant between racial violence motivated by white supremacy and the Christian principles on which the United States was founded. Grimké, like her abolitionist foremothers Angelina Grimké Weld and Sarah Grimké, explicitly connected racial injustice to a failure to uphold the religious foundation of the United States.[39] Abolitionist activists and antilynching proponents similarly incorporated a moral stance against the atrocities blacks confronted. Ideologically positioned as having a heightened moral capacity, women antilynching activists used this positioning to articulate the immorality of racial violence.

Rachel combated other gendered constraints of feminine propriety. "These constraints," according to art historian Helen Langa, "were related to socially constructed expectations of gender difference in two overlapping contexts: in response to violent social acts, and in both looking at and representing male bodies."[40] The representational choices Grimké made illuminate the constraints of feminine propriety that regulated the content of lynching plays authored by black and white women. For depicting the actual event that propels the play, Grimké chose to have the matriarch, Mrs. Loving, recollect the lynching of her husband and son. This choice complemented Grimké's stated purpose of speaking directly to mothers. Mrs. Loving laments, "They broke down the front door and made their way to our bedroom. Your father kissed me—and took up his revolver. It was always loaded. They broke down the door."[41] Her husband's possession of a loaded gun unveils a perceived need for black men to protect themselves. In Washington, this need for self-protection actualized in the 1919 race riot, in which black men in the southwest area of the city fought back against white assailants.[42] While white supremacists would have considered Mr. Loving's possession of a gun as evidence of black male criminality, Mrs. Loving's story conveys a sense fear and vulnerability that overwhelmed blacks. Mrs. Loving then proceeds to recall, "Four masked men fell—they did not move any more—after a little. (*pauses*) Your father was finally overpowered and dragged out."[43] The father resisted until defeat. Through Mrs. Loving, Grimké introduces the mob element of lynching. Mrs. Loving delves further into her memory and recounts, "In the hall—my little seventeen-year-old George tried to rescue him. Your father begged him not to interfere. He paid no attention. It ended in their dragging them both out. (*pauses*) My little George—was—a man! (*controls herself with an effort*) He never made an outcry. His last words to me were: "Ma, I am glad to go with Father." I could only nod to him."[44] The conflation of manhood with fearlessness and pride permeates this part of the matriarch's story. George's "complicity" with his fate indicates a feeling of inevitability regarding racial violence. Responding to the mob dragging her husband and son down the stairs, Mrs. Loving explains, "While they were dragging them down the steps . . . I knelt down by you [Rachel]—and covered my ears with my hands—and waited. I could not pray—I couldn't for a long time—afterwards."[45] Appealing to white Christians and speaking directly to black Christians, this portion of the story asks her audience to imagine not being able to pray. In Mrs. Loving's concluding statements of her reminiscence, she leaves her family and the audience with a cogent image. "The only sounds were the faint rustle of leaves and the 'tapping of the twig of a tree' against the window. I hear it still—sometimes in my dreams. It was the tree—where they were."[46] Actual hangings did not usually occur on trees. However, the most popular and collectively engrained image for those in support of and against lynching was a black male body swinging from a tree. Mrs. Loving's final thoughts on the lynching of her son and husband resonate with numerous highly publicized accounts and images of lynching.

While Grimké worked within dominant gender ideology by avoiding vivid depictions of lynching, she countered the dominant narratives that rendered black womanhood and motherhood invisible or insignificant. Mrs. Loving only alludes to the actual lynching. Black women writers rarely referred to such details and generally avoided narrative emphasis on lynching as public spectacles because of a prevailing expectation of feminine propriety. The emphasis on feminine propriety largely grew out of middle- and upper-class communities, although many lower- and working-class women propagated similar ideas about feminine propriety as the ideal performance of black femininity.[47] *Rachel* complicated the racial violence narrative by inserting the far-reaching consequences of lynching for African American families. By representing lynching as a form of violence that has lasting ramifications for African American families, Grimké shifts the discussion from black male victimization to the victimization of black women through the violence perpetrated against her family. The family emerges a gendered space. Black women's victimization became central to Grimké's antilynching discourse.

Rachel opened the door for what Claudia Tate describes as a new point in African American literature in which artistic depictions of racial protest became more acceptable for African Americans to produce and consume.[48] In response to *Rachel* and the emerging genre of Negro plays, Washington-based writer Willis Richardson stated, "When I say Negro plays, I do not mean merely plays with Negro characters. . . . Miss Grimké's *Rachel* is nearer the idea; still even this, with its Negro characters, is not exactly the thing I mean. It is called a propaganda play, and a great portion of it shows the manner in which Negroes are treated by white people in the United States. . . . Still there is another kind of play; the play that shows the soul of a people; and the soul of this people is truly worth showing."[49] Through the writing and production of *Rachel*, Grimké succeeded also in creating a space for an African American woman to insert her specific experiences into conversations about the harsh realities confronting African Americans. Her influence extended to aspiring writers throughout Washington. Richardson, who reviewed the play in the *Crisis* (November 1919), noted that after seeing a performance of *Rachel* he "was inspired to study the technique of drama." Her play and her commitment to using drama, fiction, and poetry as forms of activism inspired black women across the nation to "take to the pen."

While residing in D.C., Grimké worked with black women writers and supported the establishment of a space for black women playwrights in Washington. Grimké lived in close proximity to what would become the S Street Salon at 1415 Corcoran Street NW. Prior to Johnson's opening her home on Saturday nights to aspiring and prominent writers, black women in Washington frequented Grimké's home as a safe space for honing their skills as playwrights. Although known as a shy woman, Grimké served as an inspiration and a mentor to African American women in Washington, such as May Miller, seeking to voice their experiences through the dramatic arts. When Johnson commenced the Saturday night sessions at her home, Grimké was a regular attendee until she moved to New York. The July 1927 issue of the *Crisis* hailed Grimké as "a delightful addition to the salon's always-lively crowd."[50] Both her friendship with and mentoring of African American women in the S Street Salon group made her an integral figure in the New Negro women's writing community in Washington in 1920s until the passing of her father in 1930 and her relocation to New York.

Georgia Douglas Johnson, the S Street Salon, and New Negro Women's Playwrights

Rachel laid the foundation for other black women to experiment with playwriting as a viable medium for participating in the political and the cultural arenas of the New Negro movement. The publication and performance of

Grimké's *Rachel*, the establishment of the Department of Dramatic Arts at Howard University, and the emergence of literary outlets calling for African Americans to submit plays marked the arrival of a new era in black Washington women's writing and in the politicization of African American's women's expressive practices. Black women encountered unprecedented opportunities for participating in a black cultural movement that connected writing, performance, and socially, historically, and politically relevant themes. Washington women were in the center of this cultural explosion. One particular black Washington woman, Georgia Douglas Johnson, became the most prolific figure in the African American women's writing community in Washington.[51] In addition to being the most productive, Johnson opened up her home to black writers from all over the country on Saturdays for more than forty years. For black women writers and aspiring writers living in black elite circles in the nation's capital, 1461 S Street NW was arguably the most significant institution in the formation of a localized New Negro women playwriting culture.[52]

Over the course of her eighty-five years of life, Johnson achieved in a number of fields. Known primarily as an exemplary poet throughout the New Negro era, Johnson also studied the violin, piano, and vocal performance, worked as a teacher and an assistant principal, and served as the commissioner of conciliation in the Department of Labor under President Calvin Coolidge. Her dedication to crafting her skills as a writer, however, marked her life in Washington, particularly after the death of her husband, Henry Lincoln Johnson, in 1925. Inspired by her close friend Grimké's production of *Rachel* and encouraged by African American colleagues in Washington, Johnson delved into playwriting and began expanding her literary repertoire beyond poetry. Theater studies scholars have explored Johnson's career as a dramatist.[53] Literary scholars tend to focus on her work as a poet, with the notable exceptions of Kathy Perkins, Koritha Mitchell, Claudia Tate, and Judith L. Stephens.[54] Both literary and theater studies scholars credit Johnson as a leading figure in the black cultural and literary renaissance that occurred in Harlem the 1920s. Nevertheless, her centrality to New Negro women's culture in Washington remains understudied.

Grimké's foray into playwriting, particularly into writing about politically and socially relevant issues, provided a blueprint for aspiring black women playwrights in Washington to follow. Judith L. Stephens defines a lynching drama as "a play in which the threat or occurrence of a lynching, past or present, has major impact on the dramatic action."[55] This genre gained particular traction within African American writing communities in the 1920s, most notably among black women writers. Lynching plays paralleled African

American women's involvement in the Anti-Lynching Crusade of the late nineteenth and early twentieth centuries. In 1925, when Johnson completed her first known lynching drama, *A Sunday Morning in the South*, African American women participated in and led local, national, and international antilynching campaigns.[56] The most visible of these antilynching leaders was Ida B. Wells. Perkins and fellow theater studies scholar Winona Fletcher argue that Johnson explicitly connected her "plays on lynching" to the antilynching crusade and to a burgeoning awareness among African Americans regarding the potential role of drama in effecting social change.[57] Over the course of her lifetime, Johnson wrote several plays within this genre. Fannie E. Hicklen identified ten plays written by Johnson; however, only six of these plays are typically credited to Johnson: two versions of *A Sunday Morning in the South*, *Safe*, *Blue-Eyed Black Boy*, *And Still They Paused*, and *A Bill to Be Passed*.[58]

The year of 1925 also marked the first time Johnson opened the doors of her home on Saturday nights to established and aspiring African American writers. At the S Street Salon, Johnson emphasized collaboration, rigorous intellectual exchange, and the development of African American women's creative and politically active voices. Prior to Johnson beginning her Saturday night sessions, Grimké welcomed Johnson into her home as a mentor. Subsequently, Johnson embraced the role of a facilitator and mentor for black women writers in Washington who regularly attended the Saturday night sessions in the U Street Corridor. The creation of this space facilitated collaboration on lynching dramas and plays about other political and social realities confronting African Americans.

Johnson moved to Washington in 1910, after her husband received an appointment as the Recorder of Deeds from the President William Taft. Her career as a published writer preceded her move to Washington. Her first published poems, "Omnipresence" and "Beautiful Eyes," appeared in the June 1905 issue of the Atlanta-based literary journal *The Voice of the Negro*.[59] Her productivity as a poet, however, intensified after her relocation to the nation's capital. By 1916 she published the first of four volumes of poetry, *The Heart of a Woman*. Her poems also appeared in the *Crisis*.[60] Her poetry, although more widely published than her plays, did not conform to race propaganda standards. Johnson's poems captured themes of love, longing, beauty, nature, and human emotion. Her largely unpublished collection of approximately twenty-eight plays more concretely aligned with the politicization of Negro theater called for by African American leaders such as Du Bois. Her plays provided a space in which Johnson could find a distinctive, political voice as a New Negro writer.

Safe (1929), Johnson's follow-up to *A Sunday Morning in the South*, embodies the core elements of the lynching drama genre defined by African American women. *Safe* also illustrates how the plays of New Negro women playwrights in Washington subtly differed in form, content, and style from other works within the lynching drama tradition. The cadre of African American women playwrights who frequented to S Street Salon combined "stage realism" and "folk drama" techniques, comparatively rigid writing styles, and vivid descriptions of racial violence and the emotional responses they elicited. For Johnson and the black Washington women playwrights of S Street Salon, the political and social climate in Washington and across the United States necessitated realistic depictions of the horrors African Americans confronted.[61] Despite their involvement with and training from Gregory and other prominent figures in the black theater movement in Washington, these women diverged from the vision of black theater as an opportunity to showcase black humanity. Plays such as *Safe* and *Rachel* articulated a distinct historical, social, and political awareness about African American women's experiences and sought to incite meaningful social and political change.

In *Safe*, the black woman protagonist is the actual victim of violence. Johnson illuminates the horrific choices black women made in a society in which the threat of lynching loomed constantly over black families. Black-woman-as-mother characters figure prominently in *Safe*, as they did in many New Negro plays. Portraying black motherhood as the primary force in the rearing and protection of black children, Johnson, like Grimké, presents black motherhood as a vulnerable status. Black mothers had to respond to lynching as both a lived and a potential experience for their children. Johnson invested in the belief that motherhood, regardless of race, deserved protection, although not to the same extent as Grimké. Since black mothers could not protect themselves or their children from being lynched, they could not responsibly and morally fulfill their prescribed responsibilities as mothers, as they needed to do.

Liza, the main character, hears about the lynching of a black man, Sam Hosea, who is lynched because he hit a white man in a fight over a dispute about wages. The white man struck first; Sam responded in self-defense. Johnson steered away from the black-male–white-female rape argument to emphasize the pervasiveness of lynching and its link to the racial restrictions of Jim Crow. Accusations of other crimes like the one that leads to the lynching of Sam Hosea occurred more frequently than rape allegations. Liza briefly laments the death of Hosea and immediately envisions the reaction of his mother to the news of his death as well as Hosea's calling out to his mother before his fatal demise. She also considers Sam's tenacious work ethic and the close relationship Sam had with his mother. Liza says, "I been setting here thinking 'bout that poor boy Sam—him working hard to take kere of his widder mother, doing the best he kin, trying to be a man and stan up for hissef, and what do he git?"[62] This reflection leads Liza to an even more disturbing conclusion about racial violence. She thinks about the perpetual, potential violence that all African Americans face, specifically black boys, born into a white supremacist society. Her thoughts lead her to conclude that black male children are better off unborn because of the inevitability of becoming victims of racial violence.

Liza's understanding of the vulnerability of black boys and men as a group quickly spirals into a serious concern for the welfare of the unborn child she is carrying: "What's little nigger boys born for anyhow? I sho hopes mine will be a girl. I don't want no boy baby to be hounded down and kicked 'round. No, I don't want to ever have no boy chile!"[63] Despite urgings from the family and friends surrounding her that her child will be safe, Liza becomes convinced that if her unborn child is male, he will be the victim of a lynching. Her hysteria mounts as she goes into labor and thinks about her responsibility to protect her child and how she can (or cannot) fulfill that responsibility if she births a male child. Her family members and friends remain concerned as the child's birth nears. They did not anticipate how profoundly the lynching of Sam Hosea had affected Liza and her views on motherhood. The desire to protect overwhelms Liza. To represent the plight of black mothers, Johnson highlights the debilitating emotional response of an expectant mother. Liza's erratic emotional state implicitly poses a question to the audience: Would you bring a child into a world where he will be murdered? This question could reach white mothers, but it also posed a difficult question to black parents, and specifically black mothers, about the prevalence of violence against black children.

When the doctor arrives to deliver the baby, he is informed of Liza's volatile state. After the delivery, he enters the living room where Liza's family and friends wait anxiously for news. He explains, "She's all right and the baby was born all right—big and fine. You heard him cry . . ."[64] The family responds in the affirmative, and the doctor continues "And she asked me right away, 'Is it a girl?'"[65] Liza's question is full of hope. The family urges the doctor to continue relaying what transpired. It is at this point that Dr. Jenkins fully discloses what happened immediately after Liza delivered the baby. He explains,

> I said, "No, child, it's a fine boy," and then I turned my back a minute to wash in the basin. When I looked around again she had her hands about the baby's throat choking it. I tried to stop her, but its little tongue was already hanging from its mouth. It was dead! Then she began, she kept muttering over and over again: "Now he's safe—safe from the lynchers! Safe!"[66]

Liza's first actions as a mother stem from a desire to protect her child from the horrors of lynching. She also seeks to protect herself from confronting the pain of losing her child. The mere perception of the inevitability of the lynching of her newborn son leads Liza to infanticide. Her desire to fulfill her motherly duty as her child's protector enables her to commit an act resolutely outside of prevailing constructions of motherhood.

Liza decides that murdering her son is her only option for actively responding to anticipated racial violence. Johnson's use of infanticide by a black mother offers a glimpse into the psychological damage that the mere potential of lynching imposed on black mothers and families. Most likely, Johnson knew the real story of Margaret Garner, a runaway slave who killed her children to "save" them from the horrors of slavery; to some extent, Liza's actions mirror those of Garner.[67] Novels such as Harriet Beecher Stowe's *Uncle Tom's Cabin* utilize the theme of infanticide. In fact, a body of nineteenth-century literature thematically incorporated slave infanticide.[68] The fear of her son's lynching leads not only to the murder of a newborn baby but also transforms a mother into a murderer. It is quite possible that Johnson conspicuously used infanticide in her play in an attempt to revive the literary trope and also to equate the horrors of slavery with the horrors of racial violence.

Liza's actions suggest several possible meanings. From one perspective, Liza fulfills her duties as a mother by protecting her son from a fatal threat. No specific threat of violence compels her. The compulsion to act violently stems from her envisioning Hosea's murder as the future consequence for her son. In her mind, Sam Hosea represents all black boys who negotiate their manhood under white supremacy. Sam Hosea's lynching also symbolizes the inability of black boys and black men to navigate a terrain in which their humanity is denied and murderous violence is a constant threat. Liza refuses to live in fear or to have her son live in fear. Her decision, although extreme, captured the fatal effects of the mere threat of white violence against African Americans.

From another vantage point, Liza's actions aid the white supremacist agenda. During slavery, blacks were dehumanized, but their labor was highly valued. Margaret Garner's murder of her children undermined slavery: fewer black bodies meant less labor. Despite the fatality and extremity of Garner's actions, killing her children negatively affected her owner's productivity. In that sense, the deaths of her children challenged the enslavement of black children. Liza's actions, however, contribute to the vicious cycle of violence that claims the lives of African Americans. With the abolition of slavery, many whites no longer placed any value on the lives of African Americans and viewed blacks as competition. African Americans were not the property of whites, but they were wage laborers competing for the jobs that poor and working-class whites held or desired. Liza's murdering her newborn son fulfilled the desires of violent white supremacists who advocated violence against blacks. Although in her mind Liza resisted and took a radical stance against racial violence, her stance produced the same result as a lynching.

Johnson did not explicitly state why she chose infanticide as the climax of her antilynching drama. Her choice, nevertheless, comments upon the broader but less frequently discussed effects of lynching on African Americans. It also builds on the trope of infanticide in abolitionist literature. Within this body of literature, infanticide is redemptive; it is portrayed as a mother acting in her child's best interest. Using such an extreme example of Jim Crow–era racial violence facilitated a discussion about the dire circumstances that lynching as a threat and as a lived experience produced for many blacks. The jarring thought of a mother killing her own child could reach across racial lines and cause other women to think about the difficult choices and experiences black women must encounter as a result of the prevalence of white supremacist ideologies and practices. As an antilynching activist, Johnson encouraged white women to become involved in antilynching activism. Like Grimké, she embraced motherhood as a potential site for unification among black and white women. Because the protection of children was integral to both black and white motherhood, a play based on the actions of a mother spoke more personally to the concerns of women.

Both *Rachel* and *Safe* encountered mixed reactions from African American audiences, particularly from members and leaders of the NAACP, who in fact sponsored the first production of *Rachel*. While there are very few known reviews of either of the plays, Montgomery Gregory of Howard University's Department of Dramatic Arts revealed that with regard to *Rachel* and the committee that worked with Grimké on producing the play, "a minority section . . . dissented from this propagandist platform and were instrumental in founding the Howard Players organization, promoting the purely artistic approach and the folk-drama idea."[69] *Safe* confronted similar critiques because of its resolutely political tone, how it was viewed as absurd, unnecessary, and vile.[70] Playwrights and dramatists who disavowed the utility and aesthetic value of art as political propaganda most likely had negative reactions to women-authored antilynching dramas.

The reception from entities like the Federal Theater Project or from readers of *Opportunity* and the *Crisis* did not deter Grimké or Johnson from supporting other plays within the still-evolving lynching drama tradition. Additionally, Grimké and Johnson encouraged black women in Washington to explore other socially and politically relevant topics through their playwriting. Two of the most prolific black women playwrights in Washington who attended the Saturday sessions at the S Street Salon were Mary Burrill and May Miller. The relationships among Johnson, Miller, Burrill, and Grimké were rich and complicated, as mentor-mentee, teacher-student, or writer-critic. Their exchanges at the salon were also integral to the political and cultural currents occurring in Washington and in other cities and towns in the United States.

Born only one year after Johnson, Mary Burrill was Johnson's friend and playwriting colleague. Burrill graduated from M Street High School in 1901. Immediately following graduation, she enrolled in Emerson College of Oratory (which eventually became Emerson College) and graduated in 1904. In 1905 Burrill commenced her career as a teacher at her high school alma mater. Johnson worked as a substitute teacher there during Burrill's tenure, and the two subsequently formed a close personal and professional relationship. Until Burrill received a permanent assignment at the school in 1920, she taught English at both M Street and Armstrong Technical High School. In addition to her exhausting teaching responsibilities, Burrill served as the director of the School of Expression, a department within the Washington, D.C., Conservatory of Music, from 1907 to 1911; because of her formal training in oratory, Burrill taught dramatics, elocution, and public speaking. She also directed plays and musical productions throughout the city until her death in 1946. Her works appeared in publications like the *Liberator Magazine*.[71] The year before her death, the Dunbar High School senior class of 1945 dedicated their yearbook to Burrill.[72]

Burrill achieved a distinct reputation as both an exemplary teacher and a visionary director by the 1920s. Not only committed to producing her own works, Burrill also regularly organized and executed productions such as J. M. Barrie's *Quality Street*. Burrill worked for and with nearly every prominent black intellectual and cultural institution in her career. In fact, one of her best-known achievements was her narration of Howard University's annual Christmas production of *The Other Wise Men*, a locally and nationally publicized event among African Americans.[73] The breadth of her endeavors and accomplishments resulted in the formation of friendships and working relationships with the some of the most visible of the New Negro women in Washington, including Johnson. Lucy Diggs Slowe and Burrill were a prominent New Negro couple, although viewed by many as trangressive because of their identities as same-gender loving. Alice Dunbar Nelson, wife of Paul Lawrence Dunbar and a respected black Washington playwright, was also a colleague and close friend. Burrill's close relationships with black women writers in Washington such as Dunbar Nelson and Johnson and her exposure to and involvement in Washington's black theater movement at M Street High School, Howard University, and the School of Expression all led her to become one of the original and most active members of the S Street Salon group. Although Burrill wrote her two best-known plays before Johnson opened up the doors of her home to New Negro writers, Burrill continued to hone her skills as a playwright, revised one of her plays, and assisted other black women playwrights when she joined the community of New Negro playwrights meeting on Saturdays at Johnson's home.

Burrill preceded Johnson in the lynching drama tradition by six years but did not join the S Street Salon community until the late 1920s. Published in 1919, her play *Aftermath* tells the story of the lynching of a World War I soldier. Many of the lynching plays written by African American women, including *Aftermath* and *Safe*, focused on racial violence sparked by allegations of crimes other than that of alleged sexual assaults of white women. One of the only documented performances of this play occurred on May 7, 1928, in New York City. Produced and performed by the New York City Krigwa Players and the Worker's Drama League in the David Belasco Sixth Annual Little Theater Tournament held at Frolic Theater, Burrill responded negatively to this production and to the creative license the producers took with her text. She noted that "the ending tacked on by the players changed what might otherwise have been an effective dramatic close into cheap melodramatic claptrap."[74] The nine-year gap between the writing *Aftermath* and its only known staging speaks to the difficulty playwrights, particularly black women playwrights, confronted in working in the lynching drama tradition. The political nature of such plays established these women playwrights as activists, which signaled their entry into the public, political sphere and challenged existing gender expectations regarding political activism.

In September 1919 Burrill published an even more controversial play than *Aftermath. They That Sat in Darkness* focused on birth control rights for African American women. A contentious issue in African American communities, and in the United States more broadly, movements for women's reproductive rights nonetheless became more visible during the early twentieth century.[75] *They That Sat in Darkness* was published first in a special issue of Margaret Sanger's *Birth Control Review.* In 1919 Max Eastman also published the play in the *Liberator.*[76] *They That Sit in Darkness* advocates for birth control for African American women as a means to escape poverty and depicts the hardships of a woman raising children under the harsh economic conditions many African American women faced during the New Negro era. This particular issue of *Birth Control Review* was titled "The Negroes' Need for Birth Control, as Seen by Themselves." Grimké contributed her short story, "The Closing Door" for this special issue as well.[77]

The highly controversial content of Burrill's play probably explains why there is no record of its production or performance. Leading black political activists of the New Negro era, particularly those ascribing to black nationalism, fought against the reproductive rights movement, which they framed as racial eugenics and as an institutionalized form of racial violence.[78] Burrill used *They That Sit in Darkness* as a way to articulate a race- and gender-specific experience of African American women. These women confronted negative reactions from black nationalists who believed that aborting a black fetus or baby was an act of racial violence. Black women choosing to think about their rights to abortion and other reproductive rights, and specifically the necessity of birth control and reproductive health services for African American women, risked being labeled as opponents of a nascent, New Negro form of black nationalism. These agendas affirmed the necessity of strengthening the black community by increasing the number of blacks. Black men and black women alike promoted black nationalism and viewed abortion and birth control as antithetical to a progressive, racial advancement agenda.

The S Street Salon community, most notably the black women playwrights from Washington, provided Burrill a space in which she could wrestle with social and political issues that were often marginalized within New Woman and New Negro cultural and political agendas. It is unclear what the views of her fellow playwrights were regarding birth control and abortion rights, but her continued participation in the community suggests that she was not deterred from articulating an unpopular point of view. The Saturdays she spent at the S Street Salon, coupled with the intimate relationships she formed with black women Washington playwrights, situate Burrill as a central figure to a New Negro women's theater culture in the nation's capital.

As a playwright, S Street Salon participant, and teacher, Burrill touched the lives of many black women in Washington. One of the most lauded writers of the New Negro movement, May Miller, was a student of Burrill's at M Street High School. Over the course of her ninety-six-year life, Miller became the most widely published woman playwright to emerge during the New Negro era. Born on January 26, 1899, Miller came from a particularly distinguished African American family in Washington. Her father, Kelly Miller, was a famous sociologist and a professor and dean at Howard University. At age fifteen, while enrolled at M Street High School and under the tutelage of M Street teachers Grimké and Burrill, Miller wrote her play *Pandora's Box*. After graduating from M Street High School, Miller journeyed to the Hilltop for college, graduating in 1920. At graduation, Miller won the university's first playwriting award for her one-act play, *Within the Shadows*. Afterward, Miller immediately began a career as teacher of speech and English at Douglass High School in Baltimore.

Throughout her twenty-year career at Douglass, Miller also joined Du Bois's Krigwa Players and developed her talents as a performer, dramatist, and director. During the summer months, Miller furthered her playwriting studies at Columbia University under the direction of nationally recognized theater scholar Frederick Koch. In the mid- to late 1920s, Miller received a number of accolades for her plays. In 1925 *The Bog Guide* won third place in the *Opportunity* playwriting contest. The following year, in the same literary competition, Miller's *The Cussed Thing* received an honorable mention. Her experiences with Grimké, Burrill, and Johnson at M Street High School, the Howard Players and the Department of Dramatic Arts, the Baltimore Krigwa Players, Columbia University, and, eventually, her participation in the Saturday sessions at the S Street Salon all contributed to her successful career as a playwright.

Miller acknowledged the significance of the black women's playwriting community in Washington throughout her career as a writer. She described the S Street Salon as "informal . . . Maybe ten people would attend at a time . . . It was a drop-in place."[79] On any given Saturday night, Hughes, Du Bois, Fausset, Carter G. Woodson, or Richard Wright would attend and contribute to a writing community created by and predominated by African American women in Washington. At one particular Saturday session, Woodson encouraged Miller and playwright Willis Richardson to co-author an anthology of plays about black heroines and heroes. Published in 1935, the anthology, *Negro History in Thirteen Plays*, "garnered national recognition for Miller and Richardson."[80] For this collaborative effort, Miller wrote four plays, *Sojourner Truth*, *Harriet Tubman*, *Samory*, and *Christophe's Daughters*. Unlike most of her black Washington women playwriting counterparts, Miller did not write a play within the lynching drama tradition in the early part of career. *Nails and Thorns*, the sole play in Miller's entire body of work that focuses on lynching, was not published until 1933, nearly twenty years after she wrote her first play. Although Grimké, Douglass, and Burrill spoke with Miller about writing a play about lynching, a contest sponsored by the Association for Southern Women for the Prevention of Lynching in 1933 ultimately motivated Miller to author a lynching drama. Her solitary foray into this genre, however, resulted in her receiving top honors in a contest of the Association for Southern Women for the Prevention of Lynching. Before submitting a final version for the contest, her S Street Salon community offered feedback and suggested ideas and revisions for *Nails and Thorns*. Despite the accolades Miller garnered for this play, which focuses on the effects of lynching from the perspective of a white family, there is no record of the play being performed.

In *Nails and Thorns*, a white sheriff arrests a mentally handicapped black man. The sheriff's wife becomes increasingly concerned that the black prisoner may not be safe in jail, that a mob will attack the prisoner as a result of the lack of adequate security. The sheriff does not listen to his wife, and a mob attacks and lynches the black prisoner. In the aftermath of the killing, the sheriff's family devolves as a result of guilt and disgust. By centering her narrative on a white family, Miller invokes racial and gender ideologies that speak directly to whites and challenges whites to concern themselves with effects of lynching not just on black families but on white families as well. One of the last plays written in the lynching tradition by the New Negro women playwrights of Washington, *Nails and Thorns* highlights the evolution of black women writers using drama as a means to articulate African American experiences and to advocate for social change.

Conclusion

At its height in the 1920s and 1930s, the S Street Salon blossomed into a viable and welcoming space for black women writers in Washington. Although the Saturday sessions continued until Johnson's death, the collaborations and exchanges that occurred during the latter part of the New Negro era provided African American women in the nation's capital with an unprecedented opportunity to develop distinct creative and politically resonant voices. The plays of Grimké, Johnson, Burrill, and Miller exemplify how this informal space founded by a black woman facilitated the emergence of an elite, New Negro women writing culture. The combination of formal institutional support for black women's playwriting and black women's informal, local networks that solidified with the creation of S Street Salon resulted in a unique culturally expressive and politically engaged cadre of African American women in Washington. The space thrived until the 1930s, as the Great Depression directly affected the fledgling community. According to Claudia Tate, writers traveling to Washington for the S Street Salon "could no longer afford to visit Washington, D.C., with regularity, and their absence caused Johnson's Saturday Nighters Club to disband."[81] Although D.C.-centered, the S Street Salon relied on African American men and women moving in and out of the space from all over the country to contribute to the salon's unique culture.

The black women playwrights who engaged in the lynching drama tradition refused to view lynching as a phenomenon that solely affected individuals and emphasized the impact of lynching on communities, families, and, most notably, motherhood.

> But I lived in a town once where they lynched a man and I can never forget how the town and the people suffered. It wasn't what they did to the unfortunate man alone. He was out of his misery. It was what they did to every soul in that town. They crucified everything that was worthwhile—justice and pride and self-respect. For generations to come the children will be gathering the nails and thorns from the scene of that crucifixion.[82]

Playwrights created a critical lens to envision both the "strange fruit" hanging from a tree and the black and white families and communities that suffered the consequences of white terror. Female-authored antilynching plays portrayed lynching as an experience of collective victimization. The rejection of the black male subject as the sole victim of lynching is arguably the most consistent and transgressive element of this theatrical subgenre. Challenging the centrality of black men to an antiracial violence agenda provided fodder for scathing critiques from men and women. When the first known female-authored antilynching play was produced, Ida B. Wells-Barnett had already established herself as one of the most prominent antilynching activists. Wells refused to confine herself to the discussion of lynching and black men; she openly addressed black women's victimization and the effects of lynching on families and communities.

Black women playwrights such as Grimké, Johnson, Miller, and Burrill followed in her footsteps and offered other ways of examining the consequences of racial violence. Neither Wells nor the playwrights omitted the reality that black men were lynched in greater numbers than black women, and yet all of their antilynching works address the numerous victimizations that occur as a result of lynching.[83] Many of the female playwrights engaged in the antilynching drama tradition attempted to reconfigure lynching as a collective, victimizing experience that proliferated beside other distinct forms of racial violence to uphold white supremacy and patriarchy. While the success of these plays as transformative sites of social and political change cannot be measured, their existence displays a collective and interracial effort by black women to write themselves into both a masculinized political agenda and a male-centered narrative of victimization via antiblack racial violence. To varying extents, the plays of Grimké, Douglass, Burrill, and Miller engaged, manipulated, and debunked the interwoven ideologies of white supremacy and patriarchy that, together, condoned and advocated the subjugation of African Americans in the United States in the early twentieth century. The S Street Salon functioned as a literal and figurative home for elite black women in Washington using plays to insert their voices into New Negro political and social movements. Furthermore, African American women's writing from this community connected to broader trends of Washington women searching for ways to claim a distinct voice in the Jim Crow era.

Conclusion
Turn-of-the-Century Black Womanhood

Paul Lawrence Dunbar said that Washington in 1909 was "where the breeziness of the West met the refinement of the East, the warmth and grace of the South, and the culture and fine reserve of the North."[1] The nation's capital was a corridor city—a city through which distinctly Northern and Southern roots converged. Similar to Dunbar's musings about the nation's capital, Washington drew upon both the best and worst of what each U.S. region offered to blacks. The routes traveled by those relocating to Washington include folks traveling north, south, and east to create new possibilities for themselves. For many, settling in Washington offered the best of regional "worlds." For others, living in Washington rendered visible the harsh similarities between the race/sex order of the two regions. Whether moving farther south, east, or north, Washington experienced a surge of hope and possibility from the aspirations, imaginations, and dreams of its post–Civil War migrants. The sense of possibility, which connected the migrants, infused Washington with a New Negro sensibility.

From the women at Howard University during the early twentieth century to the black beauticians advertising their services in local Washington papers, African American women in Washington re-created the nation's capital as center for New Negro women's discourse. These women created and claimed new ideas about black womanhood by reconfiguring prevailing racial and gender ideologies and centering black women's right to self-articulation. They used their bodies, higher education, aesthetic and expressive practices, and political activism to situate themselves within the modern world. The desire for a modern subjectivity extended beyond political rights and equal access to educational and employment opportunities, to include purchasing products that adorned the body, rejecting intraracial gender hierarchies, and forming communities that nurtured the humanity and potential of black women. Fighting against racial discrimination and disenfranchisement and demanding access to adornment on their own terms were integral how New Negro women shaped their lives and communities. The combination of political standpoints and activities, cultural and aesthetic innovations, and educational goals and aspirations of black women in D.C. resulted in varying discourses of New Negro womanhood in the nation's capital.

Class, race, religion, urbanity, domesticity, labor, gender, sex, sexuality, and political and organizational affiliations were instrumental in the lives and rhetoric of black women during the Jim Crow era. Late-nineteenth- and early-twentieth-century Washington played a significant role in an evolving New Negro womanhood because of the city's abundant political activities, educational and professional opportunities, and cultural and expressive practices that flourished among black women in this urban space. Washington's New Negro women are important to our understanding of how ideas about how political, economic, social, and cultural agency for black women challenged New Negro's ideological focus on black men and New Woman's ideological focus on white women. Furthermore, black women of this era functioned as colored subjects, and they therefore should compel scholars who study this era to engage Colored not only as a racial category but as a gender-racial category that also encompassed class-specific and sexuality-specific implications for New Negro women and men. Notably, most of the women documented in *Colored No More* occupied elite statuses in Washington. Because of my emphasis on discourses of New Negro womanhood, I chose to focus on the archived, audible, and accessible voices of African American women in Washington. Considerable work remains with regard to excavating the stories of working-class and poor black women in Washington during the New Negro era. Allusions to and rhetoric about working-class and poor black women in Washington presented in my book should not stand as indicative of how these women conceived of themselves. I would argue, however, that the discourse of New Negro womanhood and the understanding of Colored as a gendered category of identity becomes more visible through engaging the voices of Washington women such as Terrell, Cooper, Slowe, Johnson, Burrill, and Grimké. Through their words, we arrive at new understandings of New Negro womanhood as a classed site of negotiation of intersecting identities and possibilities for African American women.

Gender, as black feminist scholar Patricia Hill Collins explicates, "has a racial face, whereby African American women, African American men, White women, and White men occupied distinct race/gender categories within an overarching social structure that proscribed their prescribed place."[2] For black women during the New Negro era, black men's experiences and perspectives were privileged and positioned as synonymous with the African American experience. Black masculinism prevailed, often with the support of black women.[3] New Negro scholars, however, must resist replicating this masculinism when chronicling this era in African American freedom and equality struggles. Beyond adding women and stirring, as warned against by historian Alice Kessler-Harris, refuting a black masculinist framing of this era means reconsidering how we periodize the New Negro era, whom we identify as New Negroes, and which arenas we explore to excavate New Negro activity. The re-periodization of the New Negro era accounts for how black women began to see themselves and how they viewed the world they navigated. By identifying the commencement of the New Negro era in the last decade of the nineteenth century, a New Negro city such as Washington becomes visible. Washington's significant influx of black migrants occurred during and after the Civil War, which meant that the seismic shifts often associated with the Great Migration and the interwar period began in Washington as early as the 1870s. By the 1890s, and more specifically by 1893 when those six black women took center stage at the Columbia Exposition, more than forty thousand black women resided in the nation's capital. The institutions, communities, organizations, and networks that arose in other New Negro cities in the early twentieth century emerged in Washington in the last decade of the nineteenth century.

New Negro women of Washington were turn-of-the-century women. The ideologies of the "New Woman" paralleled the evolution of New Negro womanhood ideologies but presumed that all women were white. In "African American Women's History and the Metalanguage of Race," Evelyn Brooks Higginbotham discusses the unstated premise of racial homogeneity (whiteness) and the subsequent universalizing of women's culture and oppression as well as the investment and complicity of white women in the oppression of African Americans, specifically African American women.[4] This presumption led to the limited visibility of racial oppression and racial particularities on the New Woman agendas. White women's neglect of their respective complicity in the oppression of black women limited the liberatory potential of New Woman ideals.[5]

New Negro womanhood encompassed black women's ideas about their own position as modern and historical subjects. As a range of ideas about black women's identities and their continual development during the late nineteenth and early twentieth centuries, New Negro womanhood was not a movement in the more traditional ways we think about African American freedom struggles or women's rights activism. More porous and mosaic than cohesive, New Negro womanhood discourse developed out of an array of concerns and perspectives extant among an increasingly diverse population of black women. Within a particular arena such as adornment, competing ideas about the modern or New Negro woman and what she represented flourished. New Negro womanhood engaged multiple standpoints and orientations regarding the lived experiences and the aspirations of black women at the turn of the twentieth century.

Although Washington, D.C., is a primary focus of this book, the city was not wholly exceptional with regard to New Negro women's identities. Black women's experiences in the nation's capital offer both a representative and a unique understanding of how black women traversed and shaped the New Negro women's era. The particularity of Washington stems from the numerous resources and institutions that supported black women's efforts to claim modern identities, places such as Howard University, M Street High School, clubs and organizations, and a dynamic community infrastructure for African Americans that dated back to the late eighteenth century. The expansion of opportunities for black women in politics, for leisure and consumption, in education, and in arts and culture, however, occurred in New York, Chicago, Paris, and numerous other cities throughout the African diaspora with existing and growing populations of people of African descent. Washington was among the first major U.S. cities profoundly shaped by New Negro women's sensibilities and is woefully understudied within New Negro era scholarship.

New Negro womanhood encapsulated the political, social, and cultural aspirations of African American attempting to participate in and configure black modern identities. The specific meanings and historical consequences of black modernity for black women reveal a distinct history of defiance, self-realization, individual and collective identity formation, and resistance and struggle. New Negro women had numerous individual and collective aspirations and desires within a modern world in which they were treated as third-class citizens. Black women in Washington, D.C., negotiated the historical entanglement of democratic ideals, white supremacist ideology, dominant patriarchy, black patriarchy, and American modernity in their daily lives. For New Negro women in Washington, the significance of claiming a space within the modern world extended beyond the civil and political rights—supposedly guaranteed, but often not protected by the Constitution and other rules of law. The women in this book articulated a desire to define themselves and their communities in a way that recognized the humanity and personhood of black women. Styling one's hair, establishing literary clubs on college campuses, or attending an after-hours blues set in Washington's U Street Corridor were varying iterations of black women striving for modern subjectivities.

From the seemingly mundane realm of hairstyles to the suffrage campaigns organized by African American women, New Negro womanhood thrived as a space in which black women could envision and create modern black womanhood at the turn of twentieth century. While still combating prevailing racist, sexist, and classist notions, New Negro women in D.C. trumpeted the importance of individual and collective affirmation and fulfillment. Their social networks, political organizations, hair salons, and leisure activities became as significant as their occupations and families in how these women perceived and identified themselves. The physical emancipation of black women from slavery did not eradicate the psychological and emotional scars of enslavement or liberate these women from the racial caste system or the gender hierarchy of the Jim Crow era. New Negro womanhood discourse strategically intervened in how black women sought to cope with Jim Crow, antiblack racial violence, black patriarchy, and the perpetuation of white cultural hegemony.

Black women in D.C. participated in institutions, movements, and daily activities that explored this newfound sense of autonomy, however limited. The realities of Jim Crow and black masculinism challenged this autonomy. Relationships between black men and black women are particularly intriguing in the context of examining black women's investment in New Negro womanhood during an era in which the plight of black men became practically synonymous with the plight of African America in its entirety. Although many black women in D.C. did not reject the idea that race trumped gender in the larger context of fighting for equality, many Washington black women vehemently fought for gender equality with comparable tenacity. These women refused silence, invisibility, and marginalization. They contested the inferiority of their racial and gender identities alike.

The migration of many black women to urban centers such as Washington offered these women new opportunities to define themselves outside of marriage and motherhood. These domestic identities remained integral to how black women perceived themselves, and yet black women in Washington openly articulated identities unrelated to their status as wives or mothers. The processes of psychological and emotional emancipation of black women opened the door for ideas about what black women could pursue, challenge, and configure. Armed with both skepticism and optimism about American democracy and racialized gender hierarchies, African American women in Washington and in urban centers throughout the African diaspora imagined new possibilities for black women in the United States through the lens of New Negro womanhood.

Scholars who study the plight of black women and, more specifically, black feminists juggle desires to explore the distinctiveness of black women's experiences and to move these experiences from the periphery to the center without displacing those already existing at the center or reifying the power of the center.[6] Broadening how we think about black women's public behavior during New Negro era opens the door for new considerations of black women's experiences. This book seeks to push the boundaries of U.S., women's, and African American history, as well as black gender studies, to include the experiences of women who challenged dominant ideologies of white supremacy and patriarchy and who confronted restrictive and limiting ideologies within communities combating these dominant ideologies. Expanding how we think about the Jim Crow–era black women allows for a thoughtful reconsideration of how we define and demarcate the New Negro era. African American women in Washington made specific claims about modern black womanhood. Using these women of the urban upper south, we broaden our understanding of pre–World War I iterations of New Negro discourse and of black women's multifaceted engagement with political and cultural currents that often marginalized their voices. The racism of many white women and the sexism of many black men compelled black women to navigate the oppressive strictures of white racism and black sexism within progressive movements for political and social change and to occupy Colored as race- and gender-specific lived experience and identity. Black women created a space where women could simultaneously address racist and sexist ideologies.

By expanding the spatial and temporal framing of the New Negro era to encompass new locations of political and cultural activity and earlier decades of African American participation in these activities, African American women become more visible as architects of New Negro discourse. Black women in Washington began fashioning themselves as new and modern as early as the 1890s. The speeches of six African American women at the World's Fair, including Washington-based Anna Julia Cooper, announced the arrival of a fledgling discourse of New Negro womanhood. The mass migration of black women to Washington largely occurred between 1860 and 1900. During the first decade of twentieth century, black women in Washington were administrators at local schools, created an alternative advertising discourse for marketing black beauty products, and reimagined their political strategies for demanding universal suffrage. I re-periodize the New Negro era to encompass new activities and perspectives of black women that emerged during the first and second waves of mass migration to the urban upper south. Using World War I as a beginning point for thinking about New Negro ideology renders invisible the prewar efforts of African American women attempting to articulate new ideas about being modern. We miss the publication and performance of *Rachel* and we miss the participation of African American women in the March 3, 1913, suffrage parade when we conceptualize New Negro within the confines of the interwar period. Not including these important texts and protests in New Negro history is damaging to the pursuit of recovering a more gender-inclusive account of New Negro discourse and activism.

The influx of black women to New York occurred later than in Washington. Consequently, privileging New York as the preeminent site for New Negro culture and consciousness relies heavily on focusing on how World War I affected African Americans. Although the Great War affected black women, it was black men who experienced the war firsthand. Positing World War I as foundational to New Negro ideology privileges black men and black masculinity as the driving force behind a New Negro movement. Black women and men, however, began envisioning and constructing new ideologies and political, social, and cultural spaces almost thirty years before U.S. victory in World War I. Washington's elite black women were central to authoring and promoting these ideologies.

At the center of this book are fundamental questions: How did New Negro women grapple simultaneously with multiple oppressive ideologies? What spaces were integral to struggling against racial and gender ideologies that relegated black women to the peripheries of political and cultural currents? How did elite black women view the modern world and their status within it? Through exploring diverse yet connected arenas of black women's culture, I ultimately define New Negro womanhood discourse as a multifaceted space of articulation for black women during the Jim Crow era. Political and cultural modernities intersected in the space of New Negro womanhood. For black women in Washington, this intersection propelled reconfigurations of self and a re-imagining of possibilities for black women.

Notes

Introduction

1. Cooper, "Discussion," 711.
2. Bolotin and Laing, *World's Columbian Exposition*.
3. Cooper, "Discussion," 712.
4. Ibid.
5. Beatty, *Revolution Gone Backward*.
6. May, *Anna Julia Cooper*.
7. "Colored" is used throughout as a historically accurate marker of racial identification. Although I use African American, I use "Colored" in specific cases in which the term reflects how particular institutions, individuals, and organizations were contemporaneously identified.
8. Clark-Lewis, *Living In, Living Out*.
9. hooks, *Ain't I a Woman*, 2.
10. Wells, Douglass, Penn, and Barnett, "Reason Why."
11. Williams, "Intellectual Progress," 696.
12. Ibid., 700.
13. Coppin, "Discussion," 718.
14. Arnesen, *Black Protest*; Trotter, *Great Migration*; Harrison, *Black Exodus*; Lemann, *Promised Land*; Marks, *Farewell*; Gregory, *Southern Diaspora*; Zieger, *For Jobs and Freedom*; Grossman, *Land of Hope*.
15. U.S. Department of Interior, Census Office, *United States Population: 1860*, table 2, p. 588; *U.S. Census of Population: 1890*, pt. 1, table 22; and U.S. Department of Commerce, Bureau of the Census, *Fifteenth Census of the United States: 1930-Population*, vol. 3, table 2, p. 99.
16. U.S. Bureau of the Census, *Thirteenth Census of the United States Taken in the Year 1910*, vol. 1, Population, General Report, and Analysis (Washington, D.C.: GPO,

1913); U.S. Bureau of the Census, *Fifteenth Census of the United States: 1930-Population*, vol. 3, pt. 1 (Washington, D.C.; GPO, 1932).

17. "Most Negroes Per Sq Mile in D.C.," *Baltimore Afro-American*, July 3, 1926.

18. Miller, "Where Is the Negro's Heaven?" 371.

19. Harley, "Black Women," 62.

20. Gates, "Trope of the New Negro."

21. Gates, "Trope of the New Negro," 132.

22. Gertrude "Ma" Rainey, "Bo-Weevil Blues," Paramount 12603-B, 1927.

23. Beemyn, *Queer Capital*, 48.

24. Baldwin, *Chicago's New Negroes*; Gill, *Beauty Shop Politics*; Mitchell. *Living with Lynching*; Sherrad-Johnson, *Portraits*; Chapman, "Prove It on Me."

25. Feimster, *Southern Horrors*.

26. Lindsey, "Post-Ferguson."

27. Chapman, "Prove It on Me," 18.

28. Jones, *All Bound Up Together*, 21.

29. Williams, "Intellectual Progress," 711.

30. Jones, *All Bound Up Together*, 175.

31. Murray and Eastwood, "Jane Crow."

32. Gilroy, *Black Atlantic*, 117.

33. Collins, *Black Sexual Politics*, 217.

34. Giddings, *When and Where I Enter*; Higginbotham, *Righteous Discontent*; Smith, *Sick and Tired*; White, *Too Heavy a Load*; Hendricks, *Gender, Race, and Politics*; Hine, *Hine Sight*; Hine, "Rape"; Lerner, "Early Community Work"; Scott, "Most Invisible of All"; Davis, *Women, Race, and Class*; Wolcott, *Remaking Respectability*; Hunter, *To 'Joy My Freedom*; Gilmore, *Gender and Jim Crow*.

35. Terborg-Penn, *African American Women*.

36. Ibid.

37. Hine, "Rape," *Signs*, 14, 4 (Summer 1989), 915.

38. Ibid.

39. Hanson, *Mary McLeod Bethune*, 22.

40. Higginbotham, "African American Women's History."

41. Gill, *Beauty Shop Politics*; Baldwin, *Chicago's New Negroes*.

Chapter 1. Climbing the Hilltop

1. Letter from Lucy D. Slowe to Dr. J. Stanley Durkee, dated May 31, 1922. Lucy Diggs Slowe Papers, Manuscript Division, box 90-2, folder 51, Moorland-Spingarn Research Center, Howard University, Washington, D.C. Hereinafter cited as Slowe Papers.

2. Ibid.

3. Wolters, *New Negro on Campus*.

4. Miller and Pruitt-Logan. *Faithful to the Task at Hand*; Perkins, "Lucy Diggs Slowe"; Harley and Terborg-Penn, *Afro-American Woman*; Bashaw, "Slowe, Lucy Diggs."

5. Beemyn, *Queer Capital*, 48.

6. Logan, *Howard University*.

7. Anderson, *Education*, 238–278.

8. Ibid.

9. Ibid., 4–32.

10. Ibid., 79–109.

11. "Genesis of Howard University," *Howard University Miscellaneous Papers*, undated, 5–6.

12. Ibid., 7.

13. Kofie, *Race*, 3–7.

14. Ruble, *Washington's U Street*; Borchert, *Alley Life in Washington*.

15. Logan, *Howard University*, 3.

16. *Annual Report of the President of Howard University*, September 2, 1869. See Dwight O.W. Holmes, "Fifty Years of Howard University: Part I," *Journal of Negro History* 3, no. 2 (April 1918): 128–38.

17. Logan, *Howard University*.

18. Johnson, *Southern Women*.

19. Slowe, "Higher Education,"356.

20. W. E. B. Du Bois, *Howard University Journal*, November 15, 1912, 1.

21. Giddings, *In Search of Sisterhood*, 47.

22. Ibid., 40.

23. Johnson, *Negro College Graduate*, 8.

24. Perkins, "Lucy Diggs Slowe," 90.

25. Mary Burrill and Anna Julia Cooper are two of the most prominent examples of this phenomenon.

26. Slowe is often not heralded alongside pioneering black women tennis players such as Althea Gibson and Ora Mae Washington. Slowe's victories opened the door for more black women to enter competitive tennis at a national level.

27. "Dean Lucy D. Slowe," Slowe Papers.

28. Miller and Pruitt-Logan, *Faithful*, 330.

29. Bashaw, "Slowe, Lucy Diggs."

30. Perkins, "National Association," 68.

31. Lester A. Walton, "Negro Women Seek to Better College Living," *The World*, April 25, 1926, in Slowe Papers, box 90-11, folder 207.

32. Ibid.

33. Perkins, "National Association," 65–75. Perkins provides a detailed history of the NACW and specifically addresses the elite class dynamics of the organization while acknowledging the ways this small group women strove to "uplift the masses" beyond the confines of their respective campuses.

34. Lucy D. Slowe, "The College Woman and Her Community," opening speech presented at the National Association of College Women, Atlanta, Georgia, April 1934; in *Howard University Alumni Journal*, Slowe Papers, box 90-6, folder 120.

35. Slowe, "The Colored Girl Enters College: What Shall She Expect?" *Opportunity Journal of Negro Life*, September, 1937, 278; in Slowe Papers, box 90-6, folder 121.

36. Ibid.

37. Logan, *Howard University*, 170.

38. Slowe, *The Hilltop*, Washington, D.C.: Howard University, May 14, 1931.

39. Ibid.

40. Miller and Pruitt-Logan, *Faithful*, 331.

41. Slowe, *The World*, April, 25, 1926.

42. Lucy Diggs Slowe, "The Dean of Women in a Modern University," in *Howard University Alumni Journal*, December 1933, 10; in Slowe Papers, box 90-6, folder 125.

43. Lucy D. Slowe, Dean of Women, Howard University, "Speech on the Occasion of the Cornerstone of the Women's Dormitories at Howard University, June 5, 1931," in Slowe Papers, box 90-6, folder 123.

44. "Howard Women Run Themselves," *Washington Afro American*, August 20th, 1932.

45. Slowe, "Higher Education," 334.

46. Ibid., 335.

47. Higginbotham, *Righteous Discontent*, and Collier-Thomas, *Jesus, Jobs, and Justice*, both detail how black women pushed the black church to rethink the role of women in the church and in society. Primarily through the politics of respectability, African American women demanded greater visibility and increased possibilities for leadership and fuller participation in black institutional culture.

48. Slowe, "Higher Education," 357.

49. McKinney, *Mordecai*.

50. Miller and Pruitt-Logan, *Faithful*, 131–206.

51. Letter, Slowe to Durkee, May 31, 1922.

52. Beemyn, *Queer Capital*, 48.

53. Ibid.

54. Mary McLeod Bethune to Slowe, Slowe Papers, November 24, 1933.

55. Charlotte Hawkins Brown to Slowe, Slowe Papers, June 6, 1936.

56. Mrs. J. C. Napier to Slowe, Slowe Papers, October 10, 1933; Ella Murphy to Slowe, Slowe Papers, March 25, 1936.

57. Beemyn, *Queer Capital*, 77–78.

58. Mollie T. Barrien to Burrill, Slowe Papers, n.d.

59. Mary Cromwell to Mary Burrill, Slowe Papers, December 29, 1937.

60. McKinney, *Mordecai*, 53–98.

61. Slowe to Howard University Board of Trustees, Slowe Papers, April 26, 1933.

62. Slowe, "Memorandum on the Mills Case," Washington, D.C., Howard University, Slowe Papers, 1927.

63. Bell-Scott, "Self-Respect," 72.

64. Clarence Mills, Letter to Slowe, Washington, D.C., Howard University, January 11, 1927.

65. Slowe, "Memorandum of the Mills Case."
66. *NAWDACS Calls to Convention*, Slowe Papers, n.d.
67. Miller and Pruitt-Logan, *Faithful*, 131–48.
68. Perkins, "Lucy Diggs Slowe," 96.
69. Church Terrell, "Progress of Colored Women."
70. Beemyn, *Queer Capital*, 84.
71. Harley, "Nannie Helen Burroughs."
72. Collier-Thomas, *Jesus, Jobs, and Justice.*
73. Slowe, "Colored Girl Enters College."

Chapter 2. Make Me Beautiful

1. Pride and Wilson, *History of the Black Press*, 97–114.
2. Gibbs, *Shadow and Light*, 367.
3. Pride and Wilson, *History of the Black Press*, 238.
4. Habermas, *Philosophical Discourses*, 7.
5. Baldwin, "Washtub to the World," 57.
6. Hanchard, "Afro-Modernity," 268.
7. Gilroy, *Black Atlantic*, x.
8. Chapman, "Prove It on Me," 78–113.
9. Cronin, *Advertising and Consumer Citizenship.*
10. Ibid.
11. Chapman, "Prove It on Me," 6.
12. Collins, *Black Feminist Thought.*
13. Harley and Terborg-Penn, *Afro-American Woman.*
14. Gill, *Beauty Shop Politics*, 3–4.
15. Baldwin, "Washtub to the World," 57.
16. Calvin Chase, *Washington Bee*, March 5, 1910. Available at http://chroniclingamerica.loc.gov/lccn/sn84025891/1910-03-05/ed-1/seq-4/#date1=1836&index=0&rows=20&words=beautifies+hair+straight&searchType=basic&sequence=0&state=&date2=1922&proxtext=straight+hair+beautifies&y=0&x=0&dateFilterType=yearRange&page=1 (col. 4).
17. Higginbotham, "African American Women's History."
18. Baldwin, *Chicago's New Negroes*, 55.
19. Banks, *Hair Matters*; Blackwelder, *Styling Jim Crow*; Byrd and Tharps, *Hair Story*; Lake, *Blue Veins and Kinky Hair*; Rooks, *Hair Raising.*
20. Blackwelder, *Styling Jim Crow*, 16.
21. White, *Ar'n't I a Woman?*; Jones, *Labor of Love.*
22. Byrd and Tharps, *Hair Story*, 14; also see Johnson, Smith, and the WGBH, *Africans in America.*
23. Blackwelder, *Styling Jim Crow*, 15.
24. Byrd and Tharps, *Hair Story*, 21.

25. Winch, *Between Slavery and Freedom.*

26. Gatewood. *Aristocrats of Color*, 39.

27. It should be noted that many blacks throughout the African diaspora engage(d) in skin lightening and hair straightening. Contemporarily, these techniques are most prominent in formerly colonized countries in Africa and in the United States. The skin-lightening industry has increased in recent years after a decline during the mid-to-late twentieth century. Many African diaspora scholars attribute the continued use of skin-lightening and hair-straightening products to "mental /psychological" colonialism and enslavement and white cultural hegemony. For an in-depth discussion of this historical and diasporic phenomenon, see Lake, *Blue Veins and Kinky Hair*; Banks, *Hair Matters*. Also, the June 2011 special issue of the *Journal of Pan-African Studies* focused on skin bleaching and white supremacy.

28. Julia Blackwelder speaks in depth about the communal exchange of black beauty practices in *Styling Jim Crow.*

29. Burrows, *Necessity of Myth.*

30. Ibid.

31. Although not easily discerned from archives because of the informality of the African American beauty industry in Washington, throughout the early twentieth century, *Boyd's Directory of the District of Columbia* identifies hundreds of colored women as hair dressers.

32. Baldwin, "From the Washtub," 74.

33. Harley, "Beyond the Classroom," 254.

34. Ibid.

35. Walker, *History of Black Business.*

36. Gill, *Beauty Shop Politics*, 32–60.

37. Available at http://chroniclingamerica.loc.gov/lccn/sn84025891/1910-01-22/ed-1/seq-3.pdf. The same page features an ad for Me-Lange, which, the copy says, "never fails; nothing like it for hair that is not naturally straight." Throughout the early twentieth century, pages such as this were quite common in black newspapers in Washington.

38. Moore, *Leading the Race*; Kerr, *Paper Bag Principle*; Kofie, *Race, Class, and Struggle*; Johnston, *Surviving Freedom*; Lesko, Babb, and Gibbs, *Black Georgetown Remembered*; Brown, *Free Negroes*; Graham, *Our Kind of People*; Gatewood, "Aristocrats of Color."

39. Baldwin, "From the Washtub," 57.

40. *Washington Bee*, March 1909.

41. *Washington Bee*, March 1909.

42. Lake, *Blue Veins and Kinky Hair*, 54.

43. "Ford's Hair Pomade," *Washington Bee*, December 29, 1906; April 27, 1907; January 25, 1908; March 12, 1910.

44. Baldwin, "From the Washtub," 61.

45. Burroughs, "Not Color, but Character."

46. Terrell, *Colored Woman*, 106.

47. Katherine Williams, "Betrayers of the Race," *Half-Century Magazine*, February 1920.

48. Ibid.

49. Rooks, *Ladies' Pages*.

50. Baldwin, "From the Washtub," 57.

51. "Skin Specialist," *Colored American*, February 1899.

52. "Ford's Hair Pomade," "The Magic," and "Her-Tru-Line," *Washington Bee*, March 12, 1910.

53. "Notice to Ladies," *Washington Bee*, March 12, 1910.

54. Rooks, *Hair Raising*, 47.

55. "Southern Beauty Culture School," *Washington Bee*, November 13, 1909; November 20, 1909; December 11, 1909; December 25, 1909; May 21, 1910; May 28, 1910; June 4, 1910; July 9, 1910.

56. "Southern Beauty Culture School," *Washington Bee*, June 4th, 1910.

57. Gill, *Beauty Shop Politics*, 46.

58. Ibid., 47.

59. Ibid., 32–60.

60. "Are We Proud of Our Black Skins and Curly Hair?" *Negro World*, August 1, 1925, cited in Gill, *Beauty Shop Politics*, 57.

61. Ibid.

62. Ibid., 56.

63. Chandler Owen, "Good Looks Supremacy: A Perspicacious Perusal of the Potencies of Pulchritude by a Noted Authority," *Messenger*, March 1924.

64. Rooks, *Hair Raising*, 23–50.

65. Ibid., 107.

66. Ibid., 41.

67. Ibid., 76–79.

68. Contemporarily, skin-lightening products and processes targeted at people of color compose a multibillion-dollar industry. Although these products are not as publicly popular among blacks in United States today as they were during the early twentieth century, African Americans are among the consumers who continue to support this industry. People in India, countries in West Africa (such as Ghana), and Brazil are among the primary consumers of skin-lightening products in the twenty-first century.

69. Gill, *Beauty Shop Politics*, 6.

70. Baldwin, "From the Washtub," 56–57.

71. Ibid., 57.

Chapter 3. Performing and Politicizing "Ladyhood"

1. Terborg-Penn, *African American Women*, 31–106.

2. Ibid., 31–80.

3. *Colored American*, February 17, 1900.

4. Terrell, *Colored Woman*; Cooper, *Voice from the South.*

5. Terborg-Penn, *African American Women*, 51–80.

6. Masur, *Example for All the Land*, 127–73. Masur discusses at length the complicated terrain of suffrage activism in the nation's capital.

7. Brown, "To Catch the Vision of Freedom."

8. Ibid., 86–87.

9. Gordon, Collier-Thomas, Bracey, Avakian, and Berkman, *African American Women*; Terborg-Penn, *African American Women*; Lerner, *Black Women in White America*; White, *Too Heavy a Load*; Wheeler, *One Woman, One Vote*; Materson, *For the Freedom of Her Race.*

10. Terborg-Penn, *African American Women*, 4–7.

11. *African American Women and the Vote, 1837–1965* (Gordon, Collier-Thomas, Bracey, Avakian, and Berkman, eds.) loosely periodizes African American women's suffrage activism. Two of the periods framed by the editors of this collection and in the extant scholarship on black women's suffrage activism are 1870–1896 and 1896–1935. These years are central to my temporal conceptualization of the New Negro era.

12. Hine and Thompson, *Shining Thread of Hope*, 29.

13. Keyssar, *Right to Vote*, 2.

14. *Dred Scott v. Sandford*, 60 U.S. 393, 573 (1856), Justice Benjamin R. Curtis, dissenting.

15. Hancock, *Essays*, 23.

16. Keyssar, *Right to Vote*, 2.

17. Litwack, "Emancipation."

18. "The Second United States Census," 1800. See https://www.archives.gov/research/census/african-american/slavery-in-dc-1800-1860.pdf.

19. Ibid.

20. Payne, *History.*

21. Brown, *Free Negroes.*

22. Sterling, *Turning the World Upside Down*, 12.

23. Ibid.

24. Ibid.

25. Faulkner, *Women's Radical Reconstruction*; Yellin and Van Horne, *Abolitionist Sisterhood*; DuBois and Ruiz, *Unequal Sisters.*

26. Elizabeth Cady Stanton, "Resolutions and Debate," First Annual Meeting of the American Equal Rights Association, New York, May 10, 1867.

27. Ibid.

28. Collier-Thomas, "Frances Ellen Watkins Harper," 50.

29. Ibid., 50–51.

30. Painter, *Sojourner Truth;* Faulkner, *Women's Radical Reconstruction*; Terborg-Penn, *African American Women.*

31. Hine and Thompson, *Shining Thread of Hope*, 157.

32. Masur, "Reconstructing the Nation's Capital"; Bercaw, *Race, Rights.*

33. Terborg-Penn, *African American Women*; DuBois, *Feminism and Suffrage*; Newman, *White Women's Rights*; Giddings, *When and Where I Enter*; Gilmore, *Gender and Jim Crow*; McPherson, *Struggle for Equality*; Edwards, *Gendered Strife and Confusion*; White, *Too Heavy a Load*; Jones, *Labor of Love.*

34. Masur, "Reconstructing the Nation's Capital," 127–73.

35. Johnston, *Surviving Freedom*, 216.

36. Masur, 127–73.

37. Johnston, *Surviving Freedom.*

38. Hine and Thompson, *Shining Thread of Hope*, 165–212.

39. Cynthia Neverdon-Morton, "Advancement of the Race," 121.

40. Giddings, *When and Where I Enter*, 120.

41. *The Colored American*, February 17, 1900.

42. Dossett, *Bridging Race Divides.*

43. *Colored American*, February 17, 1900.

44. Ibid.

45. Ibid.

46. Terrell, Mary C. "The Justice of Woman Suffrage," 1900.

47. Tillet, *Sites of Slavery*, 11.

48. Ibid.

49. Collins, *Black Feminist Thought*, 67–91. Collins discusses at length the formation and perpetuation of race/gender myths about black women. She defines them as controlling images. She also discusses how African American women contest these tropes.

50. Orlick, *Rethinking American Women's Activism*, 1–28; Adams and Keene, *Alice Paul*; Lunardini, *Equal Suffrage to Equal Rights*; Stevens and O'Hare, *Jailed for Freedom*; Clift, *Founding Sisters*; Irwin, *Story of Alice Paul.*

51. Rich, *Transcending the New Woman*, 1–36. Rich identifies the "New Woman" across ethnic communities as a cultural and literary ideal rooted in desires for autonomy.

52. Matthews, *Rise of the New Woman*, 131.

53. Davis, *Women, Race, and Class*, 114–44.

54. Ibid.

55. Adams and Keene, *Alice Paul*, 1–20.

56. *New York Times*, March 4, 1913.

57. Letter from Alice Paul to Alice Blackwell, January 15, 1913, National Woman's Party Papers, Library of Congress, box I:1, reel 1, February 12, 1891–February 5, 1913.

58. Walton, *Woman's Crusade*, 63–65.

59. Ibid., 63.

60. Ibid., 64.

61. Letter from Nellie Quander to Alice Paul, February 15, 1913, NWPP.

62. Letter from Alice Paul to Nellie Quander, February 23, NWPP.

63. Hendricks, "Ida B. Wells-Barnett," 268–9.

64. *New York Times*, March 4, 1913; *Washington Post*, March 4, 1913; *Chicago Tribune*, March 4, 1913.

65. *Chicago Tribune*, March 4, 1913.

66. *Washington Post*, March 4, 1913.

67. Mary Walton, "The Day the Deltas Marched into History," *Washington Post*, March 1, 2013.

68. *New York Times*, March 4, 1913.

69. Hendricks, "Ida B. Wells-Barnett," 270.

70. Delta Sigma Theta Sorority Inc. was founded at Howard University on January 13, 1913 by twenty-two Howard women.

71. Walton, "Deltas Marched."

72. Ibid.

73. Terborg-Penn, *African American Women.*

74. Ibid., 1–12, 107–35. Terborg-Penn details the fractured relationship between white and black women suffragists at various points in the suffrage movement. The tensions reached a breaking point after the parade on March 3, 1913.

75. Collins, *Black Feminist Thought*, 67–91.

76. Terborg-Penn, *African American Women*, 107–66.

77. Florence Toms, "The Founders' Greeting," *The Delta*, May 1963, 18.

78. Gill, *Beauty Shop Politics*, 36. Gill discusses how black women operationalized a politics of appearance through their engagement in beauty culture.

79. Miller and Pruitt-Logan, *Faithful*, 44.

80. Kerber and De Hart, *Women's America*; Wells and Royster, *Southern Horrors*; Giddings, *When and Where I Enter*; Gilmore, *Gender and Jim Crow*; Stansell, *City of Women*; Jones, *Labor of Love.*

81. Walton, *Woman's Crusade.*

82. *Colored American*, February 17, 1900.

83. Matthews, *Rise of the New Woman*, 132.

84. The work of Higginbotham, Wolcott, and Hunter are particularly salient to understanding how black women used and transformed politics of respectability.

Chapter 4. Saturday Night at the S Street Salon

1. Gatewood, *Aristocrats of Color*, 39–68; Borchert, *Alley Life*. Both Gatewood and Borchert provide detailed accounts of the social and cultural landscape of black Washington, although Gatewood focuses exclusively on the black elite.

2. Gatewood, *Aristocrats of Color*, 39–68.

3. Gregoria Fraser Goins, "History of the Treble Clef Club," Gregoria Fraser Goins Papers, Moorland-Spingarn Research Center, Howard University, notebooks 36–15, folder 149, typed transcript of recording.

4. Whitesitt, "Women as 'Keepers of Culture,'" 78.

5. "Minutes from Treble Clef Club," 1924–1928, Gregoria Fraser Goins Papers, Moorland-Spingarn Research Center, Howard University, notebooks 36–15, folder 152, April 28, 1926.

6. Locke, *New Negro.*

7. Levine, *Black Culture and Black Consciousness*; Kelley, *Race Rebels*; Lott, *Invention of Race*; Rucker, *River Flows On*; Black Public Sphere Collective, *Black Public Sphere*; Gilroy, *Small Acts*; Kelley and Lewis, *To Make Our World Anew.*

8. Barnes, "Negro Art and America," 19.

9. Perkins, *Black Female Playwrights*; Mitchell. *Living with Lynching.*

10. Perkins, *Black Female Playwrights*, 3.

11. Mitchell, *Living with Lynching.*

12. The Dramatic Arts Department at Howard University and the numerous educators who also worked as writers at M Street/Dunbar High School figured prominently in the emergence of an African American women-centered writing culture in Washington.

13. Beemyn, *Queer Capital*, 79.

14. Ibid., 74–79.

15. Perkins, *Black Female Playwrights*, 15.

16. Mitchell, *Living with Lynching*, 23–24.

17. Ibid., 23.

18. Ibid., 31.

19. Perkins and Stephens, *Strange Fruit*; Perkins, *Black Female Playwrights.*

20. "Howard Players Appear in Their Own Show," *Chicago Defender*, June 3, 1922, 5.

21. Perkins *Black Female Playwrights*, 6.

22. W. E. B. DuBois, Krigwa Players Inaugural Playbill, 1926.

23. Montgomery T. Gregory, *Howard University Newspaper*, 1921.

24. Ibid.

25. See Baker, *Modernism and the Harlem Renaissance*; Ogbar, *Harlem Renaissance Revisited*; Gates and Jarrett, *New Negro*; and Sherrard-Johnson, *Portraits of the New Negro Woman.*

26. Du Bois, Krigwa Players Inaugural Playbill, 1926.

27. Bruce, *Archibald Grimké.* Bruce provides one of the fullest accounts of the storied life of Archibald Grimké.

28. Beemyn, *Queer Capital*, 67.

29. Angelina Weld Grimké Papers, Moorland-Spingarn Collection, Howard University.

30. Mitchell, *Living with Lynching*, 12.

31. Hull, *Color, Sex, and Poetry*, 117–23.

32. Grimké, "'Rachel': The Play of the Month; The Reason and Synopsis by the Author," *Competitor* 1 (January 1920): 51–52.

33. Perkins and Stephens, *Strange Fruit*, 6.

34. *Rachel*, 1.1

35. Williams, *They Left Great Marks on Me*, 140–41. Williams details how some black men "struck back rather than allow the white men to wreak havoc on their neighborhood" (141).

36. Hall, *Revolt against Chivalry*. Hall discusses how white women mobilized around antilynching efforts and highlights how motherhood in particular was used to mobilize white women in this campaign.

37. Cott, *Bonds of Womanhood*; Bloch, "American Feminine Ideals"; Sachsman, Rushing, and Morris, *Seeking a Voice*; and Patton, *Women in Chains*.

38. Mitchell, *Living with Lynching*, 34.

39. McKivigan and Snay, *Religion*; De Caro, *"Fire from the Midst of You"*; Aymer, *First Pure, Then Peaceable*; and Speicher, *Religious World*.

40. Langa, "Two Antilynching Art Exhibitions," 30.

41. *Rachel*, 1.1.

42. Williams, *They Left Great Marks on Me*, 141. African American men, in response to antiblack racist violence, defended themselves against assault and death. The desire to and act of fighting back struck a new tone in how African Americans pushed back against white violence, particularly when it threatened black families and communities.

43. Ibid.

44. Ibid.

45. Ibid.

46. Ibid.

47. Langa, "Two Antilynching Art Exhibitions," 33.

48. Tate, Domestic *Allegories*, 210.

49. Willis Richardson, "Poetry and Drama," *Crisis*, 34 (July 1927): 158.

50. "Poetry and Drama," *Crisis* 34, (July 1927), 158.

51. Stephens, *Plays of Georgia Douglas Johnson*; Johnson, *Selected Works*. These two books capture the extensive body of work produced by Johnson and re-center the prominence of her work during the early to mid-twentieth century.

52. The S Street Salon primarily served elite black women and therefore an exclusive community for formally educated black women in Washington.

53. Fletcher, "From Genteel Poet"; Fletcher, "Georgia Douglas Johnson"; Brown-Guillroy, *Wines in the Wilderness*; Brown-Guillroy, *Their Place on the Stage*; Barlow, *Plays by American Women*; Perkins, *Black Female Playwrights*; Margaret B. Wilkerson, *9 Plays by Black Women*.

54. Hull, *Color, Sex, and Poetry*; Johnson, *Book of American Negro Poetry*; Sherrad-Johnson, *Portraits of the New Negro Woman*; Mitchell, *This Waiting for Love*; Locke, *New Negro*.

55. Stephens, "Lynching Dramas and Women." In Perkins and Stephens, *Strange Fruit*, 3–14.

56. Bay, *To Tell the Truth Freely*, 82–108. Bay, through this extensive biography, chronicles Wells's immense work with antilynching activism and her visibility as an activist around numerous issues of racial and gender injustice.

57. Fletcher, "From Genteel Poet."

58. Hicklen, "American Negro Playwright."

59. Georgia Douglas Johnson, "Omnipresence" and "Beautiful Eyes," *Voice of the Negro*, Atlanta, June 1905.

60. Georgia Douglas Johnson, "Calling Dreams," *Crisis*, January 1920; "Treasure," *Crisis*, July 1922; "To Your Eyes," *Crisis*, November 1924.

61. Stephens, "Art, Activism, and Uncompromising Attitude." Stephens situates Johnson's work as well as the genre of lynching plays written by black women in the political context of antilynching activism in the early to mid-twentieth century.

62. *Safe*, 1.1.

63. Ibid.

64. Ibid.

65. Ibid.

66. Ibid.

67. The story of Garner has a particular place within the African American women's literary canon. Toni Morrison fictionalizes the story of Margaret Garner in the widely acclaimed novel *Beloved*. Johnson was an educated and well-read woman, so it is plausible to infer that she knew the story of Garner and used it as a realistic point of departure for her fictional account of infanticide.

68. Turner, "Narrating Infanticide."

69. Gregory and Locke, *Plays of Negro Life*, 414.

70. Reader Files of the Federal Theater Project, *Safe*, box 301, Music Division, Library of Congress.

71. Mary Burrill, *Liberator Magazine*, April 1919.

72. Perkins and Stephens, *Strange Fruit*, 79–81. Perkins and Stephens provide some of the most in-depth biographical information about Burrill. There has yet to be a book-length examination of her life.

73. Ibid.

74. Letter from Mary P. Burrill to W. E. B Du Bois, May 22, 1928. The specific change in the ending, however, is not specified in the correspondence between Burrill and Du Bois.

75. Ehrenreich, *Reproductive Rights Reader*; Dixon-Mueller, *Population Policy and Women's Rights*; Nelson, *Women of Color*; Chesler, *Woman of Valor*; Coates, *Margaret Sanger*; Reed, *Birth Control Movement*; McCann, *Birth Control Politics*; Helly and Reverby, *Gendered Domains*.

76. Burrill, *They Sat in Darkness*, *The Liberator*, April 1919.

77. Brody, "Queering Racial Reproduction."

78. Hutchinson, *Harlem Renaissance*; Wilder, *In the Company of Black Men*; Allen, *Black Women Intellectuals*; Franklin and Meier, *Black Leaders*; Robinson, *Black Nationalism*.

79. May Miller, interview with Kathy Perkins, September 2, 1987. Perkins and Stephens, *Strange Fruit*, 175; the quote is from Perkins's interview with Miller on September 2, 1972.

80. Perkins and Stephens, *Strange Fruit*, 175.

81. Claudia Tate, "Introduction." In Johnson, *Selected Works*, xxxi.

82. Miller, *Nails and Thorns*, 1.1, 1933.

83. Crystal Feimster's aforementioned work challenges the prevalence of a black-men-only approach to lynching victimization. She identifies at least two hundred black women lynched during the Jim Crow era.

Conclusion

1. Paul Lawrence Dunbar, "Negro Society in Washington," *Saturday Evening Post*, December 14, 1901, 9, 18.

2. Collins, *Black Sexual Politics*, 221.

3. Chapman, "Prove It on Me," 70.

4. Higginbotham, "African American Women's History," 251–74.

5. Rich, *Transcending the New Woman*, 1–36.

6. This framing riffs on bell hooks's work, *Feminist Theory: From Margins to Center* (Boston: South End, 2000). She emphasizes how black women shaped feminist theory and movements and the importance of recovering black women's voices in women's and racial justice activism.

Bibliography

Adams, Katherine H., and Michael L. Keene. *Alice Paul and the American Suffrage Campaign*. Urbana: University of Illinois Press, 2008.

Adero, Malaika, ed. *Up South: Stories, Studies, and Letters of This Century's African American Migrations*. New York: New Press, 1993.

Albertson, Chris. *Bessie*. New York: Stein and Day, 1972.

Allen, Carol. *Black Women Intellectuals: Strategies of Nation, Family, and Neighborhood in the Works of Pauline Hopkins, Jessie Fauset, and Marita Bonner*. New York: Garland, 1998.

Anderson, James D. *The Education of Blacks in the South, 1860–1935*. Chapel Hill: University of North Carolina Press, 1988.

Anderson, Jervis. *This Was Harlem: A Cultural Portrait, 1900–1950*. New York: Farrar, Straus, and Giroux, 1982.

Aptheker, Herbert, ed. *Selections from the Crisis*. Millwood, N.Y.: Kraus-Thompson, 1985.

Arnesen, Eric. *Black Protest and the Great Migration: A Brief History with Documents*. Boston: Bedford, 2003.

Aymer, Margaret P. *First Pure, Then Peaceable: Frederick Douglass Reads James*, London: Clark, 2008.

Bachin, Robin. *Building the South Side: Urban Space and Civic Culture in Chicago, 1890–1919*. Chicago: University of Chicago Press, 2003.

Baker, Houston A., Jr. *Modernism and the Harlem Renaissance*. Chicago: University of Chicago Press, 1987.

Baldwin, Davarian L. *Chicago's New Negroes: Modernity, the Great Migration, and Black Urban Life*. Chapel Hill: University of North Carolina Press, 2007.

———. "From the Washtub to the World." In *The Modern Girl Around the World*, edited by the Modern Girl Around the World Research Group, 55–76. Durham, N.C.: Duke University Press, 2008.

Bambara, Toni C., ed. *The Black Woman Anthology*. New York: New American Library, 1970.

Banks, Ingrid. *Hair Matters: Beauty, Power, and Black Women's Consciousness*. New York: New York University Press, 2000.

Baraka, (Imamu) Amiri [LeRoi Jones]. *Blues People: Negro Music in White America*. Westport, Conn.: Greenwood, 1980.

Barlow, Judith E., ed. *Plays by American Women: 1900–1930*. New York: Applause Theatre, 1985.

Barlow, William. *Voice Over: The Making of Black Radio*. Philadelphia: Temple University Press, 1999.

Barnes, Albert. "Negro Art and America." In Locke, *New Negro*, 19–28.

Barnes, William R. "Battle for Washington: Ideology, Racism, and Self-Interest in the Controversy over Public Housing, 1943–1946." *Records of the Columbia Historical Society* 50 (1980): 452–83.

Bashaw, Carolyn. "Slowe, Lucy Diggs: Dean of Women at Howard University (1922–1937)." In *Historical Dictionary of Women's Education in the United States*, edited by Linda Eisenman, 375–77. Westport, Conn.: Greenwood, 1998.

Bates, Beth Tompkins. *Pullman Porters and the Rise of Protest Politics in Black America, 1925–1945*. Chapel Hill: University of North Carolina Press, 2001.

Bay, Mia. *To Tell the Truth Freely: The Life of Ida B. Wells*. New York: Hill and Wang, 1910.

Beatty, Bess. *A Revolution Gone Backward: The Black Response to National Politics, 1876–1896*. Westport, Conn.: Praeger, 1987.

Bederman, Gail. *Manliness and Civilization: A Cultural History of Gender and Race in the United States, 1880–1917*. Chicago: University of Chicago Press, 1995.

Beemyn, Genny. *A Queer Capital: A History of Gay Life in Washington, D.C.* New York: Routledge, 2015.

Bell-Scott, Patricia, "To Keep My Self-Respect: Dean Lucy Diggs Slowe's 1927 Memorandum on the Sexual Harassment of Black Women." *NWSA Journal* 9, no. 2 (Summer 1997): 72–90.

Bercaw, Nancy. *Race, Rights, and the Politics of Household in the Delta, 1861–1875*. Gainesville: University Press of Florida, 2003.

Berman, Marshall. *All That Is Solid Melts into Air: The Experience of Modernity*. New York: Penguin, 1982.

Best, Wallace D. *Passionately Human, No Less Divine: Religion and Culture in Black Chicago, 1915–1952*. Princeton, N.J.: Princeton University Press, 2005.

Binder, Carroll. *Chicago and the New Negro*. Chicago: Chicago Daily News, 1927.

The Black Public Sphere Collective, ed. *The Black Public Sphere*. Chicago: University of Chicago Press, 1995.

Blackwelder, Juila Kirk. *Styling Jim Crow: African American Beauty Training during Segregation*. College Station: Texas A&M University Press, 2003.

Blanchard, Michael. "Afro-Modernity: Temporality, Politics, and the African Diaspora." *Public Culture* 11, no. 1 (1999): 245–68.
Bloch, Ruth H. "American Feminine Ideals in Transition: The Rise of the Moral Mother, 1785–1815." *Feminist Studies* 4 (1978): 101–26.
Bolotin, Norman, and Christine Laing. *The World's Columbian Exposition: The Chicago World's Fair of 1893*. Reprint edition. Urbana: University of Illinois Press, 2002.
Bontemps, Arna, and Jack Conroy. *Alley Life in Washington Family, Community, Religion, and Folklife in the City, 1850–1970*. Urbana: University of Illinois Press, 1980.
———. *They Seek a City*. New York: Doubleday, Doran, 1945.
Borchert, James A. *Alley Life in Washington: Family, Community, Religion, and Folklife in the City, 1850–1970*. Urbana: University of Illinois Press, 1980.
———. "The Rise and Fall of Washington's Inhabited Alleys, 1852–1972." *Records of the Columbia Historical Society* 48 (1972): 267–88.
Bottomley, Gillian. *From Another Place: Migration and the Politics of Culture*. New York: Cambridge University Press, 1992.
Brody, Jennifer D. *Impossible Purities: Blackness, Femininity, and Victorian Culture*. Durham, N.C.: Duke University Press, 1998.
———. "Queering Racial Reproduction: 'Unnatural Acts' in Angelina Weld Grimké's 'The Closing Door.'" *Text and Performance Quarterly* 23, no. 2 (April 2003): 205–23.
Brown, Elsa Barkley. "To Catch the Vision of Freedom: Reconstructing Southern Black Women's Political History, 1865–1880." In Gordon, Collier-Thomas, Bracey, Avakian, and Berkman, *African American Women and the Vote*, 66–99.
Brown, Letitia W. *Free Negroes in the District of Columbia, 1790–1846*. New York: Oxford University Press, 1972.
Brown-Guillory, Elizabeth, ed. *Their Place on the Stage: Black Women Playwrights in America*. New York: Greenwood, 1988.
———. *Wines in the Wilderness: Plays by African American Women from the Harlem Renaissance to the Present*. New York: Greenwood, 1990.
Bruce, Dickson D., Jr. *Archibald Grimké: Portrait of a Black Independent*. Baton Rouge: Louisiana State University Press, 1993.
Bullock, Penelope L. *The Afro-American Periodical Press, 1838–1909*. Baton Rouge: Louisiana State University Press, 1981.
Bundles, A'Lelia Perry. *Madam C. J. Walker, Entrepreneur*. New York: Chelsea House, 1991.
———. *On Her Own Ground: The Life and Times of Madam C. J. Walker*. New York: Scribner, 2001.
Burroughs, Nannie H. "Not Color, but Character." *Voice of the Negro* 1, no. 6 (1904).
Burrows, John. H. *The Necessity of Myth: A History of the National Negro Business League, 1940–1945*. Auburn, Ala.: Hickory Hill, 1988.

Byrand, Karl J. *Changing Race, Changing Place: Racial, Occupational, and Residential Patterns in Shaw, Washington, D.C., 1880–1920*. College Park: University of Maryland Press, 1999.

Byrd, Ayana D., and Lori L. Tharps. *Hair Story: Untangling the Roots of Black Hair in America*. New York: St. Martin's, 2001.

Caplan, Marvin. "Eat Anywhere! A Personal Recollection of the Thompson's Restaurant Case and the Desegregation of Washington's Eating Places." *Washington History* 1, no. 1 (1989): 24–39.

Caponi, Gena Dagel, ed. *Signifyin(g), Sanctifyin', and Slam Dunking: A Reader in African America Expressive Culture*. Amherst: University of Massachusetts Press, 1999.

Carby, Hazel V. *Race Men*. Cambridge, Mass.: Harvard University Press, 1998.

———. *Reconstructing Womanhood: The Emergence of the Afro-American Woman Novelist*. New York: Oxford University Press, 1987.

Carlson, Shirley J. "Black Ideals of Womanhood in the Late Victorian Era." *Journal of Negro History* 77, no. 2 (Spring 1992): 61–73.

Cayton, Horace R., and George S. Mitchell. *Black Workers and the New Unions*. Chapel Hill: University of North Carolina Press, 1939.

Chapman, Erin. "Prove It on Me: New Negro Women Politics and Popular Culture." Phd diss., Yale University, 2006.

———. *Prove It on Me: New Negroes, Sex, and Popular Culture in the 1920s*. New York: Oxford University Press, 2012.

Chase, Hal S. "'Shelling the Citadel of Race Prejudice': William Calvin Chase and the Washington 'Bee,' 1882–1921." *Columbia Historical Society* 49 (1973): 371–91.

Chesler, Ellen. *Woman of Valor: Margaret Sanger and the Birth Control Movement*. New York: Simon and Schuster, 1992.

Clark-Lewis, Elizabeth. *Living In, Living Out: African American Domestics in Washington, D.C., 1910–1940*. Washington: Smithsonian Institution Press, 1994.

Clift, Eleanor. *Founding Sisters and the Nineteenth Amendment*. Hoboken, N.J.: Wiley, 2003.

Coates, Patricia W. *Margaret Sanger and the Origin of the Birth Control Movement, 1910–1930: The Concept of Women's Sexual Anatomy*. Lewiston, N.Y.: Mellen, 2008.

Collier-Thomas, Bettye. "Frances Ellen Watkins Harper." In Gordon, Collier-Thomas, Bracey, Avakian, and Berkman, *African American Women and the Vote*, 41–65.

———. *Jesus, Jobs, and Justice: African American Women and Religion*. New York: Knopf, 2010.

Collins, Patricia Hill. *Black Feminist Thought: Knowledge, Consciousness, and the Politics of Empowerment*. New York: Routledge, 2008.

———. *Black Sexual Politics: African Americans, Gender, and the New Racism*. New York: Routledge, 2004.

Cooper, Anna Julia. "Discussion of the Intellectual Progress of Colored Women of the United States Since the Emancipation Proclamation." *The World's Congress of Representative Women* [May 1893]. Edited by May Wright Sewall. Chicago: Rand, McNally, 1894.

———. *A Voice from the South*. London: Oxford University Press, 1990.

Coppin, Fanny Jackson. "Discussion of the Intellectual Progress of Colored Women of the United States Since the Emancipation Proclamation." *The World's Congress of Representative Women* [May 1893]. Edited by May Wright Sewall. Chicago: Rand, McNally, 1894.

Cott, Nancy. *The Bonds of Womanhood: Woman's Sphere in New England, 1780–1835*. New Haven, Conn.: Yale University Press, 1977

Crew, Spencer R. *Field to Factory: Afro-American Migration 1915–1940*. Washington: Smithsonian Institution Press, 1987.

Cripps, Thomas. *Slow Fade to Black: The Negro in American Film, 1900–1942*. New York: Oxford University Press, 1977.

Cronin, Anne M. *Advertising and Consumer Citizenship: Gender, Images, and Rights*. New York: Routledge, 2001.

Davis, Angela Y. *Blues Legacies and Black Feminism: Gertrude "Ma" Rainey, Bessie Smith, and Billie Holiday*. New York: Random House, 1998.

———. *Women, Race, and Class*. New York: Random House, 1981.

Davis, Elizabeth Lindsay. *The Story of the Illinois Federation of Colored Women's Clubs*. 1922. Reprint, London: Prentice Hall, 1997.

Davis, Francis. *The History of the Blues: The Roots, the Music, the People*. New York: Hyperion, 1995.

De Caro, Louis A., Jr. *"Fire from the Midst of You": A Religious Life of John Brown*. New York: New York University Press, 2002.

Deegan, Mary Jo, ed. *The New Woman of Color: The Collected Works of Fannie Barrier Williams, 1893–1918*. Dekalb: Northern Illinois University Press, 2002.

Detweiler, Frederick G. *The Negro Press in the United States*. Chicago: University of Chicago Press, 1922.

Deutsch, Sarah. *Women and the City: Gender, Space, Power in Boston, 1870–1940*. New York: Oxford University Press, 2000.

Dickson, Lynda F. "Toward a Broader Angle of Vision in Uncovering Women's History: Black Women's Clubs Revisited." *Frontiers: A Journal in Women's Studies* 9, no. 2 (1987): 62–68.

Dinerstein, Joel. *Swinging the Machine: Modernity, Technology, and African American Culture between the World Wars*. Amherst: University of Massachusetts Press, 2003.

Dixon-Mueller, Ruth. *Population Policy and Women's Rights: Transforming Reproductive Choice*. Westport, Conn.: Praeger, 1993.

Donalson, Melvin B. *The Representation of Afro-American Women in the Hollywood Feature Film, 1915–1949*. Ann Arbor: University Microfilm, 1984.

Dossett, Kate. *Bridging Race Divides: Black Nationalism, Feminism and Integration in the United States, 1896–1935*. Gainesville: University Press of Florida, 2008.

Drake, St. Clair, and Horace R. Cayton. *Black Metropolis: A Study of Negro Life in a Northern City*. New York: Harcourt, Brace, 1945.

DuBois, Ellen C. *Feminism and Suffrage: The Emergence of an Independent Women's Movement in America, 1848–1869*. Ithaca, N.Y.: Cornell University Press, 1978.

DuBois, Ellen C., and Vicki L. Ruiz, eds. *Unequal Sisters: A Multicultural Reader in U.S. Women's History*. New York: Routledge, 2000.

Du Bois, W. E. B. *The Black North: A Social Study*. 1901. Reprint, New York: Arno, 1969.

———. *The Souls of Black Folk*. 1903. Reprint, New York. Penguin, 1989.

duCille, Ann. *The Coupling Convention: Sex, Text, and Tradition in Black Women's Fiction*. New York: Oxford University Press, 1993.

Duster, Alfreda M., ed. *Crusade for Justice: The Autobiography of Ida B. Wells*. Chicago: University of Chicago Press, 1988.

Dyson, Walter. *The Founding of Howard University*. Washington, D.C.: Howard University Press, 1921.

———. *Howard University History, The Capstone of Negro Education, a History, 1867–1940*. Washington, D.C.: Howard University Press, 1941.

Edwards, Laura F. *Gendered Strife and Confusion: The Political Culture of Reconstruction*. Urbana: University of Illinois Press, 1997.

———. *The People and Their Peace: Legal Culture and the Transformation of Inequality in the Post-Revolutionary South*. Chapel Hill: University of North Carolina Press, 2009.

Edwards, Paul. *The Southern Urban Negro as Consumer*. 1932. Reprint, New York: Negro Universities Press, 1969.

Ehrenreich, Nancy, ed. *The Reproductive Rights Reader: Law, Medicine, and the Construction of Motherhood*. New York: New York University Press, 2008.

Erenberg, Lewis A. *Steppin' Out: New York Nightlife and the Transformation of American Culture, 1890–1930*. Chicago: University of Chicago Press, 1981.

Evans, David. *Ramblin' on My Mind: New Perspectives on the Blues*. Urbana: University of Illinois Press, 2008.

Everett, Anna. *Returning the Gaze: A Genealogy of Black Film Criticism, 1909–1949*. Durham, N.C.: Duke University Press, 2001.

Farred, Grant. *What's My Name: Black Vernacular Intellectuals*. Minneapolis: University of Minnesota Press, 2003.

Faulkner, Carol. *Women's Radical Reconstruction: The Freedmen's Aid Movement*. Philadelphia: University of Pennsylvania Press, 2004.

Favor, J. Martin. *Authentic Blackness: The Folk in the New Negro Renaissance*. Durham, N.C.: Duke University Press, 1999.

Feimster, Crystal N. *Southern Horrors: Women and the Politics of Rape and Lynching*. Cambridge, Mass.: Harvard University Press, 2011.

Fitzpatrick, Michael A. "'A Great Agitation for Business': Black Economic Development in Shaw." *Washington History* 2, no. 2 (1990): 48–73.

Fitzpatrick, Sandra McNear. "The Path to Creativity: The Life and Career of Alma W. Thomas in Washington, D.C." Master's thesis, George Washington University, Washington, D.C.

Fletcher, Winona. "From Genteel Poet to Revolutionary Playwright: Georgia Douglas Johnson." *Theatre Annual* (1985): 41–64.

———. "Georgia Douglas Johnson." In *Notable Women in the American Theater: A Biographical Dictionary*, edited by Alice Robinson, Vera M. Mowry, and Milly Barranger. New York: Greenwood, 1989.

Floyd, Samuel A. *Black Music in the Harlem Renaissance: A Collection of Essays*. New York: Greenwood, 1990.

Foley, Barbara. *Spectres of 1919: Class and Nation in the Making of the New Negro*. Urbana: University of Illinois Press, 2003.

Franklin, John Hope, and August Meier, eds. *Black Leaders of the Twentieth Century*. Urbana: University of Illinois Press, 1982.

Franklin, V. P. *Black Self-Determination: A Cultural History of the Faith of Our Fathers*. Westport, Conn.: Greenwood, 1984.

Frazier, E. Franklin. *Black Bourgeoisie: The Rise of New Middle Class*. Glencoe, Ill.: Free Press, 1957.

———. *The Negro Church in America*. New York: Schocken, 1964.

Frederickson, George. *The Black Image in the White Mind: The Debate on Afro-American Character and Destiny, 1817–1940*. New York: Harper and Row, 1971.

Gaines, Kevin. *Uplifting the Race: Black Leadership, Politics, and Culture in the Twentieth Century*. Chapel Hill: University of North Carolina Press, 1996.

Gamble, Vanessa Northington. *Making a Place for Ourselves: The Black Hospital Movement, 1920–1945*. New York: Oxford University Press, 1995.

Garfinkel, Herbert. *When Negroes March: The March on Washington Movement in the Organizational Politics for FEPC*. Glencoe, Ill.: Free Press, 1959.

Gaspar, David B., and Darlene C. Hine, eds. *More than Chattel: Black Women and Slavery in the Americas*. Bloomington: Indiana University Press, 1996.

Gates, Henry Louis, Jr. "The Trope of the New Negro and the Reconstruction of the Black." *Representations* 24, Special Issue: America Reconstructed 1840–1940 (Autumn 1988): 129–155.

Gates, Henry Louis, Jr., and Gene Andrew Jarrett, eds. *The New Negro: Readings on Race, Representation, and African American Culture, 1892–1938*. Princeton, N.J.: Princeton University Press, 2007.

Gatewood, Willard B., Jr. "Aristocrats of Color: South and North the Black Elite, 1880–1920." *Journal of Southern History* 54, no. 1 (February 1988): 3–20.

———. *Aristocrats of Color: The Black Elite, 1880–1920*. Bloomington: Indiana University Press, 1990.

Gibbs, Mifflin W. *Shadow and Light: An Autobiography*. Little Rock, Ark./Washington, D.C.: self-published, 1902.

Giddings, Paula. *In Search of Sisterhood: Delta Sigma Theta and the Challenge of the Black Sorority Movement*. New York: Morrow, 1988.

———. *When and Where I Enter: The Impact of Black Women on Race and Sex in America*. New York: Bantam, 1984.

Gill, Tiffany M. *Beauty Shop Politics: African American Women's Activism in the Beauty Industry*. Urbana: University of Illinois Press, 2010.

Gilmore, Glenda. *Gender and Jim Crow: Women and the Politics of White Supremacy in North Carolina, 1896–1920*. Chapel Hill: University of North Carolina Press, 1996.

Gilroy, Paul. *The Black Atlantic: Modernity and Double Consciousness*. Cambridge, Mass.: Harvard University Press, 1993.

———. *Small Acts: Thoughts on the Politics of Black Cultures*. London: Serpent's Tail, 1993.

Glymph, Thavolia. *Out of the House of Bondage: The Transformation of the Plantation Household*. New York: Cambridge University Press, 2008.

Goings, Kenneth W., and Raymond A. Mohl, eds. *The New African American Urban History*. Thousand Oaks, Calif.: Sage, 1996.

Gordon, Ann D., Bettye Collier-Thomas, John H. Bracey, Arlene V. Avakian, and Joyce A. Berkman, eds. *African American Women and the Vote, 1837–1965*. Boston: University of Massachusetts Press, 1997.

Gordon, Martin K. "The Black Militia in the District of Columbia, 1867–1898." *Records of the Columbia Historical Society* 48 (1972): 411–20.

Gosnell, Harold Foote. *Negro Politicians: The Rise of Negro Politics in Chicago*. Chicago: University of Chicago Press, 1935.

Graham, Lawrence O. *Our Kind of People: Inside America's Black Upper Class*. New York: HarperCollins, 1999.

Green, Constance M. *The Secret City: A History of Race Relations in the Nation's Capital*. Princeton, N.J.: Princeton University Press, 1967.

Gregory, James N. *The Southern Diaspora: How the Great Migrations of Black and White Southerners Transformed America*. Chapel Hill: University of North Carolina Press, 2005.

Gregory, Montgomery T., and Alain Locke. *Plays of Negro Life*. New York: Harper and Row, 1927.

Griffin, Farah Jasmine. *"Who Set You Flowin'?" The African-American Migration Narrative*. New York: Oxford University Press, 1995.

Grimké, Angelina Weld. "'Rachel,' the Play of the Month: The Reason and Synopsis by the Author." *The Competitor* 1, no. 1 (1920): 51–52.

Grimshaw, William J. *Bitter Fruit: Black Politics and the Chicago Machine 1931–1991*. Chicago: University of Chicago Press, 1992.

Grossman, James R. *Land of Hope: Chicago, Black Southerners, and The Great Migration*. Chicago: University of Chicago Press, 1989.

Groves, Paul A., "The Development of a Black Residential Community in Southwest Washington, 1860–1897." *Records of the Columbia Historical Society* 49: 260–75.

Guerrero, Ed. *Framing Blackness: The African American Image in Film*. Philadelphia: Temple University Press, 1993.

Habermas, Jürgen. *The Philosophical Discourses of Modernity: Twelve Lectures*. Translated by Frederick Lawrence. Cambridge, Mass.: Massachusetts Institute of Technology Press, 1987.

———. *The Structural Transformation of the Public Sphere*. Translated by Thomas Burger, with Frederick Lawrence. Cambridge: Massachusetts Institute of Technology Press, 1989.

Hall, Jacquelyn Dowd. *Revolt against Chivalry: Jessie Daniel Ames and the Women's Campaign against Lynching*. New York: Columbia University Press, 1979.

Hall, Stuart, David Held, Don Hubert, and Kenneth Thompson. *Modernity: An Introduction to Modern Societies*. London: Blackwell, 1996.

Hammond, Theresa A. *A White-Collar Profession: African American Certified Public Accountants since 1921*. Chapel Hill: University of North Carolina Press, 2002.

Hanchard, Michael. "Afro-Modernity: Temporality, Politics, and the African Diaspora." *Public Culture*. 11, no. 1 (1999): 245–68.

Hancock, John. *Essays on the Elective Franchise; or, Who Has the Right to Vote?* Philadelphia: Merrihew, 1865.

———. *The Great Question for the People! Essays on the Elective Franchise; or, Who Has the Right to Vote?* Philadelphia: Merrihew, 1865.

Hannold, Elizabeth. "'Comfort and Respectability': Washington's Philanthropic Housing Movement." *Washington History* 4, no. 2 (1992–1993): 20–39.

Hanson, Joyce A. *Mary McLeod Bethune and Black Women's Political Activism*. Columbia: University of Missouri Press, 2003.

Harley, Sharon. "Beyond the Classroom: The Organizational Lives of Black Female Educators in the District of Columbia, 1890–1930." *Journal of Negro Education* 51, no. 3 (Summer 1982): 254–65.

———. "Black Women in a Southern City: Washington, D.C., 1890–1920." In *Sex, Race, and the Role of Women in the South*, edited by Joanne V. Hawks and Sheila L. Skemp, 59–74. Jackson: University Press of Mississippi, 1983.

———. "Nannie Helen Burroughs: 'The Black Goddess of Liberty.'" *Journal of Negro History* 81 (1996): 62+.

Harley, Sharon, and Rosalyn Terborg-Penn. *The Afro-American Woman: Struggles and Images*. Baltimore, Md.: Black Classic, 1997.

Harmon, John Henry, Arnett Lindsay, and Carter G. Woodson. *The Negro as a Business Man*. 1929. Reprint, College Park, Md.: McGrath, 1969.

Harris, Abram L. *The Negro as Capitalist: A Study of Banking and Business among American Negroes*. Philadelphia: American Academy of Political and Social Sciences, 1936.

Harris, Leonard, ed. *The Philosophy of Alain Locke: Harlem Renaissance and Beyond*. Philadelphia: Temple University Press, 1989.

Harrison, Alferdteen J., ed. *Black Exodus: The Great Migration from the American South*. Jackson: University Press of Mississippi, 1991.

Harrison, Daphne Duval. *Black Pearls: Blues Queens of the 1920s*. New Brunswick, N.J.: Rutgers University Press, 1988.

Harrison, Hubert H. *When Africa Awakes: The "Inside Story" of the Stirrings and Strivings of the New Negro in the Western World*. 1920. Reprint, Baltimore, Md.: Black Classic, 1997.

Hazzard-Gordon, Katrina. *Jookin': The Rise of Social Dance Formations in African-American Culture*. Philadelphia: Temple University Press, 1990.

Helbling, Mark Irving. *The Harlem Renaissance: The One and the Many*. Westport, Conn.: Greenwood, 1999.

Helly, Dorothy O., and Susan Reverby. *Gendered Domains: Rethinking Public and Private in Women's History*. Ithaca, N.Y.: Cornell University Press, 1992.

Hendricks, Wanda A. *Gender, Race, and Politics in the Midwest: Black Club Women in Illinois*. Bloomington: Indiana University Press, 1998.

———. "Ida B. Wells-Barnett and the Alpha Suffrage Club of Chicago." In Wheeler, *One Woman, One Vote*, 263–76.

Henri, Florette. *Black Migration: Movement North, 1900–1920: The Road from Myth to Man*. New York: Anchor, 1975.

Henry, Charles P. Culture and *African American Politics*. Bloomington: Indiana University Press, 1990.

Hicklen, Fannie E. "The American Negro Playwright, 1920–1964." PhD diss., University of Wisconsin–Madison, 1965.

Higginbotham, Evelyn B. "African American Women's History and the Metalanguage of Race." *Signs* 17, no. 2 (Winter 1992): 251–74.

———. *Righteous Discontent: The Women's Movement in the Black Baptist Church, 1880–1920*. Cambridge, Mass.: Harvard University Press, 1993.

Hill, Robert A., ed. *The Marcus Garvey and Universal Negro Improvement Association Papers*. Vol. 1, *1826–August 1919*. Berkeley: University of California Press, 1983.

Hine, Darlene Clark. *Hine Sight: Black Women and the Re-Construction of American History*. Brooklyn, N.Y.: Carlson, 1994.

———. "Rape and the Inner Lives of Black Women in the Middle West: Preliminary Thoughts on the Culture of Dissemblance." *Signs* 4, no. 4 (Summer, 1989): 912–20.

———. *Speak Truth to Power: Black Professional Class in the United States*. Brooklyn: Carlson, 1996.

Hine, Darlene Clark, and Kathleen Thompson. *A Shining Thread of Hope: The History of Black Women in America*. New York: Broadway, 1998.

Hogan, Lawrence D. *A Black National News Service: The Associated Negro Press and Claude Barnett, 1919–1945*. London: Associated University Press, 1984.

hooks, bell. *Ain't I a Woman: Black Women and Feminism*. Boston: South End, 1999.

Horne, Gerald. *Race Woman: The Lives of Shirley Graham Du Bois*. New York: New York University Press, 2000.

Hull, Gloria T. *Color, Sex, and Poetry: Three Women Writers of the Harlem Renaissance*. Bloomington: Indiana University Press, 1987.

Hunter, Tera W. *To 'Joy My Freedom: Southern Black Women's Lives and Labors after the Civil War*. Cambridge, Mass.: Harvard University Press, 1997.

Hutchinson, George. *The Harlem Renaissance in Black and White*. Cambridge, Mass.: Harvard University Press, 1995.

Hutchinson, Louise Daniel. *The Anacostia Story: 1608–1930*. Washington, D.C.: Smithsonian Institution Press, 1977.

Irwin, Inez H. *Story of Alice Paul and the National Woman's Party*. Fairfax, Va.: Denlinger's, 1977.

Jackson, Jerma A. *Singing in My Soul: Black Gospel Music in a Secular Age*. Chapel Hill: University of North Carolina Press, 2004.

Janiewski, Dolores. *Sisterhood Denied: Race, Gender, and Class in a New South Community*. Philadelphia: Temple University Press, 1985.

Johnson, Abby, and Ronald Johnson. *Propaganda and Aesthetics: The Literary Politics of African-American Magazines in the Twentieth Century*. Boston: University of Massachusetts Press, 1979.

Johnson, Charles R., Patricia Smith, and the WGBH Research Team. *Africans in America: America's Journey through Slavery*. New York: Harcourt, 1998.

Johnson, Charles S. *The Negro College Graduate*. Durham, N.C.: University of North Carolina Press, 1938.

Johnson, Daniel, and Rex Campbell. *Black Migration in America: A Social and Demographic History*. Durham, N.C.: Duke University Press, 1981.

Johnson, Eloise E. *Rediscovering the Harlem Renaissance: The Politics of Exclusion*. New York: Garland, 1997.

Johnson, Georgia Douglas. *The Selected Works of Georgia Douglas Johnson*. New York: Hall, 1997.

Johnson, James W. *Black Manhattan*. 1930. Reprint, New York: Antheum, 1977.

———. *The Book of American Negro Poetry: Revised Edition*. New York: Harcourt, Brace, 1931.

Johnson, Joan Marie. *Southern Women at the Seven Sister Colleges: Feminist Values and Social Activism 1875–1915*, Athens: University of Georgia Press, 2010.

Johnson, Ronald M. "Black and White Apart: The Community Center Movement in the District of Columbia, 1915–1930." *Records of the Columbia Historical Society* 52 (1989): 1–11.

———. "Those Who Stayed: Washington Black Writers of the 1920s." *Records of the Columbia Historical Society* 50 (1980): 484–99.

Johnson, Thomas R. *The City on the Hill: Race Relations in Washington, D.C., 1865–1885*. College Park, Md.: University of Maryland Press, 1975.

———. "Reconstruction Politics in Washington: 'An Experimental Garden for Radical Plants,'" Records of the *Columbia Historical Society* 50 (1980): 180–90.

Johnston, Allan J. *Surviving Freedom: The Black Community of Washington, D.C. 1860–1880*. New York: Garland, 1993.

Jones, Jacqueline. *Labor of Love, Labor of Sorrow: Black Women, Work, and the Family from Slavery to the Present*. New York: Basic, 1985.

Jones, Martha. *All Bound Up Together: The Woman Question in African American Public Culture, 1830–1900*. Chapel Hill: University of North Carolina Press, 2007.

Jones, William. *Recreation and Amusement among Negroes in Washington, D.C.* 1927. Reprint, Westport, Conn.: Negro Universities Press, 1970.

Kelley, Robin D. G. *Race Rebels: Culture, Politics, and the Black Working Class*. New York: Free Press, 1996.

Kelley, Robin D. G., and Earl Lewis. *To Make Our World Anew: A History of African Americans*. New York: Oxford University Press, 2000.

Kennedy, Susan Estabrook. *If All We Did Was Weep at Home: A History of White Working-Class Women in America*. Bloomington: Indiana University Press, 1979.

Kerber, Linda K., and Jane Sherron De Hart, eds. *Women's America: Refocusing the Past*. New York: Oxford University Press, 2004.

Kerr, Audrey Elisa. *The Paper Bag Principle: Class, Colorism, and Rumor in the Case of Black Washington, D.C.* Knoxville: University of Tennessee Press, 2006.

Kessler-Harris, Alice. *Out to Work: A History of Wage-Earning Women in the United States*. New York: Oxford University Press, 2003.

Keyssar, Alexander. *The Right to Vote: The Contested History of Democracy in the United States*. New York: Basic, 2009

King, Deborah, "Multiple Jeopardy, Multiple Consciousness: The Context of Black Feminist Ideology." *Signs* 14, no. 2 (Autumn 1988): 42–72.

Kober, George M. *The History and Development of the Housing Movement in the City of Washington*. Washington, D.C.: Washington Sanitary Housing Companies, 1927.

Kofie, Nelson F. *Race, Class, and the Struggle for Neighborhood in Washington, D.C.* New York: Garland, 1999.

Lake, Obiagele. *Blue Veins and Kinky Hair: Naming and Color Consciousness in African America*. Westport, Conn.: Praeger, 2003.

Lamothe, Daphne. *Inventing the New Negro: Narrative, Culture, and Ethnography*. Philadelphia: University of Pennsylvania Press, 2008.

Langa, Helen. "Two Antilynching Art Exhibitions: Politicized Viewpoints, Racial Perspectives, Gendered Constraints." *American Art* 13, no. 1 (Spring 1999): 11–39.

Lemann, Nicholas. *The Promised Land: The Great Black Migration and How It Changed America*. New York: Knopf, 1991.

Lerner, Gerda. *Black Women in White America: A Documentary History*. New York: Vintage, 1997.

———. "Early Community Work of Black Club Women." *Journal of Negro History* 59, no. 2 (April 1974): 158–67.

Lesko, Kathleen M., Valerie Melissa Babb, and Carroll R. Gibbs. ed. *Black Georgetown Remembered: A History of Its Black Community from the Founding of the "Town of George" in 1751 to the Present*. Washington, D.C.: Georgetown University Press, 1991.

Levine, Lawrence W. *Black Culture and Black Consciousness: Afro-American Folk Thought from Slavery to Freedom*. Oxford: Oxford University Press, 1977.

Liebow, Eliot. *Tally's Corner: A Study of Negro Streetcorner Men*. Boston: Little, Brown, 1967.

Lincoln, C. Eric, and Lawrence H. Mamiya. *The Black Church in the African American Experience*. Durham, N.C.: Duke University Press, 1990.

Lindsey, Treva B. "Post-Ferguson: A 'Herstorical' Approach to Black Violability." *Feminist Studies* 41, no. 1 (2015): 232–37.

Litwack, Leon E., "The Emancipation of the Negro Abolitionist." In *African-American Activism Before the Civil War*, edited by Patrick Rael. New York: Routledge, 2008.
Locke, Alain. *The New Negro: Voices of the Harlem Renaissance*. Introduction by Arnold Rampersad. New York: Boni, 1925.
Logan, Rayford W. *Howard University: The First Hundred Years, 1867–1967*. New York: New York University Press, 1969.
Lott, Tommy L. *The Invention of Race: Black Culture and the Politics of Representation*. Malden, Mass.: Blackwell, 1999.
Lunardini, Christine A. *From Equal Suffrage to Equal Rights: Alice Paul and the National Woman's Party, 1910–1928*. New York: New York University Press, 1986.
Lynk, B. S. *A Complete Course in Hair Straightening and Beauty Culture*. Memphis, Tenn.: 20th Century Art, 1919.
M Street High School. *The High School Journal*. Washington, D.C.: M Street High School, 1906.
MacLean, Annie M. *Wage-Earning Women*. New York: Macmillan, 1910.
Marks, Carole B. *Farewell—We're Good and Gone: The Great Black Migration*. Bloomington: Indiana University Press, 1989.
Masur, Kate. *An Example for All the Land: Emancipation and the Struggle over Equality in Washington, D.C.* Chapel Hill, NC: University of North Carolina Press, 2012.
———. "Reconstructing the Nation's Capital: The Politics of Race and Citizenship in the District of Columbia, 1862–1878." PhD diss., University of Michigan, 2001.
Materson, Lisa G. *For the Freedom of Her Race: Black Women and Electoral Politics in Illinois, 1877–1932*. Chapel Hill: University of North Carolina Press, 2009.
Matthews, Jean. *The Rise of the New Woman: The Women's Movement in America, 1875–1930*. New York: Dee, 2004.
May, Vivian M. *Anna Julia Cooper, A Visionary Black Feminist: A Critical Introduction*. New York: Routledge, 2007.
McCann, Carole R. *Birth Control Politics in the United States,1916–1945*, Ithaca: Cornell University Press, 1994.
McKinney, Richard I. *Mordecai: The Man and His Message; The Story of Mordecai Wyatt Johnson*. Washington, D.C.: Howard University Press, 1997.
McKittrick, Katherine. *Demonic Grounds: Black Women and the Cartographies of Struggle*. Minneapolis: University of Minnesota Press, 2006.
McKivigan, John R., and Mitchell Snay, eds. *Religion and the Antebellum Debate over Slavery*. Athens: University of Georgia Press, 1998.
McPherson, James E. *The Struggle for Equality*. Princeton, N.J.: Princeton University Press, 1964.
McQuirter, Marya A. "Claiming the City: African Americans, Urbanization and Leisure in Washington, D.C., 1902–1954." PhD diss., University of Michigan, 2000.
Miller, Carol L. L., and Anne S. Pruitt-Logan. *Faithful to the Task at Hand: The Life of Lucy Diggs Slowe*. New York: SUNY Press, 2012.

Miller, Kelly. "Where Is the Negro's Heaven?" *Opportunity* 4 (December 1926): 370–73.

Miller, M. Sammye. "An Early Venture in Black Capitalism: The Capital Savings Bank in the District of Columbia." *Records of the Columbia Historical Society* 50 (1980): 359–66.

Mintz, Steven. "A Historical Ethnography of Black Washington, D.C." *Records of the Columbia Historical Society* 52 (1989): 235–53.

Mitchell, Koritha. *Living with Lynching: African American Lynching Plays, Performance, and Citizenship, 1890–1930*. Urbana: University of Illinois Press, 2012.

Mitchell, Verner D., ed. *This Waiting for Love: Helene Johnson, Poet of the Harlem Renaissance*. Amherst: University of Massachusetts Press, 2000.

Montgomery, Winfield Scott. *Historical Sketch of Education for the Colored Race in the District of Columbia*. Washington, D.C.: Smith, 1907.

Moore, Jacqueline M. *Leading the Race: The Transformation of the Black Elite in the Nation's Capital, 1880–1920*. Charlottesville: University Press of Virginia, 1999.

Murray, Pauli, and Mary O. Eastwood. "Jane Crow and the Law: Sex Discrimination and Title VII." *George Washington Law Review* 34, no. 2 (December 1965): 232–56.

Nadell, Martha Jane. *Enter the New Negroes: Images of Race in American Culture*. Cambridge, Mass.: Harvard University Press, 2004.

Nelson, Jennifer. *Women of Color and the Reproductive Rights Movement*. New York: New York University Press, 2003.

Neverdon-Morton, Cynthia. "Advancement of the Race through African American Women's Organizations in the South, 1895–1925." In Gordon, Collier-Thomas, Bracey, Avakian, and Berkman, *African American Women and the Vote*, 120–33.

———. *Afro-American Women of the South and the Advancement of the Race, 1895–1925*. Knoxville: University of Tennessee, 1991.

Newman, Louise M. *White Women's Rights: The Racial Origins of Feminism in the United States*. New York: Oxford University Press, 1999.

Null, Druscilla J. "Myrtilla Miner's 'School for Colored Girls': A Mirror on Antebellum Washington." *Records of the Columbia Historical Society* 52 (1989): 254–68.

O'Connor, Ellen M. *Myrtilla Miner, A Memoir*. New York: Arno, 1969.

Ogbar, Jeffery O. G. *The Harlem Renaissance Revisited: Politics, Arts, and Letters*. Baltimore, Md.: Johns Hopkins University Press, 2010.

Orbach, Barbara, and Nicholas Natanson. "The Mirror Image: Black Washington in World War II Era Federal Photography." *Washington History* 4, no. 1 (1992): 4–25.

Orlick, Annelise. *Rethinking American Women's Activism*. New York: Routledge, 2014.

Pacifico, Michele F. "Don't Buy Where You Can't Work: The New Negro Alliance of Washington." *Washington History* 6, no. 1 (1994): 66–88.

———. *A History of the New Negro Alliance of Washington D.C., 1933–1941*. Washington: George Washington University Press, 1983.

Painter, Nell Irvin. *Sojourner Truth: A Life, a Symbol*. New York: Norton, 1996.

Patton, Venetria K. *Women in Chains: The Legacy of Slavery in Black Women's Fiction*. Albany: State University of New York Press, 2000.

Payne, Daniel A. *A History of the African Methodist Episcopal Church*. Chapel Hill: University of North Carolina Press, 2001.

Peplow, Michael W., and Arthur P. Davis, eds. *The New Negro Renaissance: An Anthology*. New York: Holt, Reinhart and Winston, 1975.

Perkins, Kathy A., ed. *Black Female Playwrights: An Anthology of Plays before 1950*. Bloomington: 1989.

———. "Lynching Plays by Mary P. Burrill and Angelina Weld Grimké." Conference paper, Association for Theater in Higher Education Panel, Atlanta, 1992.

Perkins, Kathy A., and Judith L. Stephens, eds. *Strange Fruit: Plays on Lynching by American Women*. Bloomington: Indiana University Press, 1998.

Perkins, Linda M. "Lucy Diggs Slowe: Champion of the Self-Determination of African-American Women in Higher Education." *Journal of Negro History* 81, no. 1 (Winter-Autumn, 1996): 89–104.

———. "The National Association of College Women: Vanguard of Black Women's Leadership and Education, 1923–1954." *Journal of Education* 172, no. 3 (1990): 65–75.

Prestage, Jewel L. "In Quest of African American Political Women." *Annals of the American Academy of Political and Social Science* 515 (May 1991): 88–103.

Pride, Armistead S., and Clint C. Wilson II. *A History of the Black Press* Washington, D.C.: Howard University Press, 1997.

Rabinowitz, Howard. *Race Relations in the Urban South, 1865–1890*. New York: Oxford University Press, 1978.

Reed, James. *The Birth Control Movement and American Society: From Private Vice to Public Virtue*. Princeton, N.J.: Princeton University Press, 1978.

Rich, Charlotte J. *Transcending the New Woman: Multiethnic Narratives of the Progressive Era*. Columbia: University of Missouri Press, 2009.

Rief, Michelle. "Thinking Locally, Acting Globally: The International Agenda of African American Clubwomen, 1880–1940." *Journal of African American History* 89 (2004): 203–22.

Robinson, Dean E. *Black Nationalism in American Politics and Thought*. Cambridge: Cambridge University Press, 2001.

Robinson, Henry S. "The M Street High School, 1891–1916." *Records of the Columbia Historical Society* 51 (1984): 119–43.

Rooks, Noliwe M. *Hair Raising: Beauty, Culture, and African American Women*. New Brunswick, N.J.: Rutgers University Press, 1996.

———. *Ladies' Pages: African American Women's Magazines and the Culture That Made Them*. New Brunswick, N.J.: Rutgers University Press, 2004.

Ruble, Blair A. *Washington's U Street: A Biography*. Baltimore, Md.: Johns Hopkins University Press, 2012.

Rucker, Walter C. *The River Flows On: Black Resistance, Culture, and Identity Formation in Early America*. Baton Rouge: Louisiana State University Press, 2006.

Sachsman, David B., S. Kittrell Rushing, and Roy Morris Jr., eds. *Seeking a Voice: Images of Race and Gender in the 19th Century Press*. West Lafayette, Ind.: Purdue University Press, 2009

Scandura, Jani. *Down in the Dumps: Place, Modernity, American Depression.* Durham, N.C.: Duke University Press, 2008.

Scott, Anne Firor. "Most Invisible of All: Black Women's Voluntary Associations." *Journal of Southern History* 56, no. 1 (February 1990): 3–22.

Shaw, Stephanie J. *What a Woman Ought to Be and to Do: Black Professional Women Workers in the Jim Crow Era.* Chicago: University of Chicago Press, 1996.

Sherrard-Johnson, Cherene. *Portraits of the New Negro Woman: Visual and Literary Culture in the Harlem Renaissance.* New Brunswick, N.J.: Rutgers University Press, 2007.

Slowe, Lucy Diggs. "The Higher Education of Negro Women." *Journal of Negro Education* 2 (July 1933): 352–58.

———. *The Hilltop.* Washington, D.C.: Howard University, May 14, 1931.

———. "Mills Case." Washington, D.C.: Howard University, 1927.

Smith, Eric L. "Lillian Evanti: Washington's African American Diva." *Washington History* 11, no. 1 (1999): 24–43.

Smith, Susan Lynn. *Sick and Tired of Being Sick and Tired: Black Women's Health Activism in America, 1890–1950.* Philadelphia: University of Pennsylvania Press, 1995.

Speicher, Anna M. *The Religious World of Antislavery Women: Spirituality in the Lives of Five Abolitionists Lecturers*, Syracuse, N.Y.: Syracuse University Press, 2000.

Stansell, Christine. *City of Women: Sex and Class in New York, 1789–1860.* Urbana: University of Illinois Press, 1986.

Stephens, Judith L. "Art, Activism, and Uncompromising Attitude in Georgia Douglas Johnson's Lynching Plays." *African American Review* 29, no. 1/2 (Spring/Summer 1995): 87–102.

———. "Lynching Dramas and Women: History and Critical Context." In Perkins and Stephens, *Strange Fruit*, 3–14.

———. *The Plays of Georgia Douglas Johnson: From the New Negro Renaissance to the Civil Rights Movement.* Urbana: University of Illinois Press, 2006.

Sterling, Dorothy, ed. *Turning the World Upside Down: The Anti-Slavery Convention of American Women, Held in New York City, May 9–12, 1837.* New York: Coalition of Publishers for Employment, 1987.

Stevens, Doris, and Carol O'Hare. *Jailed for Freedom: American Women Win the Vote.* Troutdale, Ore.: NewSage, 1995.

Stewart-Baxter, Derrick. *Ma Rainey and the Classic Blues Singers.* New York: Stein and Day, 1970.

Tate, Claudia. *Domestic Allegories of Political Desire: The Black Heroine's Text at the Turn of the Century.* New York: Oxford University Press, 1992

Tentler, Leslie Woodcock. *Wage-Earning Women: Industrial Work and Family Life in the United States, 1900–1930.* New York: Oxford University Press, 1979.

Terborg-Penn, Rosalyn. *African American Women in the Struggle for the Vote, 1850–1920.* Bloomington: Indiana University Press, 1998.

Terrell, Mary Church. A *Colored Woman in a White World*. 1940. Reprint, Amherst, N.Y.: Humanity, 2005.

———. "The Justice of Woman Suffrage." Speech to the Biennial Session of the National American Suffrage Association, Washington, D.C., February 1900.

———. "The Progress of Colored Women." Speech to the National American Woman Suffrage Association Convention, Washington, D.C., February 18, 1898. Available at http://antislavery.eserver.org/legacies/the-progress-of-colored-women.

Tillet, Salamishah. *Sites of Slavery: Citizenship and Racial Democracy in the Post–Civil Rights Imagination*. Durham, N.C.: Duke University Press, 2012,

Trotter, Joe William, Jr., ed. *The Great Migration in Historical Perspective: New Dimensions of Race, Class, and Gender*. Bloomington: Indiana University Press, 1991.

Turner, Felicity. "Narrating Infanticide: Constructing the Modern Gendered State in Nineteenth-Century America." PhD diss., Duke University, 2010.

Tushnet, Mark V. *The NAACP's Legal Strategy against Segregated Education, 1925–1950*. Chapel Hill: University of North Carolina Press, 2004.

Walker, Juliet E. K. *The History of Black Business in America: Capitalism, Race, Entrepreneurship*. New York: Prenctice Hall International, 1998.

Walton, Mary. *A Woman's Crusade: Alice Paul and The Battle for the Ballot*. New York: Palgrave Macmillan, 2010.

Wells, Ida B., Frederick Douglass, Irving Garland Penn, and Ferdinand L. Barnett. "The Reason Why the Colored American Is Not in the World's Columbian Exposition." Chicago: Home of Ida B. Wells, August 30, 1893. Available at http://digital.library.upenn.edu/women/wells/exposition/exposition.html.

Wells-Barnett, Ida B., and Jacqueline Jones Royster. *Southern Horrors and Other Writings: The Anti-Lynching Campaign of Ida B. Wells, 1892–1900*. Boston: Bedford, 1997.

Wheeler, Marjorie Spruill. *One Woman, One Vote: Rediscovering the Women's Suffrage Movement*. Troutdale, Ore.: NewSage Press, 1995.

White, Deborah Gray. *Ar'n't I a Woman? Female Slaves in the Plantation South*. New York: Norton, 1999.

———. *Too Heavy a Load: Black Women in Defense of Themselves, 1894–1994* New York: Norton, 1999.

Whitesitt, Linda. "Women as 'Keepers of Culture': Music Clubs, Community Concert Series, and Symphony Orchestras." In *Cultivating Music in America: Women's Patrons and Activists Since 1860*, edited by Ralph P. Locke and Cyrilla Barr, 65–86. Berkeley: University of California Press, 1997.

Wilder, Craig Steven. *In the Company of Black Men: The African Influence on African American Culture in New York City*. New York: New York University Press, 2001.

Wilkerson, Margaret B., ed. *9 Plays by Black Women*. New York: New American Library, 1986.

Williams, Demetrius K. *An End to This Strife: The Politics of Gender in African American Churches*. Minneapolis: Fortress, 2004.

Williams, Fannie Barrier. "The Intellectual Progress of Colored Women of the United States Since the Emancipation Proclamation." *The World's Congress of Representative Women* [May 1893]. Edited by May Wright Sewall. Chicago: Rand, McNally, 1894.

Williams, Katherine. "Betrayers of the Race." *Half-Century Magazine*, February 1920.

Williams, Kidada. *They Left Great Marks On Me: African American Testimonies of Racial Violence from Emancipation to World War I*. New York: New York University Press, 2012.

Williams, Melvin R., "The Blueprint for Change: The Black Community in Washington, D.C., 1860–1870." *Records of the Columbia Historical Society* 48 (1972): 359–93.

Williamson, Joy Ann. *Radicalizing the Ebony Tower: Black Colleges and the Black Freedom Struggle in Mississippi*. New York: Teacher's College Press, 2008.

Willis, Deborah, and Jane Lusaka, eds. *Visual Journal: Harlem and D.C. in the Thirties and Forties*. Washington, D.C.: Center for African American History and Culture and Smithsonian Institution, 1996.

Winch, Julie. *Between Slavery and Freedom: Free People of Color in America from Settlement to the Civil War*. New York: Rowan and Littlefield, 2014.

Wolcott, Victoria W. *Remaking Respectability: African American Women in Interwar Detroit*. Chapel Hill: University of North Carolina Press, 2001.

Wolters, Raymond. *The New Negro on Campus: Black College Rebellions of the 1920s*. Princeton: N.J.: Princeton University Press, 1975.

Yellen, Jean Fagan, and John C. Van Horne, eds. *The Abolitionist Sisterhood: Women's Political Culture in Antebellum America*. Ithaca, N.Y.: Cornell University Press, 1994.

Zieger, Robert H. *For Jobs and Freedom: Race and Labor in America Since 1865*. Lexington: University Press of Kentucky, 2008.

Index

TREVA B. LINDSEY is an associate professor of women's, gender, and sexuality studies at The Ohio State University.

WOMEN, GENDER, AND SEXUALITY IN AMERICAN HISTORY

Women Doctors in Gilded-Age Washington: Race, Gender, and Professionalization *Gloria Moldow*

Friends and Sisters: Letters between Lucy Stone and Antoinette Brown Blackwell, 1846–93 *Edited by Carol Lasser and Marlene Deahl Merrill*

Reform, Labor, and Feminism: Margaret Dreier Robins and the Women's Trade Union League *Elizabeth Anne Payne*

Private Matters: American Attitudes toward Childbearing and Infant Nurture in the Urban North, 1800–1860 *Sylvia D. Hoffert*

Civil Wars: Women and the Crisis of Southern Nationalism *George C. Rable*

I Came a Stranger: The Story of a Hull-House Girl *Hilda Satt Polacheck; edited by Dena J. Polacheck Epstein*

Labor's Flaming Youth: Telephone Operators and Worker Militancy, 1878–1923 *Stephen H. Norwood*

Winter Friends: Women Growing Old in the New Republic, 1785–1835 *Terri L. Premo*

Better Than Second Best: Love and Work in the Life of Helen Magill *Glenn C. Altschuler*

Dishing It Out: Waitresses and Their Unions in the Twentieth Century *Dorothy Sue Cobble*

Natural Allies: Women's Associations in American History *Anne Firor Scott*

Beyond the Typewriter: Gender, Class, and the Origins of Modern American Office Work, 1900–1930 *Sharon Hartman Strom*

The Challenge of Feminist Biography: Writing the Lives of Modern American Women *Edited by Sara Alpern, Joyce Antler, Elisabeth Israels Perry, and Ingrid Winther Scobie*

Working Women of Collar City: Gender, Class, and Community in Troy, New York, 1864–86 *Carole Turbin*

Radicals of the Worst Sort: Laboring Women in Lawrence, Massachusetts, 1860–1912 *Ardis Cameron*

Visible Women: New Essays on American Activism *Edited by Nancy A. Hewitt and Suzanne Lebsock*

Mother-Work: Women, Child Welfare, and the State, 1890–1930 *Molly Ladd-Taylor*

Babe: The Life and Legend of Babe Didrikson Zaharias *Susan E. Cayleff*

Writing Out My Heart: Selections from the Journal of Frances E. Willard, 1855–96 *Edited by Carolyn De Swarte Gifford*

U.S. Women in Struggle: A *Feminist Studies* Anthology *Edited by Claire Goldberg Moses and Heidi Hartmann*

In a Generous Spirit: A First-Person Biography of Myra Page *Christina Looper Baker*

Mining Cultures: Men, Women, and Leisure in Butte, 1914–41 *Mary Murphy*

Gendered Strife and Confusion: The Political Culture of Reconstruction *Laura F. Edwards*

The Female Economy: The Millinery and Dressmaking Trades, 1860–1930 *Wendy Gamber*

Mistresses and Slaves: Plantation Women in South Carolina, 1830–80 *Marli F. Weiner*

A Hard Fight for We: Women's Transition from Slavery to Freedom in South Carolina *Leslie A. Schwalm*

The Common Ground of Womanhood: Class, Gender, and Working Girls' Clubs, 1884–1928 *Priscilla Murolo*

Purifying America: Women, Cultural Reform, and Pro-Censorship Activism, 1873–1933 *Alison M. Parker*

Marching Together: Women of the Brotherhood of Sleeping Car Porters *Melinda Chateauvert*

Creating the New Woman: The Rise of Southern Women's Progressive Culture in Texas, 1893–1918 *Judith N. McArthur*

The Business of Charity: The Woman's Exchange Movement, 1832–1900 *Kathleen Waters Sander*

The Power and Passion of M. Carey Thomas *Helen Lefkowitz Horowitz*

For Freedom's Sake: The Life of Fannie Lou Hamer *Chana Kai Lee*

Becoming Citizens: The Emergence and Development of the California Women's Movement, 1880–1911 *Gayle Gullett*

Selected Letters of Lucretia Coffin Mott *Edited by Beverly Wilson Palmer with the assistance of Holly Byers Ochoa and Carol Faulkner*

Women and the Republican Party, 1854–1924 *Melanie Susan Gustafson*

Southern Discomfort: Women's Activism in Tampa, Florida, 1880s–1920s *Nancy A. Hewitt*

The Making of "Mammy Pleasant": A Black Entrepreneur in Nineteenth-Century San Francisco *Lynn M. Hudson*

Sex Radicals and the Quest for Women's Equality *Joanne E. Passet*

"We, Too, Are Americans": African American Women in Detroit and Richmond, 1940–54 *Megan Taylor Shockley*

The Road to Seneca Falls: Elizabeth Cady Stanton and the First Woman's Rights Convention *Judith Wellman*

Reinventing Marriage: The Love and Work of Alice Freeman Palmer and George Herbert Palmer *Lori Kenschaft*

Southern Single Blessedness: Unmarried Women in the Urban South, 1800–1865 *Christine Jacobson Carter*

Widows and Orphans First: The Family Economy and Social Welfare Policy, 1865–1939 *S. J. Kleinberg*

Habits of Compassion: Irish Catholic Nuns and the Origins of the Welfare System, 1830–1920 *Maureen Fitzgerald*

The Women's Joint Congressional Committee and the Politics of Maternalism, 1920–1930 *Jan Doolittle Wilson*

"Swing the Sickle for the Harvest Is Ripe": Gender and Slavery in Antebellum Georgia *Daina Ramey Berry*

Christian Sisterhood, Race Relations, and the YWCA, 1906–46
Nancy Marie Robertson
Reading, Writing, and Segregation: A Century of Black Women Teachers in Nashville *Sonya Ramsey*
Radical Sisters: Second-Wave Feminism and Black Liberation in Washington, D.C. *Anne M. Valk*
Feminist Coalitions: Historical Perspectives on Second-Wave Feminism in the United States *Edited by Stephanie Gilmore*
Breadwinners: Working Women and Economic Independence, 1865–1920
Lara Vapnek
Beauty Shop Politics: African American Women's Activism in the Beauty Industry *Tiffany M. Gill*
Demanding Child Care: Women's Activism and the Politics of Welfare, 1940–1971 *Natalie M. Fousekis*
Rape in Chicago: Race, Myth, and the Courts *Dawn Rae Flood*
Black Women and Politics in New York City *Julie A. Gallagher*
Cold War Progressives: Women's Interracial Organizing for Peace and Freedom *Jacqueline Castledine*
No Votes for Women: The New York State Anti-Suffrage Movement *Susan Goodier*
Anna Howard Shaw: The Work of Woman Suffrage *Trisha Franzen*
Nursing Civil Rights: Gender and Race in the Army Nurse Corps *Charissa J. Threat*
Reverend Addie Wyatt: Faith and the Fight for Labor, Gender, and Racial Equality *Marcia Walker-McWilliams*
Lucretia Mott Speaks: The Essential Speeches *Edited by Christopher Densmore, Carol Faulkner, Nancy Hewitt, and Beverly Wilson Palmer*
Lost in the USA: American Identity from the Promise Keepers to the Million Mom March *Deborah Gray White*
Women against Abortion: Inside the Largest Moral Reform Movement of the Twentieth Century *Karissa Haugeberg*
Colored No More: Reinventing Black Womanhood in Washington, D.C.
Treva B. Lindsey

The University of Illinois Press
is a founding member of the
Association of American University Presses.

University of Illinois Press
1325 South Oak Street
Champaign, IL 61820-6903
www.press.uillinois.edu